CLIMAGEDDON REVIEWS

"Lawrence Wollersheim has clearly done the kind of in-depth research needed for such a complex and huge issue as climate change, and is willing to go beyond almost anyone else in presenting the hard realities that we must face and choices we must act on at this crucial juncture in history. For those of us courageous enough to take the red pill and get informed with what is really going on and the options we still have at this late date, this book is a must-read." —Vinit Allen, Executive Director, Sustainable World Coalition

"If Rachel Carson's *Silent Spring* sounded a clarion call to the harmful effects of indiscriminate use of pesticides, Lawrence Wollersheim's *Climageddon* sounds a far more urgent wake-up call to the global climate warming crisis precariously close to the tipping point. With compelling research, challenging data, and ever-escalating argument, Wollersheim paints a daunting picture about humanity's survival at the very brink. Although the situation is indeed direly urgent, he assures us it's not totally hopeless, if we can finally summon the significant individual and collective will to stem the mounting tide. *Climageddon* comes not a minute too soon to arouse that necessary will into timely action." —William Kueppers, PhD

"This thoroughly researched call-to-arms pulls no punches as it lucidly argues that the destabilizing impacts of climate change are far greater and much closer than we have been led to believe. Likely scenarios are painstakingly laid out and they only go from bad to worse. 'Which do you prefer,' writes Wollersheim, 'partial economic collapse now, or total economic collapse later, with the bonus collapse of civilization?' These options are not hyperbole; disconcertingly realistic, they are grounded in a lengthy cascade of data, charts, links, tipping points, and quotes from leading climatologists and geo-engineers. There are solutions, but they require massive collective will to initiate: 'How do we educate the people of the world that to save the future and future generations, they must now expect less, have less, and be less economically comfortable?' It's gut-check time for humanity, and the clock is ticking." —Matthew Gilbert, Founder/Curator of *Cinema Noēsis: Films for Evolving Minds*

"If you have children, grandchildren, or care for anyone of a younger generation, then you have an obligation of the heart to not only read and heed the *au courant* harbinger that is to be found in *Climageddon*, but to also be a herald of it's contents. *Climageddon* could be mankind's one and only saving grace. Are you willing to take a chance that it isn't? In my honest opinion a must-read compendium." —David T. Pike, Senior Global Warming Blog Editor

"If we ignore the issue of climate change, humanity faces certain peril, and the five billion year evolutionary experiment on this planet comes to a catastrophic turn, if not an end. This well-researched book moves beyond politics to sound science, and even proposed solutions. *Climageddon* may be the most important book of our time. Everyone needs to be informed about this." —Anodea Judith, PhD author of *The Global Heart Awakens: Eastern Body, Western Mind.*

"On any planet on which sentient life emerges and forms an industrialised civilisation, its survival will be threatened by something like global warming. A key step in surviving will be the emergence of a book that clearly identifies the problem and sets out what they must do to overcome the problem. On this planet at this time, *Climageddon* is that book." —John Stewart, author of *Evolution's Arrow*

"Wollersheim's mastery of meta-systemic analysis and his firm grasp of the crucial issue of tipping points makes his book a must-read for anyone who has the courage to face facts about climate change. His contribution to the climate debate cannot be overstated." —Byron Belitsos, author of *One World Democracy* and *Healing a Broken World*

"There is an ancient and famous question: 'Why is this book different from all other books?' Unlike the complexity that springs from a similar question asked at every Passover Seder, this one is easy to answer. This book is different from all other books because its author, Lawrence Wollersheim, has amassed the courage to look all aspects of Anthropomorphic Climate Change right in the eye, and systematically, fearlessly, pin them to his collector's boards in a frighteningly harmonious and completely understandable pattern. The result is the most honest, realistic, complete, integrated, and solution-centered summary work yet written in English on human-caused climate disruption. To fully integrate *Climaggedon* into your heart and mind will guide you, successfully, through the surrounding climatic 'Slough of Despond' that makes John Bunyan's *Pilgrim's Progress* feel like a playground game." —Michael Dietrick, MD

"*Climageddon* transcends the 'controversial' claims related to the real climate crisis by providing information from a seemingly infinite number of valid sources, and with a simple understanding of the information, we must then demand the societal mobilization that is our only sane and substantive response. However, what makes *Climageddon* a unique breakthrough, are the plausible scenarios carefully explained that we could follow that would lead us out of the climate mess and 'turn-it-around' at the last minutes we have left to lift ourselves out of the climate mire. Read *Climageddon* and see what our last great hopes are for ourselves and our living Earth." —Michael Mielke, Association for the Tree of Life

"In *Climageddon*, Lawrence Wollersheim presents a valuable discussion of the threats posed by global warming should we fail to immediately mobilize our global resources to manage and control its rapidly escalating consequences. *Climageddon* not only highlights the urgency of our task, but also discusses a range of options to help reduce our risk." —James Olson, author of *How Whole Brain Thinking Can Save the Future*

"*Climageddon* is...well written and concise when it comes to scientific facts about global warming. The information found in this book is a real eye opener for people who are unaware of the dangers and consequences we will all be facing in the near future due to our continued use of fossil fuel. The viable solutions in the latter chapters are well thought out and very doable." —Gordon Chu

"*Climageddon* is the end of denial. For the first time, a meta-study of hundreds of climate change papers puts the big picture together in plain language. It trumpets the call of Job One for Humanity. These are not politically correct views, but unvarnished truth. And it's better to know, so we can come together to force urgent change. End your personal denial and join reality!" —Grant Rudolph, neuropsychologist.

CLIMAGEDDON

THE GLOBAL WARMING
EMERGENCY AND HOW TO SURVIVE IT

LAWRENCE WOLLERSHEIM

Publisher

This book is published exclusively by Job One for Humanity, a social benefit organization, (www.JobOneforHumanity.org).

For all bulk or wholesale book purchase information contact manage@JobOneforHumanity.org or mail your request to Factnet Inc. PMB 2167, 1650 Casino Dr. Laughlin, Nevada 89029. Job One for Humanity is a DBA of Factnet, Inc. Factnet, Inc. is a 501(c)3 IRS recognized nonprofit organization in the United States.

Copyright

Parental Warning

This book is *not recommended* for children below the age of 15 due to its serious nature.

DEDICATION

Climageddon is dedicated to those brave individuals who are unafraid to follow the facts, wherever they might lead. It is also dedicated to the courageous intelligence agency analysts and directors attempting to inform their respective political leaders about the nature, danger, and the immediacy of the global warming threats as described in this book.

Climageddon is also dedicated to scientists like James E. Hansen, Kevin Anderson, and Michael E. Mann, as well as the thousands of other climate scientists who have worked tirelessly to make us aware of the escalating global warming emergency and its dangerous consequences. It is further dedicated to all past global warming activists such as Al Gore, Bill McKibben, David Spratt, and the many organizations around the world working to resolve the global warming emergency. And finally, this book is dedicated to my new family, whose future safety and security was a compelling motivation for getting this book done and shared with others.

TABLE OF CONTENTS

PREFACE

HOW *CLIMAGEDDON* CAME ABOUT

This book should have never come into being. Seven years ago, I was working for a tiny think tank called the Universe Institute and another nonprofit organization called Universe Spirit. I was doing research on how to integrate the most successful long-term patterns of biological evolution with those of universe cosmology.

Global warming was not even on my radar. By chance, I began reading a global warming book. The more I read, the more concerned I became.

After reading 10,000 pages of books and published studies, I became so concerned I stopped all research in other areas. By that time, it was clear to me that catastrophic global warming risks were still not adequately being explained to the public, and there was a growing probability of the extinction of humanity in a significantly shorter time frame than was being presented by governmental authorities.

While researching, I also learned about the brave scientists who, beginning almost 30 years ago, raised the first alarms. Their reward was retaliation in the form of academic attack or censure, lawsuits, and threats upon their persons.

Because of what I discovered, I knew I <u>had</u> to write this book.

What this book seeks to do

    a.   Inform readers about the reality that global warming is *far worse* than the media and the 28-trillion-dollar-a-year global fossil fuel industry wants them to know.

b. Help the public cut through the complexity and contradictions found in today's global warming debate.

c. Present multiple perspectives on global warming research and simplify its analysis.

d. Provide a new, analytical prediction model for the most likely progression for global warming consequences. This new model is called the *Climageddon Scenario*.

e. Help readers rethink *their* decisions about how soon global warming will affect their finances, security, and future.

f. Inform readers what they can do to resolve global warming *while we still have time left,* and help motivate the execution of the effective steps provided in the included Job One for Humanity Plan to end global warming.

g. Help readers prepare their emergency backup plan for what is coming.

h. Help ignite a vigorous public conversation on *Climageddon's* challenging new disclosures about our future.

i. Help move the polarized global warming dialog to a new place that better facilitates the rapid and effective resolution of the global warming challenge.

Who should read *Climageddon*

This book is for everyone, but especially for millennials and the younger generations who will be most adversely affected by the escalating global warming emergency. It also can be used by global warming educators and advocates, farmers, business and real estate advisors, investment bankers, market and commodity investors, city, corporate, and government planners, deep green environmentalists, intelligence agency risk and threat analysts, early adopter millennials, futurists, preppers, survivalists, and even global warming deniers.

Do not worry if you have never read anything about global warming. *Climageddon* will provide all the science needed to help you draw your own conclusions. If you are well-read on global warming, you can explore new facts, synthesize perspectives, and learn about remedial strategies not found elsewhere. If you are not sure whether global warming is an important problem directly affecting your near future or requiring replanning, *Climageddon* will convince you that it is.

If you are a global warming denier without a vested financial interest in maintaining that position, *Climageddon* is a must read! Even if you strongly doubt global warming, you have a lot more to lose than money if you do not have access to the information of this book. The chilling facts and arguments of *Climageddon* are difficult to ignore, no matter what your current worldview might be.

More than anything else, *Climageddon* is for individuals willing to follow the facts, wherever they might lead.

How the book is laid out

There are two main parts to *Climageddon*:

1. Part 1 contains facts about global warming, the climate, our current warming status, the Climageddon Scenario, and the fatal flaws of the currently accepted predictions. A few of the chapters contain information you may find complex, but you do not have to be a scientist or understand *all of it* to get the most important facts.

2. Part 2 contains the key Job One for Humanity Plan action steps designed to effectively slow and lessen the

consequences of global warming so some of us will survive. It contains a radically different approach from what other activists and organizations have presented. The Job One Plan may be our *last chance* action plan with strategies to help you and your loved ones prepare for, adapt to, and survive the upcoming disruptions.

At the beginning of some chapters, you will find:

a. a short chapter bullet point overview or

b. a short chapter introduction.

At the end of some chapters, you will find:

a. A list of bullet points summarizing the key ideas of that chapter.

b. Vaccinating positive perspectives that sometimes serve as consoling "silver linings" *essential* for coping with the difficult global warming news presented in this book.

c. Sections that delve deeper into the science being discussed. These sections are not required reading, but are recommended for a deeper understanding of complex climate and global warming issues.

d. Endnotes, which contain link sources for readers of the print copy of *Climageddon*.

Climageddon also contains a conclusion, glossary, references, and miscellaneous appendices. Its glossary familiarizes the reader with new terms not adequately or previously defined, which will allow readers to more easily understand complex climate states, conditions, and reactions.

Climate research and researcher perspectives used within this book may vary slightly in conclusions or projections. Such differences can be accounted for by slightly different research, newer research displacing older research, or different calculations or interpretations of similar or slightly different facts.

The book's biggest challenge

Climageddon seeks to rise to the challenge of candidly discussing the often distressing facts about the complex problems, dilemmas, and the immediacy of the global warming emergency. The most difficult part of this challenge is presenting so much unsettling information while still maintaining a realistic hope about what we can do so that we are motivated to act.

If the book does not create this important balance and readers can't find feasible solutions, they will respond with such statements as "what's the point," "why bother," or "it's all going to hell anyway, let's get as much as we can get while we're here, and damn the future." Hopefully, by the end of Part 2, "The New Job One for Humanity Plan to End Global Warming," you should find new solutions and hope to counter these attitudes. If you are a person who is diligent about planning their future and averting *avoidable* suffering and loss, this may be the most challenging book you have ever read through the first 9 chapters but also the most important and necessary book you may ever own.

Not just another global warming facts book

This book is not just a collection of hard-to-face facts about the escalating consequences of global warming. It is also a new way to see our challenging global warming future.

A good portion of readers may also become engaged in a cathartic process which, left to run its course, will present strong, positive attitudinal and intellectual changes, resulting in renewal and restoration. A few readers may experience a roller coaster ride of Kübler-Ross-like emotions[1] before they finally reach a new level of acceptance for the difficult predicament we find ourselves in.

Online support for you and your questions

The nonprofit organization Job One for Humanity has set up a special online *Climageddon Book Support Navigation Center* on its website.[2] This page will provide online support and the latest information and updates in the following areas:

a. A link to an evolving *Climageddon* FAQ with the most common questions and answers readers have sent to us about the book. (You can always email the author any new question that you would like to see answered in the FAQ by emailing it without attachments to Lawrence@JobOneforHumanity.org)

b. Links for individuals wanting additional information to coordinate with others on the many action steps to end global warming mentioned in the Job One Plan (found in Part 2 of the book).

c. A link to a soon-to-be created discussion forum. The facts within *Climageddon* have the capacity to create profound emotional and intellectual reactions. The safe and moderated *Climageddon* discussion forum is a place where you can share what you are experiencing and what you've learned on how to deal with it.

d. Links to new research that affects or modifies information provided in the book will be used to update future versions.

---

[1] Wikipedia contributors. "Kübler-Ross model." *Wikipedia, The Free Encyclopedia.* Apr 17, 2017. https://en.wikipedia.org/wiki/K%C3%BCbler-Ross_model

[2] Climageddon Book Support Navigation Center: http://www.joboneforhumanity.org/climageddon_book_support_navigation_center

e. Links for individuals who want to learn about the available Job One volunteering positions or to make donations to the effort.

Nerd Alert: Global warming seen from new perspectives

This book was written using a multidisciplinary meta-systemic analysis methodology not known to be previously used for overviewing the current global warming literature. This methodology examines the systems and subsystems involved in global warming as:

a. Stand-alone individual systems or subsystems (this is logical and systems thinking analysis and perspective), but also as

b. Interconnected and interdependent systems and subsystems. Global warming systems and subsystems as well as climate, human and biological systems and subsystems are constantly interacting with each other in a multitude of processes, relationships, contexts, and transformations. (This is the core way of seeing a situation from a *meta*-systemic analysis perspective.)

Seeing facts and solutions concerning global warming from a meta-systemic perspective brings to light many unique big-picture insights. It also has inspired strategies not found in the perspectives, analyses, or solutions of previous global warming books.

Because of these new meta-systemic perspectives, readers will find themselves on an exciting journey of numerous paradigm shifts[3] as they consider the facts and solutions being presented. These unexpected and often sudden perspective changes can be jarring at first, but they are integral to a more nuanced and larger understanding of the global warming threat.

The process of presenting many new perspectives may allow the information in *Climageddon* to pass more easily through any pre-existing ideological filters a reader might have. (An example of an ideological filter could be a preconceived belief or bias about the reliability of science or how facts incongruent with one's religious beliefs can't be true. Any pre-existing beliefs about global warming could act to either filter out or color any new facts being presented.)

Because of the many twists and turns of the multi-perspective journey you are about to begin, be patient as the process unfolds. What might first appear as repetition is often a lead-in to a significantly different way of seeing an earlier idea with a new and different context or perspective.

Acknowledgments

I would like to first acknowledge my wife Karen Cruz and our children for their ongoing support and insights during the creation of this book. Special thanks to Ken Burrows for his insightful and candid editing advice. Special thanks to Anne Persons for her editing and other advices and assistance. Thanks to Baraka Burrill, Lisa Winter, cover illustrator, and the chapter illustrator, Matthew A. Melillo. Special thanks to Don Morgan, Dan Shafer, David Pike, author Anodea Judith, author Byron Belitsos, author John Stewart, Michael Dietrick MD, Michael Mielke and Jean Arnold for their advice and assistance,

---

[3] Wikipedia contributors, "Paradigm," *Wikipedia, The Free Encyclopedia,* https://en.wikipedia.org/w/index.php?title=Paradigm&oldid=753106075 (accessed December 5, 2016).

and thanks to Grant Rudolph, Cindy Wollersheim, Gordon Chu, Patrick Spanner, and all the test readers for their contributions and support.

I would also like to acknowledge my late mentor, Professor Emeritus Margaret Singer, University of California, Berkeley. If not for her discovery of my unusual ability to analyse big data for errors, unseen patterns and hidden interconnections, this book would never have come into being.

I would also like to acknowledge the breakthrough work of Professor Otto Laske, who has taken the development and teaching of the *constructive developmental framework* and dialectical, meta-systemic analysis to new heights and clarity. And finally, I want to express my appreciation to the social benefit organization Job One for Humanity and its parent nonprofit organization Factnet Inc., without whose assistance this book may not have been published.

Lawrence Wollersheim
February 7, 2017

PROLOGUE

WHAT YOU DON'T KNOW WILL HURT YOU.

A wide variety of books today have documented the unsettling truth about the perils of global warming, the science behind it, and predictions for the future both near and long-term.

While these have contributed valuable and much needed knowledge, they have too often overlooked indispensable details that give a more complete and more accurate picture of the climate destabilization relentlessly unfolding before us.

Among the gaps in much of today's global warming analysis and discussion are:

- a pervasive lack of awareness in the existence of crucial tipping points and points of no return when the manifestations of global warming accelerate (such as speeding up from a linear to an exponential progression)

- an incomplete itemization of the factors feeding into global warming—some of which are measurably more dangerous than the commonly recognized culprits

- an overly narrowed time frame in which to evaluate how climate "changes"—not just over decades or even centuries but rather over millennia

- the failure to apply a meta-systemic analysis methodology, examining how interdependent human and ecological systems and subsystems interact in something as complex and dynamic as the climate.

These gaps lead to erroneous conclusions even among such widely acknowledged climate authorities as the United Nations Intergovernmental Panel on Climate Change (IPCC). As a result we proceed in a context of naive reassurances regarding current status and future projections, as though we had a rather benign climate change to deal with rather than a true climate emergency to resolve.

Climageddon breaks through this illusory naivete by filling in the gaps that have become our global warming blind spots. The book goes beyond cataloging the evidence visible in nature—melting ice sheets, dying reefs, rising sea levels, intensifying droughts, and more—to elucidate the deeper science and diverse causes underlying a steadily warming earth headed for what may be an irreversible and extinction-level fate. This provocative bigger-picture of global warming is mapped out in the book's "Climageddon Scenario," a six-phase, forewarning chronology of progressively worsening climate conditions.

Climageddon then goes on to propose what wide-ranging actions might be most effective in confronting this existential challenge, how we can and should prepare for it, how we might reverse the fateful tide, and how we may, with concerted effort and also some good fortune, escape a dystopian fate and go on instead to reestablish and sustain a safe future. This call-to-action—ambitiously global in scope yet inviting to the individual to play a part—is detailed in what the author calls the Job One for Humanity Plan.

Climageddon uncovers what has too often been missing in today's global warming books. With unflinching realism it warns of a bleak future but also illustrates how we might not only save ourselves but also in the process create a sustainable prosperity for all. It's eye-opening and unsettling. Hard-nosed yet hopeful. A must-read for our times.

CLIMAGEDDON
PART 1

Understanding the Global Warming
Emergency and the Climageddon Scenario

PART 1, CHAPTER 1

A QUICK OVERVIEW OF *CLIMAGEDDON*

With the advent of so many other forms of media to get information, many people do not read books as they used to. Today, it is common to start reading the first chapter, then go directly to the conclusion.

If they like what they read, many will then pick and choose other chapters of the book according to their interests, but fewer and fewer individuals read everything cover-to-cover. To help you navigate modern book reading and follow your key interests, here's a mini-cheat sheet:

1. If you are curious about how bad global warming is *right now*, we strongly recommend you begin with chapter 5 in Part 1 first! It is easy, interesting reading that could have been the book's first chapter as well.

2. If you want to see the key consequences coming quickly at us, read Chapter 3 in Part 1.

3. If you feel the need to peek at our last-chance solutions, read Chapter 2 in Part 2.

The above will help you get involved quickly, but it is strongly *recommended* not to skip too many of the foundational chapters in Part 1. Without reviewing the supporting facts of preceding chapters, the new Climageddon Scenario prediction model in Chapter 6 could be more difficult to understand. Without those foundational chapters it would also make it more difficult to believe the urgency behind the Job One for Humanity actions steps in Part 2.

What is Climageddon

Armageddon is a biblical term used to refer to an end-of-the-world scenario. *Climageddon's* title appropriately combines the words climate and Armageddon because global warming has evolved into a credible and imminent end-of-the-world scenario.

Climageddon contains new timetables and consequence progressions, as well as a new prediction model for how the interconnected processes and interdependent systems creating global warming will interact and unfold. Some of *Climageddon's* new premises about how our global warming future will occur are disheartening. Others offer situation-appropriate hope for the difficult consequences and choices we will soon face.

The key premises of *Climageddon* concerning global warming are:

a. We are in an *undeclared* global warming *State of Emergency!*

b. In spite of over 30 years of scientific warnings, conferences, and international agreements, global warming is *not* getting better. It is getting worse at a *far faster* rate than we are planning or preparing for.

c. We have been given inaccurate and *incomplete* predictions by the United Nations authoritative Intergovernmental Panel on Climate Change (IPCC) for when the main consequences of global warming will occur, as well as how bad those consequences will be. In part, this is happening to protect national and corporate fossil fuel economic interests.

d. Global warming has irreversibly destabilized several critical climate areas—and dangerous climate stability transition points have already been crossed.

e. The most expensive and worst consequences of global warming will not occur in 40 to 80 years as we are being told. They are already starting and many will occur in *less than half* that time.

f. Continued global warming will create economic devastation at every level. Hundreds of trillions of dollars will be lost by those individuals, businesses, and nations most uninformed and unprepared for the massive coming changes.

g. There is a clear and final global warming battle line we must not cross. It is very near, and staying on the safe side of that line will be the greatest adaptive challenge humanity has ever faced.

h. There is still time left to make prudent global warming emergency backup preparations to improve your odds of surviving this emergency (described in the Job One Plan in Part 2 of this book).

i. If we fail to act effectively to reverse escalating global warming, there is enough time left to slow down and lessen its consequences, as well as partially mitigate the mass suffering, death, and the collapse of our economic, political, and social systems. With this extra time we might find new ways to adapt.

j. If we completely fail to stop the worst consequences of escalating global warming, there is also still time left to relocate a *small* percentage of the world's population (along with essential infrastructure and supplies) north of the 45th parallel north and south of the 45th parallel south. These locations will be temporarily more survivable and civilization will continue for a while longer.

k. If we do immediately execute the actions described in the Job One for Humanity Plan and we complete those actions within the critical 2026 deadlines given, though it will be costly, painful, and difficult, humanity and our civilization should survive, and eventually our world will recover from the damage we have done.

l. We have many grave global warming problems and challenges that have barely been discovered, or only partially understood. That will be true throughout our encounter with this pivotal emergency for the 21st century. Our current global warming emergency presents a spectrum of new dilemmas that will necessitate life-and-death decisions unprecedented in human history.

m. Critical proprietary predictions and information concerning the consequences of global warming are currently unavailable outside of specialized wealth-privileged investment advisory circles or national intelligence analyst circles. *Climageddon* will disclose much of this this obscured or intentionally withheld information, and prepare you for how to evaluate and use it by providing the necessary factual foundation found within Part 1 of this book.

What's next

In the next chapter, the basics of what causes global warming, how the climate works, and what causes the climate to destabilize into dangerous conditions are explained. Fair warning: you will be amazed by how powerful and how long-lasting the worst effects of today's global warming pollution are and will become.

Part 1, Chapter 2

How Global Warming Works and Affects Our Climate

Overview:

- The concentration of the human-caused carbon pollution of our atmosphere has nearly doubled in 60 years—and it is continuing to escalate at faster and faster rates.

- Carbon in the atmosphere from fossil fuel burning isn't our only problem.

- While the situation is critical, it is still possible to slow and lessen global warming enough for the climate to establish a new, stable equilibrium. However, that equilibrium may be unlike anything previously seen in Earth's history.

To formulate your own informed global warming opinions as well as understand the new Climageddon Scenario model, it is essential to know:

a. what global warming is,

b. how it is created,

c. how the life-critical stability of the global climate is affected by global warming, and

d. how this will affect you and your future.

If you are a diligent person who is serious about planning your future and avoiding *unnecessary* suffering and loss, this may be the most important book you may ever read.

What is global warming

Global warming is a term used for the observed century-scale rise in the average temperature of the Earth's climate system and its related effects. Scientists are more than 95% certain that nearly all of global warming is caused by increasing concentrations of greenhouse gases (GHGs) and other human-caused emissions.

Within the earth's atmosphere, accumulating greenhouse gases like water vapor, carbon dioxide, methane, nitrous oxide, and ozone are the gases within the atmosphere that absorb and emit heat radiation. Increasing or decreasing amounts of greenhouse gases within the atmosphere act to either hold in or release more of the heat from the sun.

Our atmosphere is getting hotter, more turbulent, and more unpredictable because of the "boiling and churning" effect caused by the *heat-trapping* greenhouse gases within the upper layers of our atmosphere. With each increase of carbon, methane, or other greenhouse gas levels in the atmosphere, our local weather and global climate is further agitated, heated, and "boiled."

Global warming is gauged by the increase in the *average* global temperature of the Earth. Along with our currently increasing average global temperature, some parts of the Earth may actually get colder while other parts get warmer—hence the idea of *average* global temperature. Greenhouse gas-caused atmospheric heating and agitation also increase the unpredictability of the weather and climate, and dramatically increase the severity, scale, and frequency of storms, droughts, wildfires, and extreme temperatures.

Global warming can reach levels of irreversibility, and increasing levels of global warming can eventually reach an extinction level where humanity and all life on earth will end. In this book, irreversible global warming is defined as a _continuum_ of increasing temperature that causes the global climate to rapidly change until those higher temperatures becomes irreversible on practical human time scales. The eventual temperature range associated with triggering and marking the beginning of the irreversible global warming processes is an increase in average global temperature of 2.2°-4° Celsius (4°-7.2° Fahrenheit) above preindustrial levels.

Extinction level global warming is defined in this book as temperatures exceeding preindustrial levels by 5-6° Celsius (9-10.8° Fahrenheit) or the extinction of all planetary life, or the eventual loss of our atmosphere. If our atmosphere is also lost, this is referred to as runaway global warming. The result would be similar to what is thought to have happened to Venus 4 billion years ago, resulting in a carbon-rich atmosphere and minimum surface temperatures of 462 °C.

The temperature levels described above for irreversible and extinction level global warming are not hard and rigid boundaries, but boundary _ranges_ that describe the related consequences and their intensities within a certain level of global warming. These temperature boundary levels may be modified by future research. More about irreversible global warming and extinction-level global warming can come about because of complex interactions that will be explained fully in Chapter 4. Chapter 4 and Chapter 5 will set the foundation necessary to understand how we are already creating the conditions that will precipitate irreversible and extinction-level global warming if we keep going as we are now.

How long carbon dioxide remains in our atmosphere

Carbon dioxide is currently the most important greenhouse gas related to global warming. For the longest time, our scientists believed that once in the atmosphere, carbon dioxide remains there for about 100 years. New research shows that is not true. 75% of that carbon will not disappear for thousands of years. The other 25% stays forever. We are creating a serious global warming crisis that will last far longer than we ever thought possible.

> "The lifetime of fossil fuel CO_2 in the atmosphere is a few centuries, plus 25 percent that lasts essentially forever. The next time you fill your tank, reflect upon this...[the climatic impacts of releasing fossil fuel CO_2 to the atmosphere will last longer than Stonehenge... Longer than time capsules, longer than nuclear waste, far longer than the age of human civilization so far." — "Carbon is forever," Mason Inman[4]

How carbon dioxide in our atmosphere is tracked

Atmospheric carbon from fossil fuel burning is the main human-caused factor in the escalating global warming we are experiencing now. The current level of carbon in our atmosphere is tracked using what is called the Keeling curve.[5] The Keeling curve measures atmospheric carbon in parts per million (ppm).

Each year, many measurements are taken at Mauna Loa, Hawaii to determine the parts per million (ppm) of carbon in the atmosphere at that time. At the beginning of the Industrial Revolution[6] around 1880, before we began fossil fuel burning, our atmospheric carbon ppm level was at about 270. Here is the current Keeling curve graph for where we are today:

---

[4] Mason Inman. "Carbon is forever." *Nature.com*. November 20, 2008. http://www.nature.com/climate/2008/0812/full/climate.2008.122.html

[5] Wikipedia contributors. "Keeling Curve." *Wikipedia, The Free Encyclopedia*. https://en.wikipedia.org/wiki/Keeling_Curve (accessed December 20, 2016).

[6] the transition to new manufacturing processes in the period from about 1760 to sometime between 1820 and 1840. From Wikipedia contributors, "Industrial Revolution," *Wikipedia, The Free Encyclopedia*, https://en.wikipedia.org/w/index.php?title=Industrial_Revolution&oldid=755848241 (accessed December 20, 2016).

Keeling Curve Monthly CO2 graph, via Show.earth[7]

As you can see, we are not doing very well. In later chapters, you will learn what this exponentially rising carbon means to your future. You also will see other graphs that will show you how today's atmospheric carbon levels compare to those of our near and far distant past (hundreds, thousands, hundreds of thousands, and millions of years ago).

No matter what you hear in the media, if the total carbon ppm level is not going down or carbon's average ppm level *per year* is not falling or at least slowing its steep increase,[8] we are *not* making any significant progress on resolving the escalating global warming emergency. Total atmospheric carbon and carbon's average ppm level *per year* are the most dependable measurements of our progress and a predictor of what will be happening with global warming and its many consequences.

---

[7] Show.earth. "Keeling Curve Monthly CO2 Widget." *ProOxygen.*
https://www.show.earth/kc-monthly-co2-widget (accessed January 17, 2017).

[8] changes in the El Niño La Niño patterns can periodically affect annual carbon ppm levels.

How do we know if we're making honest progress in reducing carbon dioxide to reduce global warming?

There are at least two ways we will be able to tell that we are making honest progress in reducing global warming:

1. When we see our average annual increase in carbon ppm levels (currently at about 3 ppm per year) begin dropping, remaining at the current level, or at least rising at a slower rate.

2. When we start seeing the above Keeling graph levels dropping from the current carbon ppm level (approximately 407 ppm) to carbon 350-325 ppm. (More will be said about how we do this in the Job One Plan in Part 2.)

A quick look at the historic rise of carbon in the atmosphere since the Industrial Revolution

The following graph demonstrates that carbon has been rising in the atmosphere long before 1960. With the introduction of fossil fuels, carbon began rising at the beginning of the Industrial Revolution around 1880.

In the graph below, you will notice that the curve of carbon increasing in the atmosphere proceeds from about 1880 to 1950 in a gradual linear progression. From 1950 to 2000 and beyond, carbon increases in the atmosphere in a far steeper, more exponential curve.

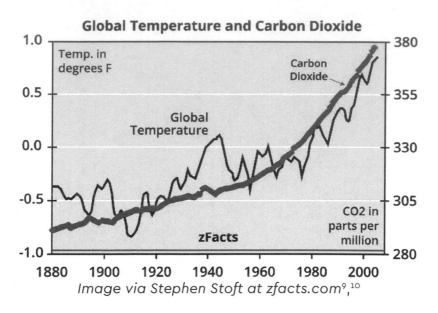

Image via Stephen Stoft at zfacts.com[9],[10]

How escalating global warming destabilizes the climate

It is important that we understand that the stability of our climate is the essential foundation for running our personal and business lives smoothly and successfully. If the global climate continues to destabilize because of escalating global warming, most people will not connect the dots to see that their normal lives will also destabilize until it is too late.

Most people do not think about:

a. What will happen when food production drops due to drought, floods, and extreme heat, which will cause food prices to soar and many foods to be scarce.

---

[9] Stephen Stoft. "Evidence that CO2 is the Cause of Global Warming." *zFacts.com*, accessed January 9, 2017, http://zfacts.com/p/226.html

[10] The slight downward trend in temperature from about 1945 until about 1975 is due to the increase in Sulfate Aerosols (SO4), largely produced by burning coal that contains sulfur. These cool the earth, and their increase during these years largely canceled the increase in CO2 during the same period.

b. How storms will continue to grow more violent, costly, and cataclysmic. Damage to homes, businesses, and infrastructure will increase, as well as occur in more and larger areas.

c. How our normal lives will gradually grind to a near halt.

It is not an overstatement to say most people do not understand how much of the stability, predictability, and success of their daily lives (and futures) are *completely dependent* upon a stable temperature range and stable climate. By and large, they take the ubiquitous general stability of the climate for granted, almost as though it could never change.

The global climate's heat-controlling systems and subsystems

Within the climate's many systems and subsystems there are factors that directly and indirectly affect the overall stability of the global climate and our temperature. One of these factors is that some climate systems and subsystems have *carbon-eating* or *carbon-releasing* qualities.

When we say something has a carbon-eating quality, we mean that it takes carbon out of the atmosphere and helps *to reduce* global warming. When we say something has a carbon-releasing quality, we mean that it puts carbon back into the atmosphere, which causes an *increase* in global warming. The climate's carbon-*eating or releasing* subsystems, which can raise or lower the Earth's average temperature and the climate's stability are:

 **Oceans with their currents, differing water temperatures, and descending and ascending layers hold absorbed carbon or heat.**[11] Initially, the oceans absorb carbon and help us. But when too much carbon is absorbed, the oceans begin the process of emitting carbon back into the atmosphere. That will raise temperatures.

 **Forests can either eat or release carbon** based on the temperature and other conditions. When trees die, their stored carbon is released back into the atmosphere. Trees normally take carbon out of the atmosphere. If certain conditions exist or it gets too warm trees will take less carbon out of the air. This will be explained further in Chapter 3.

 **Soils can also eat or release carbon** depending upon their condition under heat variables. This is due to carbon deposits from plant life. More about this will be explained in Chapter 3.

 **The carbon-eating and oxygen-producing plankton in the oceans**. If the oceans absorb too much carbon from global warming, they become acidic—specifically carbonic acid. This acidity will eventually kill some or all of the carbon-eating and oxygen-producing plankton. If we kill off these necessary plankton, we will find ourselves with insufficient oxygen in a world no one will be able to endure.

---

[11] Wikipedia contributors. "Ocean acidification." *Wikipedia, The Free Encyclopedia.* Accessed December 12, 2016. http://en.wikipedia.org/wiki/Ocean_acidification

 The **carbon and methane-releasing volcanoes**. Sustained large-scale volcanic activity can drastically affect the environment. If the volcano is large enough, such as with a supervolcano, the eruption could actually cool the planet and create two or three years of nuclear winter. Such a development creates its own extinction-level destruction in the form of severe negative impacts on agriculture and other living systems.

The climate also has systems that produce, reflect, or absorb heat. These systems can also raise or lower global temperature. Some of the climate's heat-producing, reflecting, or absorbing systems and subsystems are:

 The total amount of **heat-increasing water vapor** in the atmosphere. Atmospheric water vapor is the most important human caused greenhouse gas increasing atmospheric temperature. The higher the temperature, the more water vapor escapes into the atmosphere from evaporation, turning this cycle into a vicious self-reinforcing positive feedback loop.[12]

 The total amount of **heat-increasing carbon and methane polluting the atmosphere** from our fossil fuel burning, fracking, big agribusiness, and other uses.

 The total area of **heat-reflecting white snow and ice cover** on the planet at any one time (known as the albedo effect). This includes the glaciers and massive Arctic and Antarctic ice packs that are heat-reflecting.

---

[12] Wikipedia contributors. "Positive feedback." *Wikipedia, The Free Encyclopedia.* Accessed December 12, 2016. http://en.wikipedia.org/wiki/Positive_feedback

Positive Feedback Loop Example

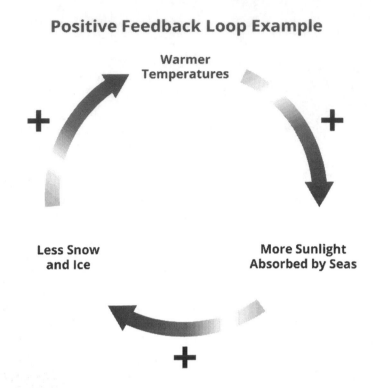

Warmer Temperatures

Less Snow and Ice

More Sunlight Absorbed by Seas

 The amount of **heat-increasing methane released by tundra and permafrost** when these methane pockets thaw.

 The amount of **heat-increasing methane released from methane clathrate crystals** from ocean bottom sediments as ocean temperatures rise. If this happens as quickly as scientists theorize it did millions of years ago, we're looking at extinction.

 The temporary **heat-reducing effects from volcanic soot** entering the atmosphere and reflecting some of the sun's heat.

Slight changes in the earth's axis position[13] that can also raise or lower the average global temperature range depending upon the angle of axis shift.[14] These temperature-affecting changes in the earth's axis are called **Milankovitch cycles**.[15] These 21,000 to 26,000 orbital cycles have an immense effect on global temperatures. Currently, we should be in a decreasing (cooling) phase of the cycle, but there are too many excess greenhouse gases in the atmosphere for the planet.[16]

Changes in the Earth's Axis

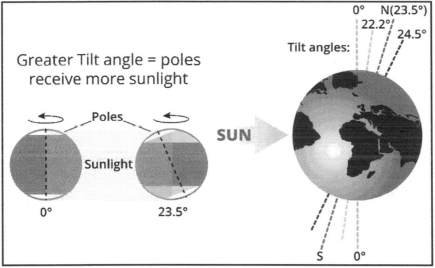

[13] Wikipedia contributors. "Climate change." *Wikipedia, The Free Encyclopedia*. http://en.wikipedia.org/wiki/Climate_change#Orbital_variations

[14] Shannon Hall, "NASA: Earth's poles are tipping thanks to climate change." April 8, 2016. *PBS.org*. http://www.pbs.org/newshour/rundown/nasa-earths-poles-are-tipping-thanks-to-climate-change/

[15] Wikipedia contributors. "Milankovitch cycles." *Wikipedia, The Free Encyclopedia*. Accessed December 12, 2016. https://en.wikipedia.org/wiki/Milankovitch_cycles

[16] "Milankovitch Cycles." *OSS Foundation*, accessed January 20, 2017. http://ossfoundation.us/projects/environment/global-warming/milankovitch-cycles

What is climate destabilization?

Now that you have a quick overview of some of the systems within the climate and how they work to increase or decrease global temperature, it's time to look at the climate reacting as a unified whole system.

The global climate system or its key subsystem processes can quickly move from one fairly stable state of dynamic balance and equilibrium into a new transitional state of instability and greater unpredictability. Eventually the global climate will settle at a new, but different, stable state of dynamic equilibrium and balance, but it will be at a new level and range (a dynamic equilibrium is not static or unchanging; it varies within a range of some climate quality, e.g., average temperature, average humidity). The preceding suggests that a useful and accurate definition for climate destabilization would be:

> "A transitional state of escalating global climate instability. This state is characterized by greater unpredictability, which lasts until the global climate eventually finds a new and different stable state of dynamic equilibrium and balance at some different level of temperature and other climate qualities from what it has held for hundreds or thousands of years." —Alexei Turchin, *The Structure of the Global Catastrophe*

The three degrees of climate destabilization

Climate destabilization can be said to come in three degrees. The three degrees defined below help individuals and organizations better understand the *relative* boundary ranges and levels of threat that is occurring or will occur based on measured increases in global warming. The temperature, carbon ppm, and loss or cost levels described below for each degree of climate destabilization are not hard and rigid boundaries, but boundary ranges designed to help you think about a set of related consequence intensities closely associated with that degree of climate destabilization. The temperature, carbon, cost, and loss boundary levels below may be modified by future research.

The three degrees and definitions for climate destabilization are:

1. *Catastrophic climate destabilization* is associated with a measurement of carbon 400-450 ppm. At the estimated current 1.2 Celsius (2.2° Fahrenheit) of temperature increase, we are already in the beginning stages of catastrophic climate destabilization. The *eventual* temperature *range* associated with catastrophic climate destabilization will be an increase in average global temperature of about 2.7° Celsius (4.9° Fahrenheit). When global warming-caused storms, floods, seasonal disruption, wildfires, and droughts begin to cost a nation 30 to 100 billion dollars per incident to repair, we will have reached the level of catastrophic climate destabilization. We are already in this phase of climate destabilization. Hurricane Sandy in New York cost the United States between 50 and 60 billion dollars to repair.

2. *Irreversible climate destabilization* is associated with a measurement beginning around carbon 425 ppm and going up to about carbon 550-600 ppm. The eventual temperature range associated with triggering irreversible climate destabilization is an increase in average global temperature of 2.2°-2.7° Celsius (4°-4.9° Fahrenheit) to 4° Celsius (7.2° Fahrenheit).

Irreversible climate destabilization occurs when we have moved away from the relatively stable dynamic equilibrium of temperature and other key weather conditions, which we have experienced during the hundreds of thousands of years of our previous cyclical Ice Ages. Once a new dynamic equilibrium finally stabilizes for the climate in these carbon ppm ranges, we will have crossed from catastrophic climate destabilization into irreversible climate destabilization.

Irreversible climate destabilization is a new average global temperature range and a set of destabilizing climate consequences we most likely will never recover from—or that could take hundreds or even thousands of years to correct or re-balance. Irreversible climate destabilization will eventually cost the nations of the world hundreds of trillions of dollars.

3. *Extinction-level climate destabilization.* Extinction-level climate destabilization as defined here is associated with beginning around the measurement of carbon parts per million in the atmosphere in the range of 600 ppm or more. The eventual temperature range associated with extinction-level climate destabilization is an increase in average global temperature of 5° to 6° Celsius (9° to 10.8° Fahrenheit).

Extinction-level climate destabilization is also defined as the eventual extinction of approximately up to half or more of the species on earth and most, if not all, of humanity. This occurs when the climate destabilizes to a level where the human species and/or other critical human support species can no longer successfully exist. Extinction-level climate destabilization has occurred several times previously during Earth's evolution.

Extinction-level climate destabilization will cost the nations of the world hundreds of trillions of dollars and potentially billions of lives—maybe the survival of the human species itself. There is a possibility that extinction-level climate destabilization may never correct or re-balance itself to some new equilibrium level. If the climate were able to correct or re-balance itself from this level of destabilization, it could take hundreds, thousands, or even hundreds of thousands of years.

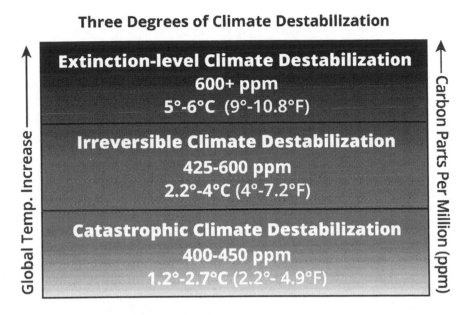

To make matters worse, every time we enter a new level of climate destabilization, the frequency, severity, and scale of global warming consequences will increase and everything becomes more unpredictable.

Today's climate destabilization can become a fatal threat to our future

Our global climate has held many different, relatively stable states over its 4.5-billion-year history. For hundreds of thousands of years, our planet's climate has moved within a fairly stable range of dynamic equilibrium, known as the cycle of Ice Ages.[17] This is an alternating pattern of an Ice Age, followed by a period of receding ice.

Humanity has flourished since the last Ice Age because of the warmer, agriculture-friendly temperatures and lack of glacial ice cover. As our current global climate moves into a human-caused destabilization period (from its previously stable state of the Ice Age to non-Ice Age cyclical periods) and into a new

[17] Wikipedia contributors. "Ice age." *Wikipedia, The Free Encyclopedia.* Accessed December 12, 2016. https://en.wikipedia.org/wiki/Ice_age

state of dynamic equilibrium, many rapid changes are occurring. These changes are characterized, in part, by droughts, floods, wildfires, superstorms, and the changing of previously established seasonal weather patterns. These changes are now also occurring with increasing unpredictability as well as with greater magnitude and frequency because of our continually escalating temperature.

We are already experiencing major changes in rainfall and snowfall, with either too much or too little at one time. These transitional conditions will remain unstable or worsen until we have completed the transition to a new, more stable, climate temperature equilibrium and range.

The long-term "good" news is that unless we hit irreversible global warming, sooner or later a destabilized global climate will seek to establish equilibrium at some new level of temperature and other climate quality states. A stable climate is generally always better than an unstable climate when it comes to our overall global climate. But . . . any new equilibrium we eventually arrive at *may not* be friendly to us as humans.

Fueled by increasing population and human-caused global warming, we have already radically increased the destabilization of our climate and our average global temperature. The climate destabilization process is already increasing the rates of reef collapse, desertification, deforestation, coastline loss, wildfires, droughts, superstorms, floods, productive soil degradation, growing season changes, water pollution, and species extinction.

It is possible[18] we may soon tip the climate into a new, fairly stable equilibrium quite unlike the 12,000-year Ice Age cycles we have been experiencing for hundreds of thousands of years. The very bad news is that billions of humans could soon be suffering and dying because this climate destabilization will

[18]Jeremy D. Shakun, Peter U. Clark, Feng He, Nathaniel A. Lifton, Zhengyu Liu, & Bette L. Otto-Bliesner. "Regional and global forcing of glacier retreat during the last deglaciation." *Nature Communications*, 5, no. 8059 (2015). doi: DOI: 10.1038/ncomms9059

also destabilize our global financial, political, agricultural, and social systems.

Now that you understand what global warming and climate destabilization are, there is a simple one-click action you can take to help improve understanding of what we are actually up against. Click here[19] to learn more about why the language you use when talking about global warming is critical.

Your next vaccination

Eventually we may be able to establish a new stable global average temperature and climate

The long-term, big-picture silver lining is that eventually, a destabilized global climate will seek to establish some new dynamic equilibrium. This means that if we keep carbon ppm and global warming below certain levels, we will eventually experience a new, stable climate and temperature equilibrium. Stable is generally much better than unstable when it comes to maintaining our global temperature, climate and civilization as we know it, but the new equilibrium might not be suitable for humans.

For a deeper perspective into the science of global warming and greenhouse gases

This is not required reading, but it is recommended. The heat absorbing and emitting process of the greenhouse gases in our atmosphere is the fundamental cause of the greenhouse effect. If you are a visual learner, see two great illustrations of the greenhouse effect by going to:

- https://en.wikipedia.org/wiki/Greenhouse_effect#/media/File:The_green_house_effect.svg

---

[19] Lawrence Wollersheim. "Pledge to Stop Saying 'climate change.'" *JobOneforHumanity.org*. Accessed December 20, 2016. http://www.joboneforhumanity.org/stop_saying_climate_change_pledge

- https://en.wikipedia.org/wiki/Greenhouse_effect#/m edia/File:Greenhouse_Effect.svg

What's next

There are many physical and financial consequences caused by escalating global warming. If you know the worst of them, you can prepare yourself, business, community, and nation and possibly avoid what is coming. The next chapter will describe the many current and future consequences of escalating global warming.

Summary

- Today's global warming emergency is not a natural disaster. It is a human-made disaster.

- A small increase in average global temperature will eventually create catastrophic change in the world.

- As climate destabilization continues, our local and national weather, as well as our global climate, will become much more unpredictable. Storms, droughts, floods, seasonal disruptions, sea level rise, and wildfires are going to become more severe, frequent, and occur at larger scales.

- As the global climate continues to destabilize, most people will not realize their lives are also destabilizing until it is too late.

- If we reach irreversible climate destabilization, it will go on much longer than our human life spans. It can last for centuries or thousands of years.

- A continually destabilizing climate will be the greatest disruptor of normal life that we have ever known— exceeding even our greatest wars.

PART 1, CHAPTER 3

HOW GLOBAL WARMING CONSEQUENCES AFFECT YOU

Overview:

- Large-scale changes to our atmosphere and environment that normally happen over thousands of years are now happening over decades.

- As our global atmosphere heats up and becomes warmer and more turbulent from fossil fuel burning and its greenhouse gas effect, our personal, business, and national lives will soon become more turbulent in many new ways.

- We could soon face a situation similar to the Paleocene–Eocene Thermal Maximum extinction event —a massive methane release that occurred 55 million years ago and killed roughly 70% of all life on the planet. We could face a similar event once we reach a 5° Celsius (9° Fahrenheit) temperature increase.

- Once temperatures surpass a 6° Celsius (10.8° Fahrenheit) increase, the ocean phytoplankton respon-sible for producing 50-80% of the atmosphere's breathable air will begin halting oxygen production and we will run out of breathable air.

In this chapter, we will present the most destructive consequences of global warming and the sequence in which some of them will likely unfold. This list of unfolding consequences will provide critical early warning signals that every prudent person should be monitoring.

Month-by-month and year-by-year, the consequences of global warming will increasingly:

a. cut into your personal, business, and national budgets,

b. change your normal day-to-day life and work in negative ways, and

c. destroy many plans for your future.

Although the list of global warming consequences is scary, there is still hope to avert the worst of it. The unhappy vision of future consequences you see unfolding occurs *only if* we fail to act immediately using effective strategies like those offered in the Job One For Humanity Plan in Part 2.

Global warming consequences across climate, human, and biological systems

Increased heat

 Human-caused carbon and methane pollution of the atmosphere from the burning of fossil fuels causes global warming. This carbon and methane pollution process traps more of the sun's solar energy in the form of heat inside our atmosphere. This increased atmospheric heat means more heat waves and many more 100+ degree days annually. During the growing season, having more than 10 days with 100+ degree temperatures is catastrophic for many of the world's five key food staples (corn, wheat, rice, soybeans, potatoes).

In many of the warmer climates, regular temperatures of 46° to 51° Celsius (115° to 125° degrees Fahrenheit) will become commonplace. During the hottest summer days in some traditionally hot places, temperatures could rise as high as 71° Celsius (160° Fahrenheit) within just decades.

What we are *not* talking about here are the large-scale changes to our atmosphere, seasons, weather, and environment that happen *normally* over thousands of years. These large-scale changes are now happening over frighteningly shorter time periods, such as decades!

It's important to understand how increasing heat will affect us personally. For instance, for every degree of Celsius temperature increase, global food production will drop 10% in many southern areas. Meanwhile the human population will continue to soar toward 9 billion.

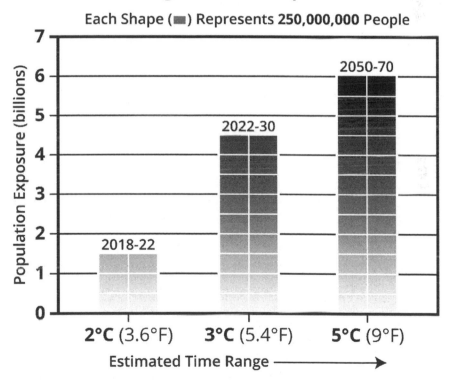

Growing Heat Wave Exposure

Each Shape (■) Represents 250,000,000 People

As we approach 2° Celsius (3.6° Fahrenheit) of global warming-caused heat increase, 1.5 billion people will be exposed to heat waves each year. At a 3° Celsius (5.4° Fahrenheit) increase, the number of heat wave exposures triples to 4.5 billion. At a 5° Celsius (9° Fahrenheit) increase, 6 billion people will be exposed. Click here[20] to see a 30-second animation called Earth's Long-Term Warming Trend, 1880-2015.

Droughts

Droughts are due to increased heat and reduced moisture over prolonged periods of time. There *will be* an increased probability and intensity of droughts. As the climate warms, experts estimate drought conditions may increase by 66 percent. Severe droughts are expected in Europe, but Africa will receive the worst of it. Less rainfall is also likely in mid-latitude and subtropical arid and semi-arid regions. For more information, read "California's Drought Could Continue for Centuries."[21]

Desertification

Desertification (the process of greener areas turning into deserts) is also caused by the increased long-term heat of global warming. It is aggravated by soil and vegetation loss. Semi-arid and sub-humid areas will likely endure a future of irreversible barrenness caused by global warming's evapotranspiration[22] and the accompanying decrease in rainfall. For more information, read "95% of Glaciers in Tibetan Plateau Have Receded."[23]

---

[20] "Earth's Long-Term Warming Trend, 1880-2015." YouTube video. 0:30, posted by "NASA.gov," January 20, 2016. https://www.youtube.com/watch?v=gGOzHVUQCw0

[21] Jacob Margolis. "California's Drought Could Continue for Centuries." *Take Two*. September 15, 2016. http://www.scpr.org/programs/take-two/2016/09/15/52133/california-s-drought-could-continue-for-centuries/

[22] Wikipedia contributors. "Evapotranspiration." *Wikipedia, The Free Encyclopedia*. Accessed December 12, 2016. http://en.wikipedia.org/wiki/Evapotranspiration

[23] Seema Sharma. "95% of Glaciers in Tibetan Plateau Have Receded." *The Times of India*. June 17, 2016. http://timesofindia.indiatimes.com/home/environment/95-of-glaciers-on-Tibetan-plateau-receded/articleshow/52799320.cms

Fires and wildfires

The potential for more fires of every kind rises dramatically as the heat of escalating global warming turns forests around the world into kindling. Fueled by the ever-increasing, long-term heat drying out the land, the Earth will experience endless wildfires increasing in magnitude and frequency with each degree of temperature increase. For more information, read "Wildfires: A Symptom of Climate Change."[24]

Jet stream disruption

Shifting jet streams will act to significantly change long-established weather patterns. This is already being witnessed in many areas of the world where the normal rains, snowfall, and seasonal temperatures are becoming more unpredictable and atypical.

In what may sound like a paradox, global warming will also produce cold waves in some areas due to changing location of jet streams and ocean currents. In some areas, winter storms have already become more frequent and intense.

At a 4° Celsius (7.2° Fahrenheit) increase, the atmospheric circulation of our jet streams is significantly affected. Jet streams commonly found in the mid latitudes are predicted to shift polewards by 1 or 2 degrees latitude in both hemispheres. For more background information or examples, click here to read "'Arctic amplification' to blame for Greenland's ice melt."[25]

---

[24] Michael Finneran. "Wildfires: A Symptom of Climate Change." *NASA.gov*. September 24, 2010. https://www.nasa.gov/topics/earth/features/wildfires.html

[25] Ben Thompson. "'Arctic amplification' to blame for Greenland's ice melt, scientists say." *The Christian Science Monitor*. June 12, 2016. http://www.csmonitor.com/Science/2016/0612/Arctic-amplification-to-blame-for-Greenland-s-ice-melt-scientists-say

Shrinking sea ice and ice shelves

 As average global temperature rises, temperatures will rise almost twice as fast in the world's northernmost and polar regions. Because of this, our ice caps are also melting at an *unprecedented* rate. For more information, see this video on the disappearance of Arctic sea ice[26] and this visualization of Arctic ice melt over the past 25 years.[27]

If the ice shelves on Greenland and Antarctica melt, sea levels could become more than 10-20 feet higher (3-6 meters) in 2100 than they are today. This would flood low-lying areas such as New York City's Lower Manhattan, Miami, and Bangladesh. This sea level rise would also be perilous for many low-elevation countries and inhabited islands.

Additionally, melting sea ice sheets also disrupt oceanic circulation patterns because they are made of fresh water, and fresh water is less dense than salt water. Because of the impact of melting fresh water on the Atlantic's meridional overturning circulation pattern,[28] Europe may become colder. (This meridional overturning circulation drives cold saltwater into the deep ocean while drawing warm water up and northward.) As the ocean currents change, they also can contribute to the shifting of jet streams and the altering of normal storm patterns.

As soon as a 2° Celsius (3.6° Fahrenheit) increase is reached, the extent of Arctic sea ice in September falls by 43% compared to long-term averages. At a 4° Celsius (7.2° Fahrenheit) increase, the Arctic would be nearly ice-free in summer. This

---

[26] "Older Arctic Sea Ice Disappearing." YouTube video. 2:35, posted by "NASA Goddard," October 28, 2016. https://www.youtube.com/watch?v=Vj1G9gqhkYA

[27] "Watch 25 Years of Arctic Sea Ice Disappear in 1 Minute." YouTube video. 1:04, posted by "climatecentral.org," December 15, 2015. https://www.youtube.com/watch?v=Fw7GfNR5PLA

[28] National Oceanic and Atmospheric Administration. "Meridional Overturning Circulation." *NOAA.gov.* Last modified November 10, 2016. http://www.aoml.noaa.gov/phod/research/moc/namoc/

could occur as early as 2035-2050. Rising sea levels will displace up to 350 million people, making the Middle East's 21st century refugee crisis seem insignificant by comparison. For more information, read "Historical Data Shows Arctic Melt of Last Two Decades is 'Unprecedented'."[29]

Shrinking glaciers and snowpack

The glaciers around the world are shrinking because of the increasing heat due to global warming. In the U.S., Montana's Glacier National Park has deteriorated over the last seven decades from 150 to just 35 glaciers.

With the approaching 2° Celsius (3.6° Fahrenheit) heat increase, glaciers will decline in global volume by as much as 55%, and snow cover in the northern hemisphere will decrease by 7%. (This excludes those on the Greenland and Antarctic ice sheets and on Antarctica's periphery.) At 4° Celsius (7.2° Fahrenheit) of heat increase, glaciers decline in global volume by as much as 85%, and snow cover in the northern hemisphere decreases by 25%.

Once most of the white sea ice, glaciers, and white snowpack melts, there is another serious consequence lurking in our dark future. The white of the glaciers and the snowpack helps reflect the heat of the sunlight back into space (the albedo effect).[30] This helps to *cool* the Earth.

But if the glaciers, ice caps, and snowpack melt, the only heat reflector left for sunlight is the ocean. The ocean, unfortunately, is much darker than white ice and snow. Darker colors do not reflect the sunlight's heat; they absorb it, further warming the

---

[29] Bob Berwyn, "Historical Data Shows Arctic Melt of Last Two Decades Is 'Unprecedented'," *InsideClimate News*, August 18, 2016.
https://insideclimatenews.org/news/18082016/arctic-sea-ice-melting-historical-data-noaa-climate-change-global-warming-greenhouse-gases

[30] Wikipedia contributors. "Albedo." *Wikipedia, The Free Encyclopedia*. Accessed December 12, 2016. https://en.wikipedia.org/wiki/Albedo

Earth in another self-reinforcing loop of ever-increasing heat. For more information, read "Crisis On High."[31]

Melting tundra and permafrost

The Arctic is warming twice as fast as the rest of the world. This warming in the far north can create another vicious, self-reinforcing cycle and positive feedback loop. This methane is 25-100 times more powerful as a global-warming greenhouse gas than carbon dioxide from fossil fuel burning.

When considering the methane problem, do not forget that the increasing methane releases from fracking and big agribusiness are dangerous on their own. However, when adding in new methane releases from loss of tundra and permafrost, this multiplying factor of methane versus carbon must once again be factored in. With methane 25 to 100 times more powerful than carbon, rising methane pollution may soon become as problematic as carbon. For more information, see here.[32]

Spreading of diseases and and pandemics

Increased heat from global warming in the atmosphere will spread more tropical diseases[33] to northern and southern areas as well as higher altitudes where they have never been before—and where most of the population has no immunity. These are tropical diseases like West Nile Disease, Zika, Rift Valley Fever, Dengue Fever, Chikungunya, *Cryptococcus Gattii* Fungus, and Chagas Disease,

---

[31] Matthew Carney. "Crisis On High." Australian Broadcasting Corporation. July 25, 2016. http://www.abc.net.au/news/2016-07-25/climate-change-the-third-pole-under-threat/7657672

[32] University of Cambridge. "Emissions from melting permafrost could cost $43 trillion." *ScienceDaily*. www.sciencedaily.com/releases/2015/09/150921112731.htm

[33] Greg Mercer. "The link between Zika and climate change." *The Atlantic*. February 24, 2016. http://www.theatlantic.com/health/archive/2016/02/zika-and-climate-change/470643/

all of which are rapidly moving north and appearing in the news on a regular basis.

 Tropical diseases rapidly spreading north and south are due to migrating humans, animals, and insects trying to escape their heat and/or water-stressed ecosystems. Other diseases likely to spread due to global warming are avian flu, cholera, plague, ebola, and tuberculosis.

There are also many infectious organisms stored in ancient sea ice and glaciers that will be released into the water system as this ice melts.[34] These may be infections for which we currently have no antibodies or medicines. Spreading diseases, both old and new, can also set the stage for global pandemics. For more information, see this warning from the White House.[35]

Increased water vapor

 For every 0.6° Celsius (1.08° Fahrenheit) rise in average global temperature, the atmosphere's capacity to hold water vapor grows by 4%. This means as global warming and water vapor increases, storms will pour forth at greater and greater magnitude.

Water vapor in the atmosphere increases every time more heat evaporates from standing water in rivers, oceans, and lakes. We are already seeing unusually heavy rains occurring at times never encountered before. More than 170 extreme weather events struck America between 1980 and 2014, disrupting daily life. Extreme weather events are defined as weather at the extremes of the historical distribution or within the *most*

---

[34] Jonathan Gornall. "Unpredictable weather raises 'zombie' diseases from the ground." *The National.* August 28, 2016. http://www.thenational.ae/world/unpredictable-weather-raises-zombie-diseases-from-the-ground

[35] Suzanne Goldenberg. "Climate change threat to public health worse than polio, White House warns." *The Guardian.* April 4, 2016. https://www.theguardian.com/environment/2016/apr/04/climate-change-public-health-threat-white-house report

unusual 10 percent in that location's recorded weather history. Extreme weather by definition is unusual, severe or unseasonal—events often thought of as close to or beyond hundred-year storm records. Eventually, increasing water vapor will become the largest indirect human-caused factor increasing global warming.

Global warming's increasing atmospheric heat energy, along with the increased water vapor, is also available for use in and by the planet's other weather systems. In particular, warmer waters are causing more hurricanes and cyclones. Global warming creates warmer ocean water, which again leads to greater evaporation. This helps to not just "prime" the creation of hurricanes and cyclones, but also to maintain their strength once they form. The destructive power of hurricanes has increased by roughly 50% in the last 30 years, a time frame closely aligned with the rising temperature of the oceans caused by global warming. For more information, read this article on 2016's Hurricane Matthew.[36]

Flooding

Many areas will become wetter due to global warming. The high latitudes and equatorial Pacific are likely to see more rainfall. Increased regular flooding represents one of the most dangerous risks to us because it destroys our crops, homes, and businesses for great lengths of time, if not permanently.

While our already existing 1.2° Celsius (2.2° Fahrenheit) temperature increase over pre-industrial levels might sound manageable, it alone will raise sea levels by at least 3 feet (0.9 meter). This will flood some of the world's richest agricultural lands and river deltas—as well as drown entire nations.

---

[36] Joe Romm. "Hurricane Matthew is super strong—because of climate change." *ThinkProgress*. October 5, 2016. https://thinkprogress.org/global-warming-hurricanes-1c3a1ddca521#.t9qojtlbe

Due to seawater salination and intrusion, many rich lands and river deltas will become unusable. For example, in Bangladesh, a 3-foot (0.9 meter) sea level rise will inundate about 15% of the land and threaten more than a million hectares of agricultural production. Additionally, the Mekong River Commission warns that a 3-foot (0.9 meter) sea level rise will wipe out nearly 40% of the Mekong Delta.

Just a 3-foot (0.9 meter) sea level rise will flood one-fourth of the Nile Delta, forcing more than 10% of Egypt's population (9.3 million people) from their homes. Because nearly half of Egypt's crops, including wheat, bananas, and rice, are grown in the delta, starvation and malnutrition will accelerate.

The damage caused by just 1° Celsius (1.8° Fahrenheit) of warming is beyond management and remediation for many nations and peoples. Even this low-level increase will quickly create more failed states among the most vulnerable nations.

For more information on the costs of flooding and sea level rise, see this article on the exponential rise of flooding costs[37] and this article on which areas in the United States will be hit hardest.[38]

Rising sea levels

 Rising sea levels are caused by factors such as the polar ice caps and glaciers melting, as well as thermal expansion. Thermal expansion occurs when global warming warms the seas. Because warmer water expands and takes up more space than cooler water, the sea's surface level rises.

Of the three causes of rising sea levels, the melting of the polar ice caps and glaciers represents the greatest threat. The

---

[37] Zahra Hirji. "Flood damage costs will rise faster than sea levels, study says." *InsideClimate News*. March 1, 2016. https://insideclimatenews.org/news/29022016/flood-damage-sea-level-rise-potsdam-institute-copenhagen-denmark

[38] Benjamin Strauss. "Sea level rise upping ante on 'sunny day' floods.' *ClimateCentral.org*. October 17, 2016. http://www.climatecentral.org/news/climate-change-increases-sunny-day-floods-20784

National Snow and Ice Data Center says that if all glaciers melted today (about 5,773,000 cubic miles of water in ice caps, glaciers, and permanent snow), the seas would steadily rise about 230 feet (70 meters) over a period of several centuries or less.[39]

On a considerably shorter time scale, a recent study by a team working with James Hansen (the scientist who first warned us about global warming 30 years ago) says that by 2050 we could see up to 10 feet (3 meters) of sea level rise.[40] This well-respected new study contradicts the 3-foot (.09 meters) maximum sea level rise by 2100 that was previously predicted by the UN's Intergovernmental Panel On Climate Change (IPCC).[41]

Rising sea levels will create huge new costs and necessitate the complete relocation of water and sewage treatment plants, refineries, electric, nuclear, and fossil fuel power stations, toxic chemical storage sites, hospitals, homes, and other businesses and institutions located near or at sea level. Low-lying or coastal communities will suffer unbearable costs[42] as well as the threat of complete destruction as the sea levels continue to rise steadily.

With the approaching 2° Celsius (3.6° Fahrenheit) heat increase, 30 million people will be affected by flooding and sea level rise each year. At 3° Celsius (5.4° Fahrenheit) of heat increase, about 60 million people a year will be affected. At 5° Celsius (9°

---

[39] "All About Glaciers." National Snow and Ice Data Center. Accessed December 10, 2016. https://nsidc.org/cryosphere/glaciers.

[40] Hansen, J., Sato, M., Hearty, P., Ruedy, R., Kelley, M., Masson-Delmotte, V., Russell, G., Tselioudis, G., Cao, J., Rignot, E., Velicogna, I., Tormey, B., Donovan, B., Kandiano, E., von Schuckmann, K., Kharecha, P., Legrande, A. N., Bauer, M., and Lo, K.-W. "Ice melt, sea level rise and superstorms: evidence from paleoclimate data, climate modeling, and modern observations that 2 °C global warming could be dangerous." *Atmos.Chem.Phys.net*, 16, (2015): doi:10.5194/acp-16-3761-2016, 2016.

[41] Intergovernmental Panel on Climate Change, ed., "Sea Level Change," in *Climate Change 2013 - The Physical Science Basis*. Cambridge University Press, Cambridge, UK and New York, NY (2013): 1137–1216, doi:10.1017/ CBO9781107415324.026

[42] Patrick Clark. Rising sea levels could cost U.S. homeowners close to $1 trillion." *Bloomberg.com*. August 2, 2016. https://www.bloomberg.com/news/articles/2016-08-02/rising-sea-levels-could-cost-u-s-homeowners-close-to-1-trillion

Fahrenheit) of heat increase, about 120 million people a year will be affected. To read how this will affect future generations, read this article on accelerating sea level rise.[43]

Toxic air pollution

 When we burn fossil fuels we create smog and soot, which is commonly known as air pollution. Some fossil fuel burning—especially coal burning—also releases toxic heavy metals, radiation, and other chemical toxins. Of the fossil fuels, coal is also the largest single source of airborne mercury poisoning.

Air pollution is the one consequence of global warming that often gets the least attention, yet in many ways it has the most impact on a personal level. This is because air pollution from fossil fuel burning is a slow and invisible cause of painful respiratory disease and death. It is also responsible for aggravating many other diseases.

Directly or indirectly, air pollution causes approximately 11 to 13% (about 1 in 8) of all deaths globally each year. According to a recent World Health Organization survey, 40 percent of deaths linked to outdoor air pollution are from heart disease; another 40 percent from stroke; 11 percent from chronic obstructive pulmonary disease (COPD); 6 percent from lung cancer,[44] and 3 percent from acute lower respiratory infections in children.

China has the most air pollution fatalities with nearly 1.4 million deaths a year. India has 645,000 and Pakistan has 110,000. To put this in perspective, air pollution kills more people each year than malaria and AIDS combined!

---

[43] PBS Newshour. "What do rising sea levels mean for future generations?" *PBS.org*. February 23, 2016. http://www.pbs.org/newshour/bb/what-do-rising-sea-levels-mean-for-future-generations-2/

[44] Maria Cheng. "WHO agency: air pollution causes cancer." *NBC News.com*. October 17, 2013. http://www.nbcnews.com/health/health-news/who-agency-air-pollution-causes-cancer f8C11410692

Because air pollution supports weed growth, it is also a major accelerator of allergy attacks. It has been directly linked to asthma. Within the past 20 years, there has been an observed doubling of pediatric asthma prevalence.

Air pollution also exacerbates pre-existing health conditions such as bronchitis, emphysema, and chronic obstructive pulmonary disease (COPD). Air pollution from fossil fuel burning also dramatically increases national and international health costs, and the burden for those increased health costs falls squarely upon individual taxpayers. Paul Epstein, with the Harvard School of Public Health, found that the hidden costs of burning fossil fuel coal in the U.S. alone to be $345 billion per year!

They calculated these costs based on public health impacts, pollution, toxic waste, and climate disruptions to people's normal lives and work. When you consider the costs of air pollution the coal industry is currently dumping onto the public without consequence, there is no offsetting net value in the electricity the coal provides!

If global warming and pollution caused by fossil fuel burning did nothing more than kill millions of people every year, that alone would make fossil fuel use a completely untenable energy generation source. Unfortunately, it does much more damage, as our continued exploration of the consequences of global warming will show. For more information, read this article on countries hit hardest by air pollution[45] and this article on the biggest threats to humanity.[46]

---

[45] Chris Mooney and Brady Dennis. "WHO: Global air pollution is worsening, and poor countries are being hit the hardest." *The Washington Post.* May 12, 2013. https://www.washingtonpost.com/news/energy-environment/wp/2016/05/12/who-global-air-pollution-is-worsening-and-poor-countries-are-being-hit-the-hardest/?utm_term=.8da44d4f601e

[46] Gabriel Samuels. "Stephen Hawking says pollution and 'stupidity' still biggest threats to mankind." *Independent.* June 28, 2016. http://www.independent.co.uk/news/science/stephen-hawking-pollution-stupidity-artifical-intelligence-warfare-biggest-threats-mankind-a7106916.html

Less food, less water, costing more

 The food consequences of escalating global warming are high and could quickly result in chaos in the world food economy. A Stanford University study analyzed the historical relationship between temperature and corn yields from 600 U.S. counties. The report concluded that each 1° Celsius (1.8° Fahrenheit) rise in temperature above the growing-season norm dropped yields 17%.

Rice, wheat, and the world's other food staples are also vulnerable to global warming's higher temperatures. With each degree of temperature rise and the consequent crop-withering heat waves, food prices will be driven up to unprecedented levels.

This will also cause shrinking harvests, malnutrition, starvation, and famine, which will increase disease, death, and conflict. As food prices and shortages grow, economically or politically unstable countries will descend into chaos. Nations that still retain good water and food resources will probably be unwilling to share these vital commodities or accept the tens or hundreds of millions of "climagees" (climate refugees) who will desperately be seeking new homes.

"The Syrian conflict was preceded by the worst long-term drought and crop failures since civilization began in the region, resulting in 800,000 people losing their livelihoods by 2009, and 2-3 million being driven into extreme poverty." (From *Climate Reality Check* by David Spratt.[47])

The Syrian drought initially triggered a migration of about 1,500,000+ climagees into Europe. Europe as a whole is struggling to deal with them. The Syrian and other Middle

---

[47] David Spratt. "Climate Reality Check." *Breakthrough - National Centre for Climate Restoration.* March 2016.
http://media.wix.com/ugd/148cb0_4868352168ba49d89358a8a01bc5f8of.pdf

Eastern drought climagees are only a tiny preview of the migration tidal wave that is coming.

With the approaching 2° Celsius (3.6° Fahrenheit) of temperature increase, 1.5 billion people will be exposed to increased water stress. At 3° Celsius (5.4° Fahrenheit) of temperature increase, there will be significant negative consequences on production of major crops including corn, rice, and wheat. In temperate and tropical regions, 1.75 billion people will be exposed to increased water stress, and there will be 5.7 million square kilometers (2.2 million square miles) of cropland decline. For more information on water stress, see this article on which areas will be hit hardest[48] and this article on worsening water pollution.[49]

At a 4° Celsius (7.2° Fahrenheit) increase, it will be hot and humid enough for parts of the year in some areas to compromise day-to-day human work activities such as working outdoors or growing food. At a 5° Celsius (9° Fahrenheit) increase, about 2 billion people will be exposed to increased water stress, and 7.6 million km² (2.9 million mi²) of cropland will decline. By the end of the century, some states in the U.S. Midwest, Southeast, and lower Great Plains risk up to a 70 percent loss in average annual crop yields.

Mass climagee migrations

The previously mentioned worsening global warming conditions combined with dwindling resources will lead not only to the massive migration of animals and insects, but also to massive waves of global warming and climate destabilization-driven human migration. These

[48] Suzanne Goldenburg. "Global water shortages to deliver 'severe hit' to economies, World Bank warns." *The Guardian*. May 3, 2016.
https://www.theguardian.com/environment/2016/may/03/climate-change-water-shortage-middle-east-asia-africa-world-bank

[49] Chris Mooney. "Air and water problems are worsening on a global scale, U.N. says." *The Washington Post*. May 23, 2016. https://www.washingtonpost.com/news/energy-environment/wp/2016/05/23/the-pace-of-environmental-damage-is-intensifying-across-the-globe-u-n-agency-says/?utm_term=.1fad1f5490ce&wpisrc=nl_daily202&wpmm=1

individuals will be the new climagees.

Millions will migrate at a 2° Celsius (3.6° Fahrenheit) temperature increase, hundreds of millions at a 4 degrees increase, and eventually billions of climagees will be desperately on the move as we approach a 5°-6° Celsius (9°-10.8° Fahrenheit) temperature increase. They will seek out already overcrowded urban areas in the northernmost countries of the world.

These mass migrations will cost nations more of their resources and cause continual increases in citizen taxes to deal with the ever-growing influxes of new climagees. The northernmost nations will face a compassion dilemma. The more climagees they allow in and support, the more will come in a self-reinforcing cycle that will further diminish emergency resources and budgets for both their own population and the other newly arriving climagees.

Problems with cultural integration will also cause fear and tensions with the nation's existing citizens. Growing tensions between the indigenous national citizens and the new climagees have already resulted in nationalist backlashes all over Europe.

Today, global warming-related migrations are only in their earliest stages. As the climagee migration pressure continues to increase, tensions will also arise among the wealthy northern countries that do not do their fair share and allow entry for as many climagees as other wealthy northern countries allow. The growing tensions of climagee migration into vulnerable areas and nations will also likely lead to more conflicts. For more information, read this article on an Alaskan community[50] and this article on a Louisiana community[51] forced to migrate due to flooding.

---

[50] Victoria Herrrmann. "America's climate refugee crisis has already begun." *LA Times.* January 25, 2016. http://www.latimes.com/opinion/op-ed/la-oe-0125-herrmann-climate-refugees-20160125-story.html

Conflict and wars

 An ecological crisis such as global warming and violence are inextricably entangled. Nations suffering from climate catastrophes, food shortages and/or crop failure, water shortages, or mass migrations become highly vulnerable to security challenges, including regional panic, instability, and aggression. In another deadly self-reinforcing positive feedback loop, diminished quantities of food, water, and arable land invariably further increase *mass migrations*, global security threats, conflicts, and war.

Escalating global warming started out as an ecological threat. It has now become the *world's greatest security threat and threat multiplier*. Over time, one of the most costly consequences of escalating global warming will be the conflicts and wars it will create, intensify, or prolong. As these global warming-induced migration, resource, and land conflicts expand or worsen, they can quickly escalate from conventional weapons and warfare to small-scale tactical nuclear weapons— possibly even full-scale nuclear war. For more information on the increasing tensions of armed conflict and global warming, read this article.[52]

Ocean acidification and marine death

 The oceans absorb roughly 30% of all human-caused carbon dioxide from the atmosphere. As global warming increases average temperature, the process of absorbing carbon dioxide increases both the average ocean temperature as well as the acidification of the

[51] Hannah Thomas-Peter. "Isle De Jean Charles: Louisiana community to be climate change refugees." *Sky News*. August 30, 2016. http://news.sky.com/story/isle-de-jean-charles-louisiana-community-to-be-climate-change-refugees-10556485

[52] Alejandro Dávila Fragoso. "The link between armed conflict and climate change just got a bit stronger." *ThinkProgress.org*. July 26, 2016. https://thinkprogress.org/the-link-between-armed-conflict-and-climate-change-just-got-a-bit-stronger-87193e5391da#.xmqq4bh1e

oceans. (Acidification is simply the ocean becoming more acidic from the absorbed carbon, creating carbonic acid.)

The reproductive cycles in many ocean species will be dramatically harmed by the combination of warmer oceans and ocean acidification. A strong connection has already been observed between ocean warming and increases in mortality rates, as well as declines in reproduction among seals, sea lions, and seabirds. The shells of most crustaceans (crabs, lobsters, shrimp, mussels, clams) are destroyed as acidification increases in the oceans. Because of this escalating ocean warming and ocean acidification, ocean fish food stocks will be dramatically reduced beyond their current threatened levels and remaining ocean fish food stocks will increase in price.

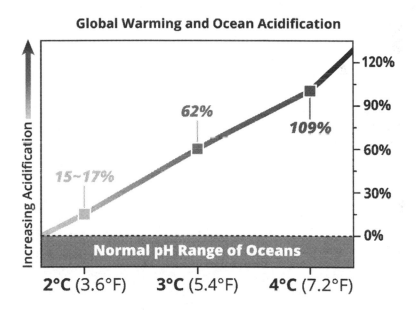

Global Warming and Ocean Acidification

At a 2° Celsius (3.6° Fahrenheit) increase, the oceans become more acidic with the surface ocean pH decreasing by 15-17%. (pH is a numeric scale used to specify the acidity or basicity [alkalinity] of a solution.) At a 3° Celsius (5.4° Fahrenheit) increase, ocean acidification is much greater, with surface pH decreasing up to 62%. At a 4° Celsius (7.2° Fahrenheit) increase, ocean acidification accelerates hugely, with surface pH decreasing up to 109%. For more information on ocean acidification, read this article about its effects on the Atlantic ocean [53] and this article on how it is already affecting phytoplankton.[54]

Loss of breathable air from phytoplankton

Ocean phytoplankton create oxygen that rises into our atmosphere and creates breathable air. Ocean phytoplankton are responsible for up to 50 to 80% of all the oxygen we breathe! One of the most critical longer-term consequences of ocean warming and ocean acidification is the reduction of ocean phytoplankton. These are living microalgae are also indispensable to the ocean's marine food cycle.

A study published in the Bulletin of Mathematical Biology calculated how unrestrained global warming could affect phytoplankton and thus the ocean's ability to generate breathable air. Their computer models looked at what would happen to phytoplankton's ability to photosynthesize at different temperatures. According to the Bulletin study, if global emissions continue unabated, and if the world's oceans warmed[55] by 6° Celsius (10.8° Fahrenheit), the phytoplankton would halt oxygen production! What this means is that if we cross over the 6° Celsius global warming tipping point, the oceans will stop producing breathable oxygen and we will run out of breathable air.[56]

---

[53] Sean Greene. "The damage wrought by acidic oceans hurts more than marine life and lasts longer than you think." *LA Times*. July 8, 2016. http://www.latimes.com/science/sciencenow/la-sci-sn-phytoplankton-acidic-oceans-20160708-snap-story.html

[54] Emily J. Gertz. "The Atlantic ocean is acidifying at a rapid rate." *TakePart*. February 3, 2016. http://www.takepart.com/article/2016/02/03/atlantic-ocean-now-acidifying-at-a-rapid-rate

[55] Taylor Hill. "The West Coast's massive algal bloom could be the toxic wave of the future." *TakePart*. June 19, 2015. http://www.takepart.com/article/2015/06/19/toxic-algal-bloom-climate-change-rising-water-west-coast

[56] Taylor Hill. "Report: the world will run out of breathable air unless carbon is cut." *TakePart*. December 5, 2015. http://www.takepart.com/article/2015/12/03/climate-change-oxygen-ocean

Destruction of ecosystems

Many of the world's critical ecosystems face catastrophic degradation due to the increasing heat of escalating global warming. As coral reefs bleach, deserts expand, soils become unproductive, and the oceans warm, we will lose the critical productivity of the ecosystems we depend upon for food and other critical resources we and other lifeforms need.

Loss of biodiversity

As our ecosystems degrade with escalating global warming, current animal habitats become inhospitable to increasing numbers of insect, aquatic, and other animal species. For example, animals that are entirely dependent on colder or cold ecosystems will move to more northerly ecosystems. This animal migration will lead to competitive encroachment upon other ecosystems and the possible displacement or elimination of other animals from their natural colder habitats.

If average temperatures rise more than 1.1° to 6.4° Celsius (2°-11.5° Fahrenheit), as much as 30 percent of all plant and animal species alive today risk extinction by or before 2050. Some biologists have already stated we are experiencing what is being called the beginning of the Sixth Great Extinction Event.[57]

Animal attacks

As animal habitats degrade or are lost, animals will be forced to migrate to new areas. In these new habitats, they often come into contact with humans. This in turn leads to an increase in animal attacks. For instance, we are already

---

[57] Nadia Drake. "Will humans survive the Sixth Great Extinction?" *National Geographic.* June 23, 2015. http://news.nationalgeographic.com/2015/06/150623-sixth-extinction-kolbert-animals-conservation-science-world/

seeing this happen with bears when residential development encroaches on urban-forest interfaces.

At a 2° Celsius (3.6° Fahrenheit) increase, many species and ecosystems with limited ability to adapt to higher temperatures will be subject to very high risks. At a 3° Celsius (5.4° Fahrenheit) increase, most small mammals without high ground to escape to will not be able to keep up with the rate of climate change. At a 4°Celsius (7.2° Fahrenheit) increase, wildlife and ecosystems will be hit by severe and widespread impacts, with substantial numbers of species going extinct.

Increased volcanic activity

The shifting weights of melting glaciers over the planet's surface can initiate episodes of volcanic activity. Sustained large-scale volcanic activity can have a catastrophic effect on human life. If the volcano is large enough, such as a supervolcano, the eruption could cool the planet and create two or three years of nuclear winter. Such a development creates its own extinction-level destruction in the form of severe negative impacts on agriculture and other living systems.

Tsunamis

Glacial ice sheets apply massive pressure to the surface beneath them. As glaciers melt from global warming, their massive weight decreases—lessening the total weight over the tectonic plates below them. As the tectonic plates move and shift, this unweighting can lead to volcanic activity and earthquakes. Whenever these tectonic plates move significantly, they are also capable of creating deadly tsunamis.

Methane time bomb, and extinction event

In addition to the many consequences listed above, there is one additional consequence that could rapidly turn into a mass extinction event. See more about this and the Paleocene–

Eocene Thermal Maximum (PETM) extinction event in Chapter 2 and Chapter 6.

This theory suggests that a self-reinforcing positive feedback loop between permafrost-melting methane emissions and warming of methane clathrate crystals on the bottom of the ocean created a massive and rapid global warming temperature surge. As the ocean temperatures rose, gigatons of frozen methane hydrate crystals trapped along the continental shelves of our oceans thawed. This caused a *sudden and dramatic* release of carbon into the atmosphere (from melted methane hydrate crystals.) This caused another sudden heat increase. As a result, roughly 70 percent of all life on the planet was killed off.

An extinction event of this scale happening today would decimate populations so completely that either there would be no survivors or there might be as few as 200 million surviving close to the poles. The onset of this PETM extinction event has been linked to an initial 5° Celsius (9° Fahrenheit) temperature increase and extreme changes in Earth's carbon-eating and carbon-releasing cycles. To read more about how today's carbon levels mimic those from about 56 million years ago, read this article.[58]

Financial losses and collapse

 If temperatures continue to rise as they are doing now and rise only as over "optimistically" projected by current global warming authorities until the turn-of-the-century:

a. Average global income will shrink by 23%.[59]

---

[58] Alister Doyle. "Carbon emissions highest in 66 million years, since dinosaur age." *Reuters.* March 21, 2016. http://www.reuters.com/article/us-climatechange-carbon-idUSKCN0WN1QR

[59] Ben Gruber. "Unmitigated climate change to shrink global economy by 23 percent, researchers find." *Reuters.* November 16, 2015. http://www.reuters.com/article/us-climatechange-climate-economy-idUSKCN0T524X20151116

b. U.S. gross domestic product per person will drop by 36%.[60]

c. Global warming will facilitate a massive transfer of value and wealth from the hotter parts of the earth to the cooler parts. At least initially, countries like Russia, Mongolia, Canada, and possibly the northernmost parts of the U.S. will see large economic benefits. Most of Europe will do slightly better even though parts of it will suffer severe droughts. The U.S. and China will do slightly worse, mostly because the southern and western parts of the United States will be in a heat and/or drought crisis. All of Africa, Asia, South America, and the Middle East will be economically ravaged.

d. Inflation will continually rise (reaching up to 100% in the final phases of the Climageddon Scenario).[61] This rising inflation is due to having to repair the ever-escalating, near continuous damage from ever-more global warming related natural disasters as they continue to expand across, local, regional, national and global areas. Repairing these continuous and escalating natural disasters will create an ever-increasing need for resources that will grow ever-scarcer. The needed repairs and the resource scarcity will continually push prices and inflation higher and higher. (More will be said about global warming-caused inflation in Chapter 8.)

The financial costs of global warming will go up with each rising degree of average global temperature. It is highly

---

[60] Kenneth Rapoza. "Climate change will be disastrous for these economies." *Forbes.* October 26, 2015. http://www.forbes.com/sites/kenrapoza/2015/10/26/climate-change-will-be-disastrous-for-these-economies/#246817eb4052

[61] Tim Garrett, interview by Alex Smith, *Radio Ecoshock*, October 19, 2011, transcript. http://www.ecoshock.org/downloads/climate2010/ES_Garrett_101119_LoFi.mp3

probable that global warming costs will not rise in a linear fashion, but more likely in a rapidly rising exponential curve.

The estimated differences in total global warming costs are derived from different inputs, assumptions, and computer models. As you will soon discover, no matter what estimates you choose to use, the escalating costs of global warming will put an unbearable, steadily increasing burden on the citizens and nations of the world. When you read these cost estimates, keep in mind that none of these estimates places any dollar value on the massive predicted loss of human life.

Obviously it will be horrendously costly to repair, rebuild, relocate, or construct for the first time both current and new infrastructure, homes, and businesses. The Stern Review done in 2006 estimated that the rising costs of escalating global warming will grow to 5% or more of the gross domestic product of all the nations on Earth. (Gross domestic product [GDP] is a monetary measure of the value of all goods and services produced in a given period of time [quarterly or yearly].)

This means that 5% of the the world's total gross domestic product will be lost to emergency recovery from global warming-related consequences. For an economic comparison and perspective, consider that the Great Depression of the 1930s in the United States was the result of *only a 4% loss* in U.S. gross domestic product.

Newer studies from 2015 project that if the average global temperature increase reaches 6° Celsius (10.8° Fahrenheit) by the end of the century, the nations of the world will be spending from 10% up to a possible 30% of their total gross domestic product recovering from an endless stream of mega global warming-related consequences and catastrophes on the final road to extinction. The current GDP of the world is about $80 trillion a year; by 2100 it may double or triple that. This means we could be spending one-third of the world's GDP in 2100—about $100 trillion a year—just to try to survive extinction from global warming.

If we are able to avoid global warming extinction, the total estimated costs of all related global warming destruction could be in the range of $400-$600 trillion—about eight years of the current total gross domestic product for every nation on Earth. To put this in perspective, this means that if we fail to successfully resolve global warming now, farther down the road we will have to dedicate 5 to 8 times the total current value of all annual global human productivity to try to recover from the global warming consequences.

Worse yet, that is only what we may have to pay if we are lucky. If we go into irreversible or extinction-level climate destabilization, what will the cost be then?

Additionally, all of the related financial costs of global warming-related catastrophes and emergencies will rapidly diminish any existing national emergency recovery safety nets. This will cause unthinkable suffering among those who are not prepared and who will consequently have no governmental safety net.

It is clear that no person, corporation or nation will be able to cope with these ever-increasing levels of economic losses caused by global warming.

Here is only a small sample of costs happening already with global warming-influenced extreme weather. The National Oceanic and Atmospheric Administration (NOAA), which tracks U.S. billion-dollar disaster events resulting from extreme weather, has found that severe storms caused losses of $8 billion in the 1980s, $26 billion in the 1990s, $43 billion in the 2000s, and $78 billion thus far in the 2010s.[62] In the past few years, the United States has experienced nearly 50 climate-related disasters, each costing taxpayers over $1 billion.

If we continue on the path of escalating global warming, we will soon be facing a new kind of superstorm, what can be

---

[62] NOAA National Centers for Environmental Information. "U.S. Billion-Dollar Weather and Climate Disasters." *NOAA.gov.* 2016. https://www.ncdc.noaa.gov/billions/

called a *millennial superstorm*. Millennial superstorms are storms of such severity that they have not been present on Earth for thousands of years. These new millennial superstorms are important to consider because almost all of our infrastructure has been built on the basis of surviving the worst storm that occurs *about once every 100 years*. Our current infrastructure is in no way prepared to survive these 1,000-year millennial superstorms. For more data on increasingly extreme storms, read this article by Paul Douglas.[63]

Who are the big financial losers?

There will be very big financial losers as global warming escalates. A few of the big losers will be:

a. Home and business owners in catastrophe zones. Those living near river or lake floodplains or close to oceans, or areas vulnerable to wildfires, droughts, hurricanes, or tornadoes will be subject to huge real estate valuation losses and insurance premium increases. Insurance companies will be forced to raise prices 1-5% per year for any customers in the escalating global warming high danger zones, or they will cancel policies and offload the risks and the unpredictable costs onto national government relief programs and safety nets.

It would also not be unreasonable to estimate that real estate prices in affected global warming high-risk areas will soon begin dropping 1-3% per year as savvy buyers realize the risk and potential losses involved in such properties. In extremely high-risk areas, real estate prices could crash drastically, similar to the way the prices of homes and businesses crashed when toxic pollution was discovered in the water and soils at Love Canal, New York.[64]

---

[63] Paul Douglas. "Meteorologists are seeing global warming's effect on the weather." *The Guardian*. May 27, 2016. https://www.theguardian.com/environment/climate-consensus-97-per-cent/2016/may/27/meteorologists-are-seeing-global-warmings-effect-on-the-weather

[64] Wikipedia contributors. "Love Canal." *Wikipedia, the Free Encyclopedia.* https://en.wikipedia.org/wiki/Love_Canal

b. Fossil fuel companies and related industries will not be able to hide or secretly offload the pollution and health costs onto unsuspecting taxpayers for the worst effects of their products. Fossil fuel subsidies that now total $5.3 trillion a year will soon disappear, and special global warming reduction carbon tax fees from $40-$100 a ton or more will be added to their operational costs.

Green energy will become highly subsidized, and fossil fuel energy generation will become highly unprofitable by comparison. This does not take into consideration the momentum building behind the rapidly growing movement to divest from fossil fuel holdings.

c. Countries in the Southern hemisphere will be most affected by the worst of escalating global warming. They will experience soaring heat, the rapid spread of tropical diseases, as well as economic, social, and political instability. Needless to say, such countries whose economies are dependent on tourism will see those revenues steadily disappear. The irony here is that many of the undeveloped nations that have produced only a tiny fraction of total global warming will get poorer as northern countries responsible for most of the global warming will initially get richer and experience other benefits.

d. Millennials and the younger generations will be financially punished the most by escalating global warming. Click here to learn more about the trillions of dollars the younger generations will lose.[65]

e. Average individuals from every generation will watch their monthly budgets, reserves, and personal and business equity be destroyed. This is because global

---

[65] Maria Gallucci. "Climate change could be worse than student debt, Great Recession for millennials' income." *Mashable.* August 22, 2016. http://mashable.com/2016/08/22/climate-change-cost-millennials-trillions/#MPVks6RnU8q6

warming-related inflation and "natural" disasters and their recovery costs will continue rising as the temperature rises. Part of the reason for this loss of equity is that as the emergency worsens, individuals will not be able to find relief from either insurance or government emergency programs because eventually those funds will also be exhausted by the ever-widening drain in the bathtub of global warming costs. To add further hardship, these individuals will endure steadily increasing new taxes, which their governments will be forced to impose as insurance companies go bankrupt due to the continuous, worsening "natural" disasters caused by global warming.

f. The poor and the middle class will be the first to suffer and they will suffer the most. In addition to the pain of dwindling personal equity and rapidly increasing taxes from ever-escalating global warming disasters, the poor and the middle class will also watch their government social security and safety net benefits continually cut back and finally disappear as their governments try to cope with dwindling and overburdened resources themselves (i.e. retirement and unemployment benefits, food assistance, assistance for the elderly or physically or mentally handicapped, worker's compensation, etc.). Click here to see a small glimpse of how bad it will get for the poor.[66]

In the early to mid phases of the Climageddon Scenario described in Chapter 6, it is fair to say that almost everyone will begin watching the process of their personal wealth dwindling and disappearing. More will be said about the many costs of escalating global warming in Chapter 6.

The overall destabilization of climate

---

[66] Megan Darby. "Climate change could push 100m into extreme poverty." *Climate Change News*. August 11, 2015. http://www.climatechangenews.com/2015/11/08/climate-change-could-push-100m-into-extreme-poverty/

Global Warming Consequences Destabilizing our Climate and Lives

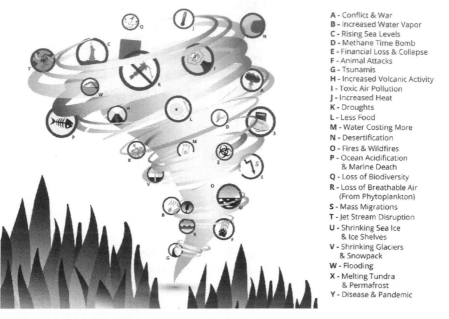

A - Conflict & War
B - Increased Water Vapor
C - Rising Sea Levels
D - Methane Time Bomb
E - Financial Loss & Collapse
F - Animal Attacks
G - Tsunamis
H - Increased Volcanic Activity
I - Toxic Air Pollution
J - Increased Heat
K - Droughts
L - Less Food
M - Water Costing More
N - Desertification
O - Fires & Wildfires
P - Ocean Acidification
    & Marine Death
Q - Loss of Biodiversity
R - Loss of Breathable Air
    (From Phytoplankton)
S - Mass Migrations
T - Jet Stream Disruption
U - Shrinking Sea Ice
    & Ice Shelves
V - Shrinking Glaciers
    & Snowpack
W - Flooding
X - Melting Tundra
    & Permafrost
Y - Disease & Pandemic

Far beyond what we generally understand to be the painful individual consequences of global warming is its effect on the overall global climate as well as the ensuing destabilization within our human and biological systems. This is what takes place when many of the global warming consequences continue to increase in magnitude, as well as interact with each other in an accelerating and multiplying way *as a whole system*.

To further break down what this means, know that as global warming consequences unfold at greater magnitude, the climate destabilizes, which then destabilizes everything else dependent on the climate. To see how this process unfolds, see the illustration below. (For more on climate destabilization, revisit the previous chapter.)

How the collective consequences of global warming will unfold to destabilize the climate as well as human and biological systems

With each degree of increased temperature, our weather will become considerably more unpredictable and violent. An exact year time frame of when many of the worst global warming consequences mentioned above will occur is still being researched. How global warming will unfold as a process is much better established.

With each degree of increased temperature, global warming's destabilization consequences will almost always increase in their severity, scope of affected areas, and frequency. Global warming consequences in terms of climate, human, and biological systems such as floods, droughts, heat waves, wildfires, economic recessions or depressions, spread of disease, species die-offs, seasonal disruptions, and catastrophic superstorms will unfold irregularly.

As most of the world warms, a few places will get colder. Seasons will not feel like they used to anymore. Monsoons will be too short and come at the wrong time. Winters will last too long or springs will come too early. Winter snows or monsoon moisture will run off long before it can be captured in properly positioned reservoirs for spring and summer use by our farmers. Crops will fail and people will starve and migrate.

As more critical global warming tipping points are crossed, there will be sudden, more extreme and larger-scale chains of negative weather, human, and biological system consequences will be drastically greater than ever before experienced.

Global Warming Critical Warning Signals

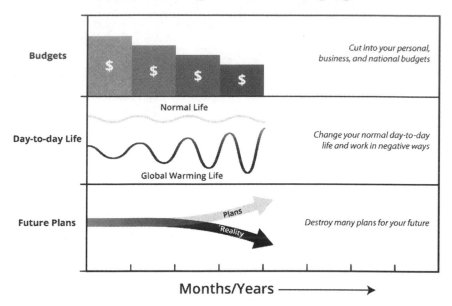

Budgets — Cut into your personal, business, and national budgets

Day-to-day Life
Normal Life
Global Warming Life
— Change your normal day-to-day life and work in negative ways

Future Plans
Plans
Reality
— Destroy many plans for your future

Months/Years ⟶

Our normal day-to-day lives will experience more unpleasant changes such as less spendable money in our budgets, more volatility and instability in our physical environments, and less future planning predictability. (Note: Global warming "tipping points" are explained fully in Chapter 4.)

Eventually, the exponential growth of carbon and methane pollution in the atmosphere will cause the dynamic climate balance that has existed for hundreds of thousands of years to destabilize and collapse into some new unknown state. The normal cycle of glacial and non-glacial periods may *never* return as they were.

If this happens, the new climate conditions may no longer be suitable for human life as it is now. If the climate collapses and destabilizes to a new condition unsuitable for maintaining almost eight billion human beings, war and conflict will escalate radically in the fight for scarce remaining resources, and martial law will be quickly imposed in every climate-stressed nation. This would unfortunately cancel out centuries of hard-won, traditional protections of civil rights.

As the escalating individual consequences of global warming tumble further into human and biological systems we will face many costly and painful catastrophes within those systems (economics, politics, pandemics, mass species die-offs, etc.). When this happens, consequences will be multiplied and we will have created what is properly called the *perfect storm of perfect storms,* which is described in the next chapter and in the later phases of the Climageddon Scenario (see Part 1, Chapter 6).

Your next vaccination

Overcoming the global warming emergency will force us to grow in maturity *as one human global society*

How we *collectively* face the adaptive challenge of the escalating global warming emergency may become humanity's greatest evolutionary teacher to date, producing unforeseen benefits, as well as severe consequences. It's not the disasters of global warming that are beneficial, of course.

What's positive is the potential innovation, cooperation, and community building we will have to develop in order to overcome these unfolding disasters. This will, when achieved, directly expand our evolutionary maturity as a *global society.*

What's next

In the next chapter, you will explore the single most dangerous and unpredictable factor of the Climageddon Scenario: crossing global warming tipping points and points of no return. Tipping points occur not just in the climate, but everywhere in life. Understanding how they develop can save you untold pain and suffering. If we cross over more global warming tipping points, our whole world will drastically change for the worse faster than anyone is prepared to live through. Knowing which global warming tipping points we are most likely to cross, *and when,* will be indispensable to your individual, business, or national survival.

Summary

- Global warming started out as an environmental problem. It has now evolved into the world's largest, continually escalating economic and security problem.

- Our air pollution caused by fossil fuel burning has been linked to autism, learning disabilities, and developmental problems in brains and lungs in babies and children.

- The continuously rising costs of escalating global warming act like a gaping hole in the bottom of a bathtub, draining our resources. By 2100 we may be spending one-third of our whole global GDP—about $100 trillion a year—just to cope with global warming disasters.

- Most of the consequences of global warming are interconnected and interdependent. Understanding the relationships of these consequences and how their processes affect each other as well as how they affect the overall climate, and human and biological systems is essential to understanding the nearly unimaginable destructiveness inherent within the now unfolding Climageddon Scenario.

- The escalating consequences of global warming are grossly unfair to millennials and today's younger generations in particular. If escalating global warming continues as it is now, they are robbed of any legitimate economic or survival optimism concerning the future.

- Knowing the global warming consequences and how they are unfolding will serve as critical warning signs about the future quality of your life and future.

PART 1, CHAPTER 4

CROSSING MORE GLOBAL WARMING TIPPING POINTS WILL STEAL OUR FUTURE

Overview:

- Irreversible global warming, also known as the runaway greenhouse effect, can lead to the climate and environment permanently destabilizing and our planet losing its atmosphere.

- A keystone tipping point will be the most likely trigger for irreversible global warming.

- Positive feedback loops—endless, self-reinforcing cycles—can speed a global warming process to jump from a gradual, linear progression to a steep, exponential progression.

- If we can determine the point of no return for global warming tipping points, we can better prepare and predict future catastrophes, as well as locate other tipping points.

Tipping points do not occur only within the climate. They can and will occur in almost any area of life, causing large and unexpected changes. Knowing when they're coming is essential if you do not want to be blindsided by catastrophic global warming consequences.

This chapter contains everything you need to know about global warming-related tipping points. Because of the complexity of tipping points and their initiating processes, this chapter may be more challenging, but you *do not* have to understand everything about tipping points *perfectly!*

By the time you finish this chapter, you will have gleaned enough about the critical and dangerous role of global warming tipping points to understand their high potential impacts both on your present day-to-day life and your future. To make this chapter a bit more manageable, the most complex science has been placed just before the end along with a humorous 11-minute animation link to help you visualize important tipping points and principles.

Although this is a science-filled chapter, it *is* essential reading to understand the depth of our current global warming emergency (presented in Chapter 5) and the Climageddon Scenario global warming prediction model (presented in Chapter 6).

What is a global warming tipping point?

The simple definition of a global warming tipping point is:

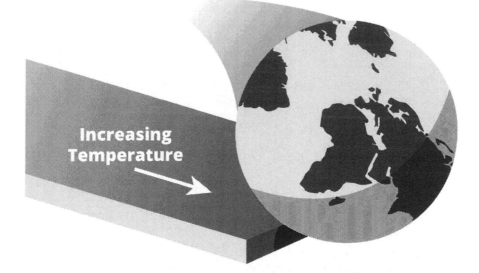

**Global Warming Tipping Points
Will Push Us Over Climate Cliff**

the point where some process or new stimulus causes a sudden and significant change in the status of the ongoing process or system, causing it to jump from one state to a new, *significantly different* state. This sudden change is not only significant; it is often extreme!

As an example of a sudden and significant change, imagine a wine glass tipping over and going from the state of being full to empty. After the wine glass tipping point has been passed, a transition to a new state quickly occurs.

Like the falling of the wine glass, tipping points can often lead to the sudden collapse of a process. If you think about a tipping point on a graph causing a steep slope change, you will understand why knowing when tipping points will occur is so important. (See the Tipping Points Have Points of No Return graph below for what a tipping point does to the slope of a graph line.)

Tipping points are often also irreversible, comparable to wine spilling from the glass. No matter how hard you try, standing up the wine glass will not put the wine back into it. Similarly, many global warming tipping points are also irreversible or almost irreversible *in any time frame relative to a human lifespan!*

For example, the West Antarctic ice shelf appears to have passed its tipping point and is now in an *irreversible* melting process. Once escalating global warming is finally ended, it may take tens of thousands of years to restore that ice shelf—if it ever could even happen.

Points of no return

Before a tipping point is reached, there is another key milestone in the process. It is the point of *irreversible process momentum* toward that tipping point, or what is commonly known as the *point of no return*. In simple mechanical systems like in the wine glass example, the point of no return can occur very close to the actual tipping point. Even though the point of no return may be close to its tipping point, the two are separate parts of the tipping point process.

In complex climate, human, biological or geological systems, the *point of no return* can occur *long before* the actual tipping point. This is because global warming and our climate are complex adaptive systems. The developmental processes that eventually trigger a tipping point usually involve many factors and many processes beyond a single mechanical balance point or a simple mechanical falling process as in the wine glass spilling example. (If you're curious, at the end of this chapter you will find a section that provides more information about the complex qualities and nature of complex adaptive systems.)

In the wine glass example, the point of no return is the moment of *directional motion and momentum* where the forward-falling glass is no longer able to teeter backwards and maintain or return to its original upright position and stability. In the wine glass tipping scenario, the point of no return is quite visible. Once it falls past this last balancing point of *still reversible* direction and momentum and crosses its point of no return, it can no longer stop itself from falling further and crossing the wine glass's last *balancing* point, thus irreversibly tipping and spilling the wine out of the glass.

By contrast, global warming points of no return tend to be largely *invisible*—i.e., irreversible fates are set in motion before we know they are happening. However, *if* you can determine the point of no return for any global warming tipping point, you can "buy" yourself critical forecasting capabilities that can give you some warning for approximately when that tipping point will be crossed. Being aware of global warming process points of no return will be extremely useful in preparing for and predicting global warming tipping points and catastrophes.

> "Tipping points are so dangerous because if you pass them, the climate is out of humanity's control: if an ice sheet disintegrates and starts to slide into the ocean there's nothing we can do about that." —James Hansen

Tipping Points Have Points of No Return

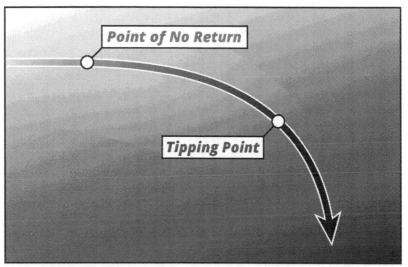

Tipping Point Developmental Process Over Time

Contrary to what many people believe, tipping points are not just rare high-impact events. Knowing global warming, climate, human and biological tipping points as well as how and when they will occur will be the key to creating all future planning as global warming escalates, and our global climate continues to destabilize.

The *global warming* tipping points within the climate, human, and biological systems

There are many global warming system and subsystem tipping points within the climate, human, and biological systems. The key process that directly or indirectly causes the global warming tipping points to be crossed is *increasing heat*, as is implied in the term global warming.

When global warming tipping points are crossed, one or more of them can trigger processes leading to:

a. sudden large scale catastrophes in climate, human, and biological systems,
b. irreversible global warming,

    c. irreversible climate destabilization, and/or

    d. extinction-level climate destabilization.

Global warming tipping points within interacting climate, human, and biological systems are:

1. *The total amount of melting ice.* Increased heat melts more sea ice, ice shelves, and glaciers, resulting in more water flowing into our oceans and increasing sea levels. This process repeats with each increase in temperature in an endless, self-reinforcing cycle—a positive feedback loop. At some point, this positive feedback loop triggers a tipping point, and the increased heat and ice melting process can go from a gradual linear progression (1, 2, 3 ,4, 5, 6, 7, 8, 9, 10) to a far steeper exponential progression (2, 4, 8, 16, 32, 64, 128, 256, 512, 1,024, 2,048, 4,096, 8,192, 16,384).

2. *The albedo effect.* The whiteness of polar ice reflects heat away from the planet. This is called the albedo effect. As the polar ice melts, significant areas darken and therefore absorb more heat rather than reflecting it outward. At some point in this melting process, a self-reinforcing positive feedback loop occurs, which again reduces the albedo effect's total heat-reflecting capabilities. This in turn further increases global warming. As before, this self-reinforcing cycle of loss of reflectivity and increasing heat will eventually move from a gradual linear progression to a steep exponential heat increasing progression.

3. *The release of methane from the warming of polar permafrost and tundra.* As temperature continues to increase, a self-reinforcing positive feedback loop triggers a permafrost and tundra methane release tipping point, leading eventually to the exponential

progression mentioned before. This could be a very critical tipping point because methane produces 20 to 100 times the heat-creating effect in the atmosphere as compared to carbon dioxide. This increased methane within our atmosphere will also remain there from three years to decades before it decays back into simple carbon. To emphasize how dangerous this is for our future, in February 2013, scientists using radiometric dating techniques on Russian cave formations to measure melting rates warned that a 1.5° Celsius (2.7° Fahrenheit) global rise in temperature compared to pre-industrial levels was enough to start a general permafrost melt. (From David Spratt's *Climate Reality Check*.) As you will read in Chapter 5, we are almost at 1.5° Celsius right now, and even higher temperatures are inevitable.

4. *The total amount of water vapor in the atmosphere.* Water vapor is the gaseous state of water. It is the *most important* natural greenhouse gas. When it condenses onto a surface, a net warming occurs on that surface. In the atmosphere, water vapor increases as heat increases. Increased heat evaporates more water from oceans, lakes, and rivers, which creates more water vapor and heat in an endless self-reinforcing cycle— another positive feedback loop. At some point, this positive feedback loop triggers a tipping point, and the process goes from a gradual linear heat producing progression into a steeper exponential progression. The result is that the average global temperature increases even faster.

5. *The die-offs of carbon-eating and oxygen-producing sea plankton* because of the warming, carbonization, and acidification of the oceans. As this continues to

intensify, it also creates a self-reinforcing positive feedback loop, which triggers a tipping point, and the die-off process goes from a gradual linear progression into a steeper exponential progression. This results in sudden and rapidly increasing die-offs in the ocean fish populations that live on this plankton, as well as sudden and rapidly increasing drop-offs in the ocean's oxygen-producing capabilities. (Oxygen-producing plankton are critical to our future. They produce 50% - 80% of the world's total oxygen supply.)

6. *The ever-increasing atmospheric heat captured and stored by the oceans and sent to lower levels of the ocean.* These captured and stored masses of *deep warm water* can suddenly rise to the surface again. This will release a massive amount of additional heat directly into the atmosphere and quickly spike average global temperature.

7. *The loss of the atmospheric carbon-eating forests because of heat, drought, wildfires, and timber-harvesting or agriculture-related clearcutting.* As temperatures rise and droughts, heat, forest fires and clearcutting kill trees, we lose our essential carbon-eating forests, which increases the carbon and heat in the atmosphere. This process eventually triggers a tipping point and the forests' loss of carbon-eating capabilities goes from a gradual linear progression into a steep exponential progression of forest loss and escalating carbon in the atmosphere. This results in a sudden additional spike upward in average global temperature.

8. *Soils that normally absorb carbon begin releasing it back into the atmosphere* from their previously stored

or inherent carbon because of the escalating heat. This increasing heat-induced release of carbon by the soils creates a self-reinforcing positive feedback loop. This triggers a soil carbon release tipping point and the process goes into a more exponential progression. This also results in a rapid increase in average global temperature.

9. *The changes in major ocean currents that help to stabilize our weather and seasons.* Research is now expanding on how increasing heat will affect currents like the North Atlantic current. Because of global warming, if the North Atlantic current were slowed down or diverted from its presently established pathway, it would create very significant changes in weather patterns, which would affect growing seasons, rain, snowfall, and temperature—all of which have strong effects on vital crop yields.

10. *The global warming-caused pandemic potential.* When ancient ice, glaciers, permafrost, or frozen tundra melts, it releases still-living bacteria and viruses never seen before. This means we could soon be unleashing the ultimate global pandemic. So many different types of new bacteria and viruses could be released *at once* that even our best scientists would not be able to create and distribute the vaccines needed in time to contain disease outbreaks or a growing global pandemic.

11. *Total weight of rising seas and melting ice shifting.* Although research is sparse in this area, it has been posited that the total massive weight change from all ice melt areas (where ice covers land masses) as well as the heating, expanding and shifting weight effect on seas caused by global warming *can move* existing tectonic plates. This plate motion could cause

earthquakes and volcanic eruptions at an unprecedented scale. If the shifting of these tectonic plates causes numerous or massive volcanic eruptions around the planet, we could also go into a volcanic winter. If the shifting of tectonic plates triggers a supervolcano-like eruption, the years that the sun would be blocked could kill off most of the human population.

Why understanding global warming tipping points is critical to your future

To demonstrate why understanding tipping points is so important, it is necessary to also understand the many dangers found within the complex interactions, processes, and consequences of the global warming tipping points. When you understand these additional dangers, you will also understand how the phases of the Climageddon Scenario (detailed in Chapter 6) build upon each other.

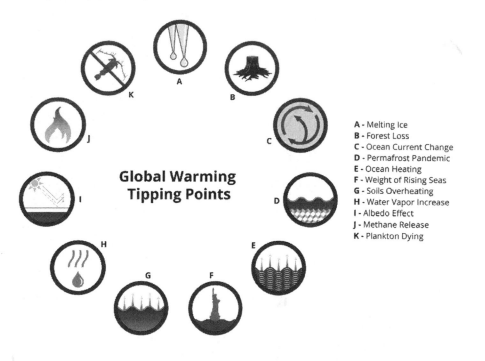

Global Warming Tipping Points

A - Melting Ice
B - Forest Loss
C - Ocean Current Change
D - Permafrost Pandemic
E - Ocean Heating
F - Weight of Rising Seas
G - Soils Overheating
H - Water Vapor Increase
I - Albedo Effect
J - Methane Release
K - Plankton Dying

Overview of the biggest dangers of global warming tipping points:

a) Exponential expansion: Once a tipping point is crossed, its consequences will cease progressing in a steady, gradual, and linear way (1, 2. 3 ,4, 5, 6, 7, 8, 9, 10) and will typically shift into a steep, nonlinear, exponential progression (2, 4, 8, 16, 32, 64, 128, 256, 512, 1024). Notably, one of the hardest things for individuals to do is visualize real-life scenarios of the difference in results between a linear and an exponential progression. Using the sample above, in just the 10 *linear* steps, the last *linear* progression number noted is 10. That is about *100 times less* than the last and 10th step of the above sample *exponential* progression.

b) Crossed tipping points create more crossed tipping points: As average global temperature continues to rise, we will cross more of the global warming tipping points. When any interconnected or interdependent global warming tipping point within the system or subsystems is crossed, it makes it *significantly more likely* that more tipping points will inevitably also be crossed in other interconnected or interdependent systems or subsystems. Once this domino-like process starts, we could eventually cross many of the global warming tipping points. (See the lighted match Keystone Tipping Point illustration below.)

c) Colliding multiple tipping points can accelerate us into the last phases of the Climageddon Scenario: Colliding crossed multiple tipping points means that each tipping point's vulnerability is also subject to the powerful triggering influence of other crossed tipping points. Tipping points crashing into other interconnected or interdependent areas can quickly trigger other tipping points, creating a cascading meltdown across both climate and human system tipping points. Crossing more global warming tipping points may *collectively* be enough to throw us into irreversible climate destabilization or even extinction-level climate destabilization. (The Climageddon Scenario is discussed in Chapter 6.)

d) <u>Crossed global warming tipping points will accelerate the crossing of vulnerable human and biological system tipping points:</u> Crossed global warming tipping points within the numerous global warming climate systems or subsystems can also unpredictably collide back and forth to create a *system-wide,* cascading chain reaction of numerous self-reinforcing positive feedback loops. Once this cascading meltdown process begins, crossing more tipping points occurs at a faster and faster rate and it will eventually accelerate crossing over into our many vulnerable human and biological system tipping points (economy, politics, society, war and conflict, etc.).

e) <u>Quick collapse and slow recovery:</u> The greatest dangers of crossing tipping points is that they can suddenly cause *severe, unpredictable,* and *irreversible* changes, even complete system collapses. In most cases, if the system or subsystem crashes or collapses, recovery from these crashes or collapses is very slow and difficult, if not impossible!

If recovery is possible, not only will it be slow and difficult, but there is also the higher likelihood that it will not be adequate to restore the original stability, range, or level of the collapsed system (or subsystem). This difficult recovery leads instead to some new stability range—a level that will likely be significantly different. After we cross one or more tipping points, this could mean that when our temperature eventually restabilizes, it could be at a range or level either unfriendly to life as we know it, or completely incompatible.

f) <u>Crossed tipping points can have both linear cause-and-effect relationships as well as dangerous and currently unpredictable nonlinear cause-and-effect</u>

relationships. These nonlinear relationships can occur between global warming tipping points and human and biological system tipping points (economy, politics, mass species die offs, war, and conflict) as well as within and between any other part of the climate system and its subsystems. The presence of counter-intuitive, nonlinear tipping point and system relationships mean that *causes and effects* within climate and global warming systems and subsystems are sometimes not logically connected, clear *or predictable.* This means that within a complex adaptive system like global warming and the climate, an area that happens to be a part of its system or its subsystems can create an *effect* in some other completely different system or subsystem where there seems to be *no apparent* cause and effect relationship between the two systems or subsystems. The huge danger here is that if a global warming tipping point triggers a nonlinear reaction in another climate or human system or subsystem, we could quickly find ourselves caught in a catastrophic situation without ever being able to predict it or prepare for it.

Unpredictable Nonlinear Reactions

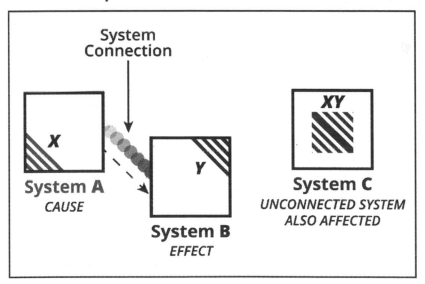

A complex adaptive system such as the climate reacts with its subsystems in both predictable and unpredictable ways. In the illustration above, an action X in system A causes the obvious linear effect Y in system B, but it can also cause a seemingly unconnected nonlinear XY reaction in system C. It is this nonlinear unpredictability in other interconnected and interdependent systems which also should cause us great concern as we add more fossil fuel carbon to the atmosphere.

g) <u>Hidden points of no return can occur long before tipping points are crossed:</u> A major factor working against the resolution of the global warming emergency is that with each degree of temperature increase, *developmental momentum* within the processes of that particular global warming area will push relevant tipping points toward their points of no return, which makes crossing of such tipping points inevitable.

In the case of global warming systems and subsystems, these points of no return are often hidden, sometimes occurring long before the actual tipping point is crossed. Generally, they are even less researched and understood. Unfortunately, if we want to avoid the global warming tipping points, we not only have to do more research on the actual tipping points, but we also have to do more research on these points of no return.

A good example of the dangers of crossing any point of no return is found within the West Antarctic Ice Sheet. Recent research has shown that the West Antarctic Ice Sheet has already entered the irreversible collapse process. This was caused first by warmer water and, secondly, by the melting of its ice shelves from above and below because of warmer air temperatures.

At some point, as the warmer water and the warmer air melted the massive ice sheet, the ice sheet's point of no return was crossed. This then set up the final scenario leading to the tipping point of irreversible melting.

This crossed tipping point is a huge problem because this particular ice sheet and its shelves contain enough ice to raise sea levels by another 10-13 feet (roughly 3-4 meters). Even worse, these ice sheets and shelves act as essential flying buttresses, keeping the rest of Antarctica's massive ice stores locked on land instead of sliding off and melting into the sea and passing their own point of no return, which, if it occurred, would spike sea levels massively higher.

h) Invisible momentum and inertia factors: It's important to understand the technical meaning of momentum and inertia to understand their important relationship to global warming tipping points. In classical mechanics, momentum is the product of the mass and velocity of an object. For example, a heavy truck moving rapidly has momentum—it takes a large or prolonged force (generally an engine and fuel) to get the truck up to speed, and it also takes a large or prolonged force to bring it to a stop afterwards (brakes). If the truck were lighter or moving more slowly, it would have *less momentum* and it would take less force to get it moving or to stop it.

Inertia is defined as the resistance of any physical object to any change in its state of motion (this includes changes to its speed, direction, or state of rest). It is the tendency of objects to *keep moving* in a straight line at constant velocity or to *stay in the state they are in.*

Global warming tipping points can have inherent momentum and/or inertia factors within their processes. These two factors can cause either a time accelerator—pushing a process over a tipping point faster, or a *time delay*—helping to prevent a process from going over a tipping point.

Including both momentum and inertia factors is critical to the *accurate prediction* of global warming, climate, human, and biological systems outcomes. For example, the momentum or inertia factors in global warming tipping points for ocean heat capture or release are regulated by atmospheric heat. Oceans take up and release atmospheric heat very slowly, and they pass that heat to deep ocean layers slowly. There is an inertia-related time lag due to that slow absorption rate. This is due to the ocean's pre-existing water temperature. It also has inertia-related time lag as it seeks to maintain its current temperature by changing slowly.

There is also a *momentum* factor for how the ocean eventually releases its previously captured atmospheric heat back into the atmosphere, which would once again spike average global temperatures. It appears that once deep warm water is released, it builds its own momentum, eventually rising to the surface and then quickly releasing its heat. Once a certain temperature or set of conditions is triggered, nothing will stop this inherent momentum from the rising of the warmer water from deep ocean layers.

i) *Crossing multiple tipping points will lead to the later phases of the Climageddon Scenario*. In addition to increasing unpredictability and leading us into the later phases of the Climageddon Scenario, crossing multiple tipping points can create a dramatic acceleration of consequence time frames. It will <u>drastically</u> increase the scale, severity, and frequency of the consequences within the related global warming systems and subsystems involved.

Interacting Global Warming Tipping Points

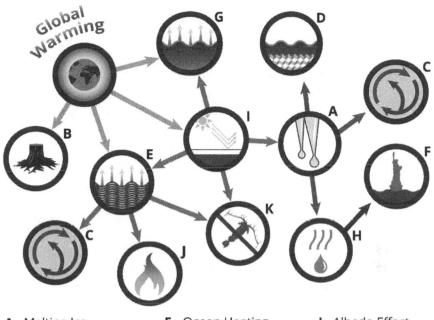

A - Melting Ice   **E** - Ocean Heating   **I** - Albedo Effect
B - Forest Loss   **F** - Weight of Rising Seas **J** - Methane Release
C - Ocean Current Change **G** - Soils Overheating   **K** - Plankton Dying
D - Permafrost Pandemic   **H** - Water Vapor Increase

Now that you understand what the main tipping points are and their dangers to our future, there are other essential facts about tipping points important to know.

What is a *keystone* tipping point

There is a uniquely important type of tipping point relevant to global warming and the climate. It is called a keystone tipping point.

If you have seen a Roman architectural arch, you already know a little about what a keystone is. It is the central, usually triangular-shaped stone at the top center of the arch. It is also the critical supporting stone that holds all the other stones in place and maintains the integrity and strength of the arch.

If you pull a keystone out of a Roman arch, the whole arch immediately crumbles and completely falls in on itself. Like the keystone in the Roman arch, if we cross any keystone global warming tipping point, all dependent or interconnected global warming systems and subsystems can also begin collapsing faster than we can be prepared for or recover from. If we cross any currently unknown or known keystone tipping point, every projected time frame relating to global warming consequences would suddenly and radically change for the worse. Consequences that were predicted to be many decades away could now become just one or two decades away *or less.*

You're probably curious about which of the previously mentioned global warming tipping points are keystone tipping points. The difficult truth is that increasing heat itself, as well as all of the previously mentioned tipping points (except the pandemic tipping point caused by melting ice and permafrost), could become keystone tipping points. The painful truth is that if the conditions surrounding any global warming tipping point worsen enough, it could act as and become a *keystone tipping point,* which could ignite a cascading meltdown and triggering of multiple other tipping points, leading to sudden and catastrophic results.

Keystone Tipping Point Process

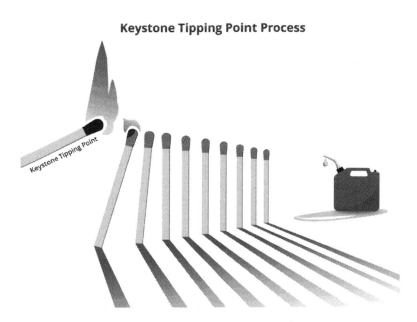

Keystone Tipping Point

A keystone tipping point will also be the most likely trigger for the *irreversible* global warming process

Irreversible global warming (aka runaway climate change or the *runaway greenhouse effect*) is defined by its processes and what will happen after we cross any keystone tipping point (or we cross multiple important tipping points, which will cumulatively act like a keystone tipping point). The crossed irreversible global warming tipping point then causes the global climate to dramatically change—this is the climate destabilization process in action. But, keep in mind that irreversible climate destabilization and irreversible global warming are different things.

Warning signs that a tipping point may soon be crossed

Many times, just before a tipping point is crossed and crashes, it experiences a period of increasing oscillations, "flipping" more rapidly from one state to another. Not only does it oscillate from one state to another, but the *severity* of the oscillations also increases. Finally, the *frequency* of the oscillation swings also begins to accelerate in close time proximity.

We are already seeing these pre-tipping-point oscillation warnings occurring in our more frequent and severe weather swings over larger and larger areas—going from cold to warm, summer- to winter-like conditions, and from droughts to deluges. Whenever you see this type of intensified oscillation pattern occurring, whether it's in climate or biological systems or the stock market, it is the harbinger of big changes.

In general, the further up the local, regional, national, or global climate that climate, human, or biological systems or subsystems are:

a. oscillating,
b. tipping points are being crossed, or

c. extreme weather problems are expanding, the more trouble we are in! If the *global* climate is oscillating more frequently and severely, we are in a a lot more trouble than if it is *only* our local climate that is oscillating similarly. Additionally, *smaller* systems and subsystems will move to a state of chaos *more readily* than larger systems and subsystems due to smaller systems and subsystems usually having less inertia to resist the change.

Tipping Points/Crash Warning Signs

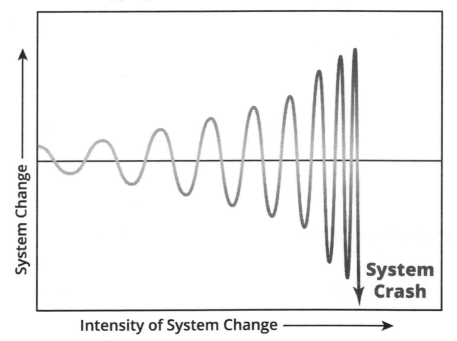

Which global warming tipping points will most likely be crossed first

While it is difficult to set specific dates for crossing a tipping point, in general, the melting of sea and glacial ice around the world—particularly in the polar regions—appears to be the tipping point area of greatest immediacy and concern. There are a few key reasons for this:

a. At the far north and far south, global warming has seen double the temperature increases as compared to increased temperatures elsewhere on the planet.

b. Ice melting directly or indirectly links to other critical tipping points: the albedo effect, methane releases from melting permafrost and tundra, changes in ocean currents, deep and surface level ocean temperature increases, die-offs in ocean life, and potential pandemics caused by ancient viruses and bacteria being released from the permafrost.

This melting-ice-related cluster of interconnected and interdependent tipping points of itself can usher in the end of humanity or hell on Earth. The next group of tipping points to monitor would be the total global water vapor levels and the carbon-releasing and carbon-eating condition of trees and soils. The last and slowest developing risk will be from increased earthquakes and volcanoes due to changing glacier-related weight over the Earth's tectonic plates.

More detailed time estimates on when we will cross more climate, human and biological systems tipping points will be found in the Climageddon Scenario in Chapter 6. Estimates for exactly when we will cross the many global warming tipping points will continuously evolve as new research is released.

In general, if temperatures continue rising, the time frames in which we will be crossing more tipping points will get shorter. (There is an easy way to educate yourself about this as new global warming research comes out that can and will affect you, your business, and nation. If you have not done so already, sign up for the Global Warming blog RSS feed.[67] By doing so, you will automatically receive a weekly or biweekly email with the latest headline news on national and international global warming reduction successes and losses.)

---

[67] Job One for Humanity. "Blog Signup Page." *JobOneforHumanity.org.* http://www.joboneforhumanity.org/blog_signup_page

A carbon level we should be most concerned about

Above and beyond keystone tipping points, there is another important danger level. It exists as a *collection* of crossed tipping points.

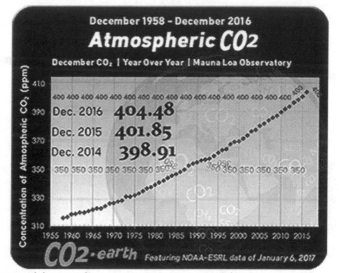

"Monthly Keeling Curving CO2 Widget" courtesy of Show.Earth[68]

A dangerous collective juncture of several crossed tipping points from different areas of the climate system interacting with each other is highly probable once we reach the carbon 425-450 ppm level. This danger level aligns with climate researcher James Hansen's statements that even a carbon 450 ppm level (which will occur in about 10-15 years at present carbon pollution rates) would eventually correspond to an average global temperature increase of 6° Celsius (10.8° Fahrenheit) in this century and the end of human civilization as

---

[68] Show.earth. "Keeling Curve Monthly CO2 Widget." *ProOxygen*. Accessed January 17, 2017 from https://www.show.earth/kc-monthly-co2-widget

we've come to know it.[69] More will be said about this critical danger level in later chapters.

Which global warming tipping points are likely to be crossed the soonest

New research and evidence suggest that more systems and subsystems within the interconnected and interdependent climate system may be heading toward global warming tipping points or experiencing worrisome qualitative change toward their points of no return. These global warming-related climate systems include:

a. accelerating ice mass loss from Antarctic ice shelves and the vulnerability of East Antarctic glaciers;

b. the vulnerability of Arctic permafrost, exemplified in part by the proliferation of Siberian methane craters;

c. rapid thinning of Arctic sea-ice;

d. declining carbon efficiency of the Amazon forests and other carbon sinks (oceans, soils etc;) and

e. the slowing of the major sea current known as the Atlantic conveyor, likely as a result of global warming.

In late 2015, a chilling report[70] released by the International Cryosphere Climate Initiative warned that the 2015 Paris commitments from the IPCC conference:

"... will not prevent our 'crossing into the zone of irreversible thresholds' in our polar and mountain glacier regions, and that crossing these boundaries may result

---

[69] Hansen, James, et al. "Target atmospheric CO2: Where should humanity aim?" *The Open Atmospheric Science Journal* 2, no. 1 (2008): 217-231. DOI: 10.2174/1874282300802010217

[70] International Cryosphere Climate Initiative. *Thresholds and Closing Windows*. ICCI.org. December 2015. http://iccinet.org/wp-content/uploads/2015/11/ICCI_thresholds_v6b_151203_high_res.pdf

in processes that cannot be halted unless temperatures return to levels below pre-industrial."

And in a similar vein, the *Climate Reality Check* stated:

"To put it most bluntly, only a new 'Little Ice Age' may re-establish some of today's mountain glaciers and their reliable water resources for millions of people; or halt melting polar ice sheets that, once started, irrevocably would set the world on course to an ultimate sea-level rise of between 4–10 metres or more...some of these cryosphere thresholds, including potential fisheries and ecosystem loss from polar ocean acidification, cannot be reversed at all." —From David Spratt's *Climate Reality Check*.[71]

Crossing global warming tipping points is not going to happen far off in the future. It is happening now!

How global warming tipping points are unfolding

What we do know is that:

a. We are already crossing important tipping points in the Arctic and Antarctic regions.

b. As we approach the carbon 425 to 450 ppm levels, crossing more tipping points and points of no return in global warming systems and subsystems will accelerate.

c. Unknowingly, we may have already crossed multiple global warming tipping points or points of no return.

d. In general, with each new global warming tipping point crossed, the *momentum* increases toward more global warming tipping points being crossed in other climate,

---

[71] David Spratt. "Climate Reality Check." *Breakthrough - National Centre for Climate Restoration.* March 2016.
http://media.wix.com/ugd/148cb0_4868352168ba49d89358a8a01bc5f8of.pdf

human, and biological systems and subsystems. This is a tipping point *momentum* we allow to happen at our *extreme peril.*

What we do not know:

a. At this time, no exact sequential order has been researched to show when each global warming tipping point will be crossed.

b. Which specific global warming tipping point will act as the *keystone tipping point* that will trigger other tipping points, creating irreversible global warming and setting off the end-of-the-world Climageddon Scenario.

Our exponential exposure and vulnerability as we cross more global warming tipping points

Crossing any global warming tipping point creates an extreme vulnerability and exposure because the danger is *neither* singular nor constant. It is not a *singular threat* because at a minimum, many tipping points and points of no return reside within the climate, human, and biological systems and subsystems—any of which could be crossed and feed back into other interconnected systems or subsystems, triggering a *cascading meltdown* of more crossed global warming tipping points across more and more systems.

There is not just the threat of a *single* keystone tipping point. There are potentially *many* tipping points that, if *collectively crossed*, could act like a keystone tipping point and lead to the final phases of the Climageddon Scenario. Crossing tipping points is also not a linear steady threat. With each rising degree of average global temperature, the threat, vulnerability, and exposure boils and rises *exponentially!* See boiling pot illustration below.

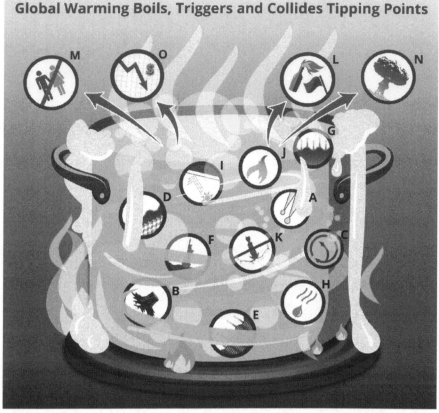

Global Warming Boils, Triggers and Collides Tipping Points

A - Melting Ice	**F** - Weight of Rising Seas	**K** - Plankton Dying
B - Forest Loss	**G** - Soils Overheating	**L** - National Instability
C - Ocean Current Change	**H** - Water Vapor Increase	**M** - Social Instability
D - Permafrost Pandemic	**I** - Albedo Effect	**N** - War & Conflict
E - Ocean Heating	**J** - Methane Release	**O** - Economic Loss & Collapse

Our estimated risk level for going over more global warming tipping points

To better evaluate risk, let's first put the scope and intensity of the irreversible global warming risk in a comparative context. From the standpoint of total cumulative harm to be wreaked, consider that a 40% risk for a series of global warming millennial superstorms costing $1 trillion each actually presents a comparatively smaller risk of harm than a 1/100th of 1% risk of irreversible global warming with its end-of-the-world consequences. Yes, this means that a 40% risk of millennial superstorms poses far less of a risk of destructive consequences than a 1/100th of 1% risk of irreversible global warming.

We've already experienced global warming-related extreme storms and know the damage and havoc they leave in their wake. What we are seeing now pales in comparison to irreversible global warming's potential for global destruction and chaos. This helps put the enormity of risk into a comparative perspective, which helps drive home how utterly serious and urgent the global warming emergency is.

To further help quantify this global warming tipping point risk level, now consider that one of our most respected climate scientists, Michael Mann, has estimated the current risk level for going over a global warming tipping point at not 1/100th of 1%, not 1%, but at approximately 10%![72] If one of our best climate scientists has set a 10% risk level for us crossing more global warming tipping points, how should *you* begin to think about this level of risk to your future? (Keep in mind that any global warming tipping point also has the potential to become a keystone tipping point.)

It's reasonable to suppose the nations of the world would not allow even a fraction of 1% of a risk level for global thermonuclear war to go less than 100% managed and controlled. So how should we be managing our tipping point risks? How can we rationally continue to allow a 10% risk level of crossing more global warming tipping points to still go unmanaged when it can quickly lead directly to the extinction of humanity and the end of civilization?

Because of the difficulty of quantifying known and unknown factors involved within developing points of no return and tipping points themselves, the risk of going over more global

---

[72] Micheal E. Mann. "The fat tail of climate change risk." *Huffington Post*. September 11, 2015. http://www.huffingtonpost.com/michael-e-mann/the-fat-tail-of-climate-change-risk_b_8116264.html (In this article, professor Mann uses the terminology "fat tail" to describe global warming tipping point events.)

warming tipping points is likely much higher than 10%. (More will be said about this in Chapter 9 and the conclusion.)

Understanding the many unique dangers of global warming and crossing its tipping points is critical to your future quality of life. Once you understand tipping point risks are real and how they work, you are hopefully more likely to use the information in this book for managing them.

More about irreversible global warming, climate destabilization and tipping points

Global warming causes climate destabilization, but climate destabilization can also cause global warming. These processes can work both ways. For example, already destabilized burned forests and acidified oceans can't absorb as much carbon. Because they cannot absorb as much carbon, more carbon stays in the atmosphere, causing more global warming heat.

There are also hopeful transition points between the processes of irreversible global warming and the levels of climate destabilization. Climate destabilization transforms into irreversible warming only if there is a cascading meltdown of many tipping points, or a keystone tipping point is crossed.

Tipping points and the worst level of irreversible global warming—extinction level global warming

Astronomers use the expression *runaway greenhouse effect* or runaway global warming to define the worst scenario of extinction-level global warming. Runaway global warming occurs as the climate crosses a final critical or keystone tipping point and deviates and destabilizes catastrophically and *permanently* from its original state. This is what scientists think happened on Venus about 4 billion years ago. Solar winds blew all its water vapor and atmosphere off into space.

We currently do not know what tipping point level of greenhouse gases have to be present in our atmosphere before Earth could suffer the same runaway greenhouse effect and extinction-level global warming, which will cause our water and atmosphere to boil and burn off like the Venus event. In Earth's distant past, carbon levels have exceeded 1200 ppm without losing our atmosphere, but with the acceleration of carbon entering the atmosphere, there is no telling when we may reach or exceed those levels.

Only if we can keep global warming from becoming irreversible do we have a reasonable chance of making it through this emergency and avoiding extinction-level global warming (Phase 6 of the Climageddon Scenario in Chapter 6).

One more tipping point shocker

When you get to Chapter 7, you will be shocked by how dangerously global warming tipping points are being mishandled and consequently hidden by the world's recognized authority on the climate. More cannot be said about this now because you will need the information of the following chapters to prepare you.

A humorous 11-minute tipping point animation

Once you have finished this chapter, take 11 minutes to watch "Wake Up, Freak Out - Then Get a Grip."[73] Pay particular attention to the animation's excellent explanation of the various critical global warming tipping points. This video has been viewed over 1 million times and has been translated into 22 different languages. One note: this video gives temperature degrees in Celsius. A rough Fahrenheit temperature conversion is double the Celsius amount. Near its end, the video presents a somewhat polarized viewpoint. Though the informational and tipping point content is good, the Job One for Humanity organization that is publishing this book puts a higher priority on *collaborative approaches* in lieu of polarized ones.

A deeper perspective into the science of exponential

---

[73] "Wake Up, Freak Out - then Get a Grip." Vimeo video. 11:34, posted by "Leo Murray," September 11, 2008. http://vimeo.com/1709110

progressions

We are facing an exponentially rising threat. If you are not fully grasping the critical difference between linear progressions and exponential progressions, it is highly recommended to view this YouTube video [74] on the nature of exponential progressions. It has been watched 5 *million times*. It should help you better visualize what "exponential" means in relation to the potential of the coming drastic rise in the magnitude at every level of coming global warming consequences.

Deeper tipping point and climate science

The following two deeper science perspective sections are not required reading. They can be helpful if you are further exploring the validity of the premises forwarded in this book, or if you would like to know more of the reasoning behind the statements in this and later chapters.

A deeper perspective on climate science when seen as a complex system that is adaptive

The following presents some basics of systems theory and complex systems that are adaptive (also known as complex adaptive systems) for those who want a deeper understanding of:

a. the nature of the global climate,
b. the processes of climate destabilization,
c. how human, climate and biological systems might react, and
d. global warming as a complex adaptive system.

Envisioning how complex adaptive systems interact with each other through their many interconnections, interdependencies, nonlinear processes, and contextual relationships and

[74] "The Most IMPORTANT Video You'll Ever See." YouTube video. 9:17, posted by "wonderingmind42," June 16, 2007. https://www.youtube.com/watch?v=F-QA2rkpBSY

transformations has indeed been challenging for everyone involved in this book.

To illustrate this challenge, imagine each global warming subsystem within the master climate system as a tangle of *cooked spaghetti*. Now imagine several such tangles of spaghetti interconnected by most of their strands. Sorting out what the connections are would be quite the challenge, yes?

Viewing the Interactions of the Climageddon Scenario is Challenging

Although that's not the best image for the overall complexity and interconnectedness of global warming, the climate, and our human and biological systems and subsystems, it will at least open the door to envisioning the research and prediction challenges climate scientists face. In spite of this inherent complexity, it is well worth the extra effort to understand the context and principles behind these relationships, processes and transformations within global warming processes, the climate, and our human and biological systems and subsystems.

To better grasp the nature of this "spaghetti," it is useful to understand global warming, the climate and human and biological systems *as complex adaptive systems.*

Complex adaptive systems by nature:

1. Are *complex* (multifaceted, multilayered, etc.)

2. Are *self-organizing* (can organize themselves into new states or make changes without involvement or actions from outside the system. Self-organization occurs in response to some change in the environment or mutation. This also dramatically increases the unpredictability potentials of the system.)

3. *Evolve and adapt* (they can respond with both reactive and adaptive changes as needed to maintain internal balance and system integrity and stability.)

4. *Contain elements of spontaneous emergence* (something coming into being that was not predicted or completely unpredictable.)

5. *Can contain tipping points* (points of sudden significant change or collapse.)

6. *Can contain points of no return* (where the momentum of some process will sooner or later trigger the tipping point.)

7. *Contain linear and nonlinear cause-and-effect relationships* between the various parts of the system and its subsystems.

8. *Can change rapidly and are highly unpredictable.*

In summary, complex adaptive systems, like global warming, the climate, and our human and biological systems, are highly unpredictable, self-organizing, and often include spontaneous or nonlinear unexpected outcomes. Sometimes they also contain high-impact, *nonlinear* relationships and tipping points, causing radical, sudden, and completely unforeseen consequences.

The presence of these often counter-intuitive, linear and nonlinear relationships and processes as described above means that *causes and effects* within climate, global warming human and biological systems and subsystems are sometimes not logically connected, clear, *or predictable*. Within a complex adaptive system like global warming, the climate, and our human and biological systems, one area can affect a completely different system or subsystem where there seems to be *no apparent,* direct or connected cause and effect relationship between these numerous interacting and interrelated systems or subsystems.

Your next vaccination

Now that you understand the powerful Implications of how crossing global warming tipping points will wreak havoc on the future, this next "big picture" vaccination Is a must to restore balance.

A big-picture perspective on the challenge before us

The escalating global warming crisis has become the greatest adaptive challenge and evolutionary adventure in human history. Paradoxically, while it is the greatest current challenge, if you step back and look at this crisis from the long evolutionary sweep of human history, this crisis is just another evolutionary challenge like the many we have overcome in the past.

The following Great Bottleneck story should help you better frame the difficult challenge in front of us.

The human species has almost gone extinct at least once before. This occurred about 72,000 years ago. This incident has been called the Great Evolutionary Bottleneck.

A supervolcano called Toba erupted and blocked the sun for about 6 years. It also covered the earth with 6 inches of ash. Because of this supervolcano eruption and the resultant volcanic ash blocking the sunlight, global temperature was dramatically lowered. This volcano-related temperature lowering occurred on top of an already existing Ice Age.

Under the cold and darkened skies, humanity as a whole was reduced to as few as 1,000 mating pairs. Some research suggests even fewer survivors. Maybe as few as 200 mating pairs were all that survived of humanity.

This supervolcano eruption has been called an evolutionary bottleneck because during this time the total early global human population fell from an estimated 18-26,000 individuals with reproductive capabilities to 1,000 or fewer reproducing pairs. That was roughly a 90% reduction in total global population. If some other catastrophe had also occurred at the same time, humanity itself might have gone extinct.

Up until now, the Toba eruption has been the single greatest adaptive challenge to the survival of the whole of the human species. Unfortunately, today we are facing a new and far greater adaptive challenge.

This second great bottleneck is different, yet in some ways similar to the first great evolutionary bottleneck. This second bottleneck contains a global warming threat opposite to that of the colder temperatures of the first great evolutionary bottleneck. Unlike the first great bottleneck, which was caused by nature, the second is *human-caused* due to increasing carbon and methane atmospheric pollution and the steadily rising average global temperature.

This increasing global warming is causing a destabilization of our climate from its previously fairly stable temperature range level. This increasing destabilization will lead to some higher temperature range that may not be suitable for the survival of a majority of the 7 billion-plus people alive today. It may not be suitable for preserving *any* of the human species over time.

This means that together as a single human species, we are facing a new great adaptive challenge in the form of the second great evolutionary bottleneck. If we are going to come through this second evolutionary bottleneck, more will need to be done faster with more people cooperating on greater levels than has ever been achieved in human history.

Whenever you feel overwhelmed by the global warming challenge in front of us, never forget that humanity made it through the first great evolutionary bottleneck with far less cooperation, technology, and resources. Yes, today's challenge will still be more difficult than any humanity has previously overcome. But, in the process of overcoming it, we will not only ensure our own future, but our effort will also provide each of us, both young and old, the opportunity to participate in the greatest evolutionary adventure in human history. Participating in such a challenge and adventure will create a deeply meaningful and purpose-filled life.

> "The ultimate measure of a man is not where he stands in moments of comfort and convenience, but where he stands at times of challenge and controversy."
>
> — Martin Luther King, Jr.,
> American civil rights leader

What's next

Our current global warming condition is not good at all. The next chapter will help you see how deep a hole we have dug for ourselves. It is important to face these painful facts because in order to get to where you want to go, it is vital to know exactly where you are starting from.

Summary

- Crossed tipping points can cause sudden and unpredictable severe changes and immediate or complete system crash or collapse.

- Crossing global warming tipping points is not as rare as the fossil fuel industry would like you to believe. We have already crossed several global warming tipping points and it is likely we will cross more.

- In general, when a tipping point is crossed, unpredictability increases along with the speed of change. Our ability to control the disruption of a tipping point and reverse it drops radically as the system tumbles towards collapse.

- Once a point of no return is crossed, it is just a matter of time before its tipping point is crossed.

- Because the climate and global warming are complex adaptive systems, when any global warming tipping point is crossed, it makes it significantly more likely that more tipping points will also be crossed in interconnected or interdependent systems or subsystems.

- Because of inherent pre-existing momentum or inertia factors within one or more of the global warming tipping points, and the possibility that points of no return have already been crossed, we may have already crossed more of the global warming tipping points and be inevitably locked into crossing even more tipping points no matter what we do.

- At this point, at the least what we must do is prevent our crossing more tipping points or any keystone tipping point, which would bring on irreversible global warming and the later stages of the Climageddon Scenario.

- Any global warming remedial plan based on everything going perfectly will become the perfect plan for failure.

- The most important process that directly or indirectly causes global warming tipping points to be crossed is increasing heat.

- Humanity successfully survived the first great evolutionary bottleneck. We have many more advantages today, which should be of help in getting us through the current emergency we are facing.

PART 1, CHAPTER 5

WHY AREN'T WE BEING TOLD WE ARE IN A GLOBAL WARMING *STATE OF EMERGENCY*

Overview:

- Life on Earth has flourished best when carbon levels were in a range of 200-270 ppm (in the pre-industrial age).

- The battle to keep global warming less than 2° Celsius (3.6 degrees Fahrenheit) has already been lost.

- The Intergovernmental Panel on Climate Change (IPCC) has failed to properly educate global leaders and has significantly underestimated timetables, which in turn has dangerously diminished awareness of the emergency we are in.

- It is highly probable carbon parts per million (ppm) in the atmosphere will rise beyond the carbon 550 ppm total, which translates to a 3° to 4°+ Celsius increase (5.4° to 7.2°+ Fahrenheit) in average global temperature—Hell on Earth. A 6° Celsius (10.8° Fahrenheit) increase is also a realistic projection, and it could occur *long before* 2100.

- If we resolve global warming, we also create a green Third Industrial Revolution. This will directly and indirectly create millions of new green energy-related jobs worldwide to replace lost fossil fuel industry jobs.

How bad is global warming right now

In order to see our current global warming condition as an undeclared but real *State of Emergency*, it is essential to explore how bad global warming has become. To put current warming conditions in their proper context, it is wise to compare our current temperatures and conditions with historic temperatures and conditions of the past.

Prepare yourself to be shocked while reading this not-so-happy overview, but do not forget that all temperature projections in this chapter do not include how much higher temperatures will rise, or how quickly, if we cross *any more* of the global warming tipping points (Chapter 4). Numerous graphs and illustrations have been provided to help make the depth of this emergency abundantly clear. (All graphs found below are for carbon dioxide only and do not include *any* of the atmospheric methane pollution, which is also a greenhouse heat-increasing gas.) This chapter does contain some complex science, but like the previous chapter, you do not have to understand everything perfectly. Just by reading it, you will gather enough essential information for the following chapters. Let's review the facts.

Thirty years of failure

In spite of 30 years of warnings by credible scientists, plus the work of the environmental movement, plus a preponderance of collaborating scientific evidence as well as numerous conferences and previous treaties, the carbon dioxide and methane pollution of the atmosphere has not stopped, slowed, or even leveled off. On the contrary, *it is getting worse faster than ever before!*

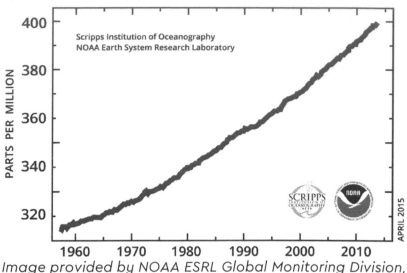

Atmospheric CO$_2$ at Mauna Loa Observatory

Image provided by NOAA ESRL Global Monitoring Division, Boulder, Colorado, USA (http://esrl.noaa.gov/gmd/)[75]

Leading climate scientists like James Hansen, who originally warned us about the global warming danger 30 years ago, say we would remain safe if carbon in the atmosphere did not go over 350 parts per million (ppm). As of August 2016, carbon was near 407 ppm[76] and increasing at about 3 ppm per year in a near exponential progression.

When you combine the heating effect of carbon with the other greenhouse gases, it is called the CO2e ppm rating. CO2e, or carbon dioxide equivalent, is a standard unit for measuring all greenhouse gases in terms of the amount of warming they create compared to carbon dioxide alone. When you include atmospheric methane and the other greenhouse gas pollutants, our current adjusted CO2e rating has already risen to the shocking level of 430 ppmv of CO2e! Worse yet, we will be at

---

[75] "Atmospheric CO2 at Mauna Loa Observatory," *Nation Oceanic & Atmospheric Administration*, accessed January 18, 2017, https://www.esrl.noaa.gov/gmd/ccgg/trends/full.html.

[76] Natasha Geiling. "The Earth just passed a major climate milestone." *ThinkProgress.* September 28, 2016. https://thinkprogress.org/world-passes-400-ppm-threshold-fade7f48e025#.30ibi2rvc

carbon 450 ppm in 10 years or less when we include atmospheric methane in our calculations.

To put this in a time-lapse perspective, from 1850 to about 1950, the increase in carbon pollution was steady at about 1 ppm per year. From 1950 to 2000, the increase rose to 2 ppm per year, and now in its current exponential curve, it is at about 3 ppm per year and rising rapidly toward 3-4 ppm per year. If carbon continues to rise in this exponential, *nonlinear* way, virtually unchecked by our ineffective previous actions, the increase could easily reach a level of 4-5 ppm per year by 2025.

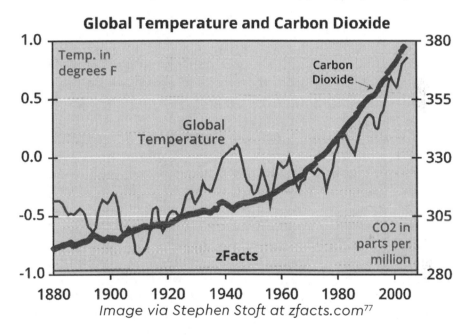

Image via Stephen Stoft at zfacts.com[77]

According to James Hansen, a carbon 450 ppm level would *eventually* correspond and develop into an average global temperature increase of 6° Celsius (10.8° Fahrenheit) in this century and the end of human civilization as we've come to know it.[78] Based on carbon ppm levels already in the system,

[77] Stephen Stoft. "Evidence that CO2 is the Cause of Global Warming." *zFacts.com*, accessed January 9, 2017, zfacts.com/p/226.html

[78] Hansen, J., et al.. "Ice melt, sea level rise and superstorms: evidence from paleoclimate data, climate modeling, and modern observations that 2 °C global warming could be dangerous." *Atmos.Chem.Phys.net*, 16, (2015): doi:10.5194/acp-16-3761-2016, 2016.

and reaching the 450 mark, this also means at least another 2.7° Celsius (4.9° Fahrenheit) global temperature increase beyond where we are now is the eventual and inescapable future reality.[79]

This 2.7° Celsius would also be the most realistic *minimal* temperature increase to project as part of any future planning over the next 10-30 years. Bear in mind that even this scenario applies only if everything goes perfectly and we cross no additional global warming tipping points.

Unfortunately, it is highly probable that because of our ongoing denial and delay in addressing escalating global warming, atmospheric carbon parts per million will most likely continue to rapidly rise beyond the carbon 450-550 ppm total, which translates to a 3° to 4° Celsius increase (5.4° to 7.2°+ Fahrenheit) up to as much as a 6° Celsius (10.8° Fahrenheit) increase in average global temperature. (A 4° Celsius increase [7.2° Fahrenheit] in average global temperature would become "Hell on earth" as Mark Lynas, author of *Six Degrees: Our Future on a Hotter Planet*, has stated.)

Hansen's projections for ending human civilization as we know it" are *not* the same as *mass human extinction* as we approach the 5° or 6° Celsius (9° to 10.8° Fahrenheit) temperature levels. In Hansen's 6° Celsius rise coming from eventually crossing the carbon 450 ppm mark, what would be considered normal, comfortable, or predictable daily life in developed nations will be severely impaired. In undeveloped nations, there will be a level of chaos and breakdown that will rapidly render most of these nations politically and economically unsustainable. As it is already occurring, the chaos of existing less-developed nations destabilized by factors such as war and the global warming emergency will affect the more developed and stable nations *far beyond* just the current massive migrations of those escaping the suffering.

---

[79] Climate research and researcher perspectives used within the book may not always precisely agree. Such differences can be accounted for by using different research, different formulas, different time horizons, newer research studies displacing older research, or slightly different interpretations of similar data by different climate researchers.

In spite of all the media PR, 21 UN / IPCC climate conferences, endless warnings from credible scientists over the last 30 years, and national reduction pledges and treaties, things are worsening in a nearly *exponential* progression (2,4,8,16, etc.) There is no way to deny we are not only losing the escalating global warming battle, but losing it at a progressively faster rate!

Instead of enacting the needed changes when they were far easier, more gradual, and far less costly, we must now take radical, painful, and costly *tough medicine* if we are going to save the future. The changes that would have been inconvenient 30 years ago will now become nearly unbearable.

Some of today's most disturbing global warming facts

1. We are not receiving adequate accurate facts about how bad escalating global warming is now, or how bad it will become. The heavily lobbied global media decline alarming us to the real dangers in order to allow the fossil fuel industry to continue business as usual.

2. Current atmospheric fossil fuel burning-related carbon ppm values are now at 410. This is higher than at any other time in the last 1 million years (possibly higher than any time in the last 25 million years). This new carbon pollution record represents an increase of 85 carbon ppm in the 55 years since David Keeling began making his revolutionary atmospheric carbon pollution measurements at Mauna Loa. (See graphs in this and previous chapters).

3. Carbon pollution accumulating in the atmosphere has been increasing even faster over the last few decades. It is now nearly certain that if we refuse to take

immediate, effective measures to resolve global warming, future increases will happen *at even faster rates*.

4. Global average temperatures have the potential to rise far faster than what we normally experience. For example, about 9600 BC, in the Boreal climatic phase,[80] global temperatures rose 7° C (12.6° F) in *less than a decade*, pushing the ice sheets into rapid collapse and sending sea levels soaring.[81]

Our 30-year inability to control the global warming emergency is due in part to:

1. The lack of national and international verifiable and enforceable international laws that would make continued large-scale carbon and methane pollution of the atmosphere a strongly punished activity or crime.

2. The physical time lags in developing and deploying the infrastructure needed for the new green energy technologies. As we are progressing now, it will likely take another 30-50 years.

But, if everyone on the planet and every government simultaneously agreed to scale up green energy generation immediately and there were *no budgetary or resource restrictions* in completing this life-critical project, it could take just 10 years to put that infrastructure in place.

If escalating global warming and its consequent climate destabilization proceed to the levels currently being predicted, it will eventually cost the global society hundreds of trillions of

---

[80] Wikipedia. "Boreal (age)." *Wikipedia.org*. Last modified November 6 2016. https://en.wikipedia.org/wiki/Boreal_(age)

[81] Alley, Richard B., *The Two-Mile Time Machine: Ice cores, abrupt climate change, and our future* (Princeton University Press; 2000.)

dollars in crisis recovery, as well as soaring insurance rates, massive real estate losses and depreciation, and massive coastal and other infrastructure losses, in addition to the vast amount of human suffering and death.

Right now, most nations are struggling with debt and their economies are in trouble with anemic annual growth. How will many of these nations, particularly the weakest ones, remain politically or financially viable, stable, or even continue to exist if another 5% or more of their total GDP (the Stern Review[82]) is drained off each year into the continually escalating costs of global warming-caused climate destabilization? Current estimates from a book called *Climate Shock*[83] project all global warming consequences will cost 10 percent and maybe far more of the world's total GDP by 2100.

The global warming emergency is already here! Its superstorms, flooding, seasonal disruptions, wildfires, heat waves, migrating insect infestations, and droughts will continue increasing in magnitude and frequency. According to a recent analysis from scientists at the National Center for Atmospheric Research (NCAR), "[t]he worst case projections for global warming may be the most likely."[84]

The next battle now lies in keeping global warming from becoming irreversible or rising to an extinction-level event where human-caused carbon dioxide and methane levels in the atmosphere push the global temperature increases to 4°-6° Celsius (7.2°-10.8° Fahrenheit) above preindustrial levels *and beyond.*

---

[82] Nicholas Stern. "Stern Review on the Economics of Climate Change." *UK Government Web Archive*. Last modified July 4, 2010. http://webarchive.nationalarchives.gov.uk/20100407172811/http://www.hm-treasury.gov.uk/stern_review_report.htm

[83] Gernot Wagner and Martin Weitzman, *Climate Shock* (Princeton University Press; April 2016).

[84] Common Dreams. "Worst case climate projections likely: Study." *CommonDreams.org*. November 9, 2012. http://www.commondreams.org/news/2012/11/09/worst-case-climate-projections-likely-study

An already "baked-in" future of higher temperatures no matter what we do

A 2° Celsius (3.6° Fahrenheit) increase in global average temperature by year 2100 has been the official estimate of the Intergovernmental Panel On Climate Change (IPCC). But it is low and overly optimistic. This 2° Celsius IPCC estimate is based on the operating premise that everything happening in the very complex and highly interconnected climate system will always work *perfectly* as predicted, *in our favor*, and no more known or unknown climate tipping points will be crossed.

Coming Soon, Superstorms, Extreme Droughts, Floods & Wildfires

Planning for everything to go perfectly is the perfect plan for failure, and there's a dangerous global warming shocker hidden within these low temperature estimates. The first wave of escalating global warming superstorms or "millennial storms" (storm severity levels that have not been seen for thousands or tens of thousands of years) will be coming much sooner than we are planning for. When you include crossing more of the critical global warming tipping points and adjust projections in evaluating the current climate data, it suggests all types of extreme weather such as millennial superstorms, super droughts, super floods, and super wildfires could begin replacing our current waves of extreme weather in as little as 15 to 30 years.

Unfortunately, there's more bad news. Even if we stopped emitting all carbon dioxide and methane greenhouse gases today, we face considerably more global warming than the IPCC has publicly stated. According to Michael Mann, Distinguished Professor of Meteorology at the University of Pennsylvania State, we are already on track for a total rise in temperature of 1.7° Celsius [85] (about 3° Fahrenheit) in the northern hemisphere, *no matter what we now* do to slow or stop global warming. In part, this is because there is future global warming already "baked into" the warming pipeline.

This is what it is called "committed warming." Committed warming is inevitable, delayed only by the lag time for the oceans to heat up, owing to the slow ocean warming response to greenhouse gases.

The temperature increase of 1.7° Celsius (3° Fahrenheit) is already committed. This is baked-in global warming and it is *really bad news*.

Worse yet, the computer modeling used to create the 1.7° Celsius prediction also does not include the possibility that we have unconsciously already crossed or could very soon cross more global warming tipping points. If that has happened or will happen soon, the calculation for already committed global warming could be significantly above 1.7° Celsius. We could

[85]Michael E. Mann. "How close are we to dangerous planetary warming." *The Huffington Post*. December 23, 2015. http://www.huffingtonpost.com/michael-e-mann/how-close-are-we-to-dangerous-planetary-warming_b_8841534.html

rapidly move through an increase of 2° or 3° Celsius (3.6° to 5.4° Fahrenheit) and beyond.

Additionally, after all of the atmospheric fossil fuel-related soot is gone, global temperatures are estimated to go up an additional .2 to .5° Celsius (0.36°-1° Fahrenheit), depending upon the atmospheric soot levels in your area of the world.

This additional calculation for how average global temperature will go up as we rapidly shut down the aerosol soot created by fossil fuel burning *is significant*. This implies that planning your personal or business future using *only* 1.7° Celsius (3° Fahrenheit) of *already committed* and "baked-in" average global warming is also a faulty and dangerous future planning assumption.

It would be far wiser to assume an increase in average global temperature of 1.9° to 2.2° Celsius (about 3.4° to 4° Fahrenheit) as a long-term planning *starting point*. While 1.9° to 2.2° Celsius is more realistic, it is still not as good as the most realistic 2.7° Celsius increase for longer-term planning. This is because the 1.7° to 2.2° Celsius (3° to 4° Fahrenheit) previous temperature planning starting point also *does not* include any calculations regarding crossing more global warming and climate system or subsystem tipping points, which is highly likely to happen.

To put this *already committed*, non tipping point inclusive temperature range increase of 1.7° to 2.2° Celsius into another comparative perspective, the IPCC at the last Paris conference in December 2015 still pushed hard promoting that global warming should not not rise above 1.5° Celsius (2.7° Fahrenheit). This is because they already know a 1.5° Celsius increase heralds an unending chain of horrific disasters for many of the world's poorest countries. Why the IPPC promoted a global temperature target that was below the already known baked-in increase is hard to comprehend, and it will be indirectly addressed in chapter 7.

According to Professor Mann, when we hit 405 parts per million (ppm) of carbon in the atmosphere, we have now committed ourselves to a 2° Celsius (3.6° Fahrenheit) increase in global temperature. Now add in the fact that none of the above *already committed* global warming calculations except the 2.7°C (4.9° Fahrenheit) projection include any possibility that we have already unknowingly crossed or will cross more global warming tipping points. We are in deep trouble already!

From the preceding, it would be unrealistic to keep promoting that we can realistically keep the average global temperature increase below 2° Celsius. Yet, that is exactly what the IPCC promoted to world's nations at its 2015, Paris conference in addition to promoting its lower 1.5° Celsius (2.7° Fahrenheit) target.

It is time to face bitter facts. The battle to keep warming from rising less than 2° Celsius (3.6° Fahrenheit) has been lost!

In reality, if we include crossing more tipping points we face a baked-in 2.7° degrees Celsius (4.9° Fahrenheit) average global temperature rise as we approach carbon 425 to 450 ppm. We need to immediately begin preparing for these severe temperature increases while we still have time!

It is also important to be aware that even though the 2.7° degrees Celsius temperature is already baked in and committed also because of previously mentioned momentum and inertia issues, it does not mean these higher temperatures will occur immediately. It could take a decade or more for these baked-in temperature rises to be fully realized.

Additionally, when we extrapolate from the IPCC's own current worst case projections using what you have learned so far, a 6° Celsius (10.8° Fahrenheit) increase occurring *much sooner* than 2100 becomes a real probability. This eventual 6° Celsius temperature increase prediction is based on these highly probable assumptions:

1. We continue business as usual, increasing the carbon pollution of the atmosphere at our current exponentially rising levels of carbon 3-4+ ppm per year,

2. Methane continues rising as it has over the last several decades because of the fracking boom, big agribusiness and other factors, and

3. We have unknowingly already crossed or will soon cross more known or unknown global warming tipping points within any of the critical systems or subsystems of the climate system. For example, in May of 2014, we crossed another dangerous climate tipping point when scientists discovered that the West Antarctic Ice Shelf has gone into an *irreversible* and escalating melt.

According to the climate author Mark Lynas, if we let our planet's temperature increase by 6° Celsius (10.8° Fahrenheit), "it would cause a mass extinction of almost all life and probably reduce humanity to a few struggling groups of embattled survivors clinging to life near the poles."[86]

In order for humanity to endure, we now have no other prudent choice but to do whatever we can to try to lessen and slow the long-term pain of this emergency so that global warming does not become irreversible. We may still have enough time to prepare families, businesses, nations, and ourselves for the tremendous stress that escalating global warming will cause—but only if we begin preparing for it now!

Putting only a 2° Celsius temperature rise in perspective using carbon levels and temperature fluctuations from Earth's past

Seeing the global warming emergency from as many perspectives as possible will help you better grasp the depth

---

[86] Mark Lynas, *Six Degrees*. (National Geographic; January, 2008.)

and seriousness of the crisis we are in. For example, the Earth's geologic past not only verifies that specific outcomes of *global warming* have occurred, but also gives us vital information about what similar consequences *will likely occur* as we duplicate the carbon dioxide levels, atmospheric temperatures, and other conditions of our distant and not-so-distant past.

According to a 2015 paper in *Science*, about three million years ago:

1. The average global temperature was about 1.7°-2.7° Celsius (3°-5° Fahrenheit) warmer than today.

2. The Arctic regions of the planet were about 7° Celsius (12.6° Fahrenheit) warmer.

3. Carbon dioxide levels were about as high as today.

4. Sea levels stood *at least* 20 feet (6-7 meters) above today's level.[87]

In our more recent geological past, around 400,000 and 125,000 years ago, average global temperatures were respectively about 2° Celsius (3.6° Fahrenheit) and about 1° Celsius (1.8° Fahrenheit) above pre-Industrial times. During those two separate time periods, the upper bounds for sea level rise were estimated to be up to 42 feet higher (13 meters) than present. As you can imagine, at those temperatures— close to the temperature increases currently predicted—either of the sea level rises (20-foot or 42-foot) would be a nightmare for world shorelines and their populations if they were to occur today.

Unfortunately, that is exactly what we are racing toward—*and beyond*. According to the same *Science* article, even if we managed to limit average global warming to just 2° Celsius

---

[87] A. Dutton, A. E. Carlson, A. J. Long, G. A. Milne, P. U. Clark, R. Deconto, B. P. Horton, S. Rahmstorf, M. E. Raymo, "Sea-level rise due to polar ice-sheet mass loss during past warm periods." *Science*, July 10, 2015.
http://science.sciencemag.org/content/349/6244/aaa4019

(3.6° Fahrenheit), sea levels may still eventually rise at least 20 feet (6 meters) above their current levels.

The illustration below will be useful for mid range planning (the next 10-15 years) for any industry, individual, or nation whose future plans will be affected by the previously discussed consequences of escalating global warming. Keep in mind, this illustration with its estimated time frames does not include crossing *any* additional tipping points.

Baked In Temperature Increases

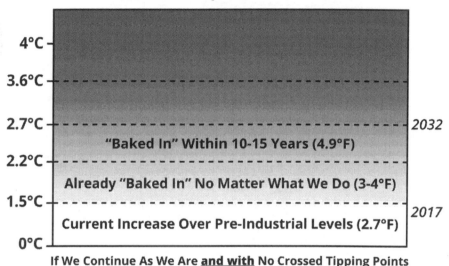

If We Continue As We Are **and with** No Crossed Tipping Points

Why the global warming State of Emergency isn't being discussed by our political leaders

To help you see where and why we are currently in a losing battle to end global warming, we have provided the following Keeling-styled graphs for the atmospheric carbon level data in different parts of this chapter.

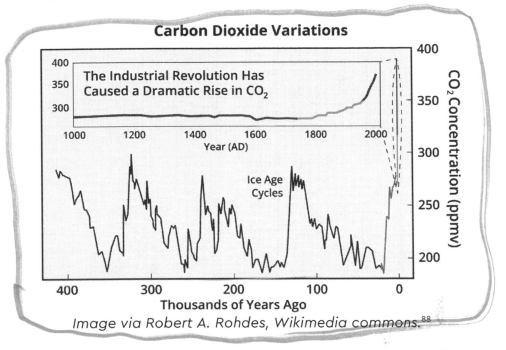

Image via Robert A. Rohdes, Wikimedia commons.[88]

The above graph shows variations in concentration of carbon dioxide in the atmosphere during the last 400 thousand years. It also helps to illustrate the carbon pollution data progressing from the Industrial Revolution of the 1880s to the present day. Other data also show the carbon ppm levels for the last several hundred thousand to millions of years. This way, you can see the modern spike in today's carbon pollution emergency in a historical, and especially post-Industrial, context.

More carbon in the atmosphere equals more heat

It is important to notice in the graph above that the *long-term average* carbon parts per million (ppm) never rose much above 270 ppm until the Industrial Revolution. For hundreds of thousands of years, carbon ppm stayed in a general range significantly below where it is today. Only hundreds of millions of years ago were carbon ppm levels much higher, during Earth's turbulent developmental and volcanic periods.

---

[88] Rohdes, Robert A. "Variations in concentration of carbon dioxide in the atmosphere during the last 400 thousand years." Digital image. Wikimedia Commons. December 21, 2009. Accessed January 11, 2017.
https://commons.wikimedia.org/wiki/File:Carbon_Dioxide_400kyr.png.

ing has radically changed in carbon ppm atmospheric since the beginning of the fossil fuel-powered Industrial lution of the 1880s. For the first time in hundreds of thousands of years, we have now crossed the unprecedented carbon 400 ppm level. Today's carbon ppm 410+ level is now nearly double the carbon 200-270 ppm range it held consistently for hundreds of thousands of years. This radical change in such a short period of geological time can and will have serious consequences!

Even if we do not cross any other global warming tipping points, which avoidance is *highly unlikely,* just by extrapolation using the current exponential rise per year and cumulative carbon levels, we could be at carbon 550 ppm in 30-40 years...*or sooner*. If we hit carbon 550 ppm, which translates to a temperature increase range of about 3° to 4°+ Celsius increase (5.4° to 7.2°+ Fahrenheit), as it appears we will, this "seals the deal" on destructive changes for most life on Earth (as described in Phase 3 of the Climageddon Scenario in the next chapter).

Extrapolating from the carbon ppm and average global temperature graph shown below, it appears that in spite of everything that we are doing now to slow escalating global warming, the current global average temperature is increasing by approximately 1/2 degree for about every 25 additional parts per million of carbon going into the atmosphere.

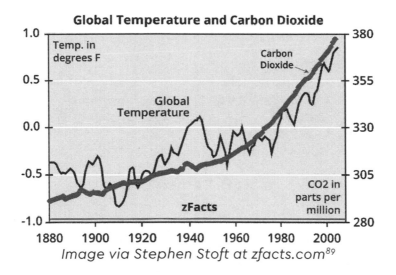

Image via Stephen Stoft at zfacts.com[89]

The above graph provides evidence that CO2 is a contributing cause of global warming. This ongoing or increasing fossil fuel use will increase carbon ppm, which then increases average global temperature. This increased or decreased carbon ppm in the atmosphere appears to have a direct or near direct relationship to rising and falling temperature all the way back to Earth's earliest times.

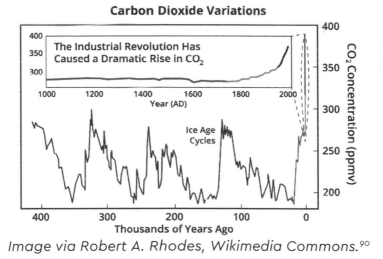

Image via Robert A. Rhodes, Wikimedia Commons.[90]

[89] Stephen Stoft. "Evidence that CO2 is the Cause of Global Warming." zFacts.com, accessed January 9, 2017, http://zfacts.com/p/226.html

In the next graph below, one can see carbon pollution levels hundreds of millions of years into our past. As you can extrapolate from the carbon ppm range disclosed near the bottom of the far lower left of the graph, modern life forms as we know them today appear to exist and function best when atmospheric carbon levels are quite low in about the 200-270 ppm range. Life on Earth was much different with the higher carbon levels seen hundreds of millions of years ago.

Phanerozoic Carbon Dioxide

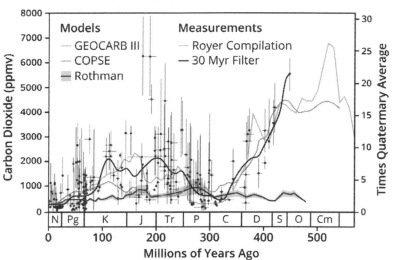

(Here, COPSE, GEOCARB III, and Rothman illustrate the findings from geochemical models for tracking CO2 levels in the past. Abbreviations at the bottom stand for the Neogene, Paleogene, Cretaceous, Jurassic, Triassic, Permian, Carboniferous, Devonian, Silurian, Ordovician, and Cambrian periods in geologic history. Image via Robert A. Rohdes, Wikimedia Commons.[91])

---

[90] Robert A. Rohdes. "Carbon Dioxide Variations." Digital image. Global Warming Art Project (defunct), archived at Wikimedia Commons. Accessed January 11, 2017. https://commons.wikimedia.org/wiki/File:Carbon_Dioxide_400kyr.png

[91] Robert A. Rohdes, "Phanerozoic_Carbon_Dioxide.png." Digital image. *Global Warming Art Project* (defunct). February 25, 2006. Accessed January 2017. https://commons.wikimedia.org/wiki/File:Phanerozoic_Carbon_Dioxide.png

How human systems contribute to the global warming State of Emergency

It would not be fair to discuss over 30 years of continuous global warming warnings without also describing some of the problems of inertia within our human systems. Inertia is defined as the resistance of any physical object to any change in its current state of motion (including changes to its speed, direction or state of rest or motion).

Our current global society is locked into the grip of almost a century and a half of change resistance (inertia) that favors using more and more fossil fuel. Part of the reason for this resistance is that fossil fuel use directly or indirectly is also responsible for about one-third of the world's gross domestic product (GDP).

The fossil fuel industry engenders a powerful human system resistance to change that we will have to overcome in order to successfully change over to green energy generation systems. The fossil fuel industry is constantly fighting the needed evolution of our energy generation systems. But even if we ended all fossil fuel use today, it is estimated that it would take 30 to 50 years to replace all of the current fossil fuel generation and distribution infrastructure.

Unfortunately, there is nothing close to unanimous agreement to act now, and we don't have another 30 to 50 years to fight the resistance of various fossil-fueled nations and fossil fuel-related corporations. Therefore, it is completely fair to say that the fossil fuel industry resistance and inertia are significant factors explaining why after 30 years of warnings, global warming is actually getting worse and not better!

In addition to the inertia and resistance of the fossil fuel industry working against efforts to end the use of polluting fossil fuels, here are other significant human system resistance (inertia) factors for why global warming is escalating faster than ever before in spite of all previous warnings:

1) *Human evolutionary psychology:* We are designed to react to immediate and obvious threats with the flight or fight response. Escalating global warming is slow, almost invisible, and it is generally believed to be far off in the future. Also, for many individuals, it is so complex that it can't be comprehended as the single most serious international security threat of the 21st century.

2) *Human political evolution:* Human society has not yet evolved a global government with transnational enforcement and verification powers over all the member nations of our world. Global warming is a *transnational problem* that *has to have* a *transnational solution.*

3) *Human legal evolution:* Humanity has not evolved viable global courts to work out the inherent international justice issues relating to the developed countries that caused the pollution and will likely benefit from it in the short term. We really have no international justice process for dealing with the fact that *undeveloped* countries that didn't cause the pollution are expected to suffer nearly equally in the costs and efforts of resolving it.

4) *Global political evolution:* The designated world authority, the UN's Intergovernmental Panel on Climate Change (the IPCC), failing to properly educate global leaders on all critical global warming risks, along with providing significantly underestimated timetables, has dangerously diminished a global sense of collective urgency and public awareness. This has significantly reduced the demand for change even though strong warnings were initiated over 30 years ago.

There are other reasons why we have failed for 30 years and still face a daunting challenge to end the global warming emergency, which will be covered in Chapters 7 and 8.

A difficult truth

Before facing a difficult truth, it is important to review the definitions of climate and weather. Climate is the statistics of weather, usually *over a 30-year interval*. It is measured by assessing the patterns of variation in temperature, humidity, atmospheric pressure, wind, precipitation, atmospheric particle count, and other meteorological variables in a given region over long periods of time. Climate differs from weather, in that weather only describes the short-term conditions of these variables in a given region. (From Wikipedia.[92])

Fossil fuel lobbyists like to intentionally confuse us by directing our attention to the far shorter time cycles of climate and weather, whereas global warming cycles occur over far longer time cycles (as seen in the graphs depicting hundreds, thousands, and millions of years.) When we compare the current global warming cycle and temperature range to past global warming cycles and temperature ranges rather than tiny 30 year climate cycles, we can see what's really happening and how dangerous global warming is to our future.

From the preceding, it is not difficult for any rational person to see that we are dealing with far more than garden-variety seasonal changes in the weather or the the normal 30-year climate cycle. We are dealing with a full blown and yet undeclared global warming emergency.

In truth, we have wasted over 30 years of valid warnings, and now there is no time left to make the gradual changes that we should have begun over 30 years ago. Immediate, radical, and painful change must happen now. Our global warming emergency is not off in the future 25, 50 or 100 years from now as you have been deceived into believing. Our global warming emergency is now.

---

[92] Wikipedia contributors, "Climate," *Wikipedia, The Free Encyclopedia*, https://en.wikipedia.org/w/index.php?title=Climate&oldid=764370642 (accessed February 14, 2017).

per dive into the science

This is optional reading.

1. In order to help you better visualize the global warming tipping point risks, as well as why we are not effectively acting to end the extreme risks of the global warming State of Emergency, we strongly recommend you view *The Most Terrifying Video You'll Ever See 2*. It has been watched almost 7 million times. recheck other chapters for this[93] to watch that video now.

2. If you are still not yet convinced we are really in a global warming state of emergency, or you want to see more detailed science on this issue, please recheck other chapters for this.[94]

Your next vaccination

In the process of resolving global warming, we also can create the foundation for a long-term *sustainable prosperity*

It's not all bad news now that we know exactly where we are in the global warming emergency. This accurate knowledge will motivate rational and mature individuals to make the needed changes toward a more sustainable future.

By being forced toward a sustainable future, we will create tens of millions of new great paying jobs as we act to end the carbon and methane fossil fuel-related pollution that has been steadily added to the atmosphere since the beginning of the Industrial Revolution of the 1880s.

---

[93] "The Most Terrifying Video You'll Ever See." YouTube video. 9:33, posted by "wonderingmind42," June 8, 2007. https://www.youtube.com/watch?v=zORv8wwiadQ

[94] David Spratt. "Climate Reality Check." Breakthrough - National Centre for Climate Restoration. March 2016. http://media.wix.com/ugd/148cb0_4868352168ba49d89358a8a01bc5f8of.pdf

For added motivation, consider that by 2050 sea levels may rise 6-10 feet (1.8-3 meters) or more, depending on how many tipping points we cross. This sea level rise will, of itself, help generate the greatest single construction project in human history. We will soon need to begin to move *all* coastal homes and businesses, as well as all essential water, electrical, transportation, and waste and sewage infrastructure at least 13-20 feet (3.9-6 meters) above the current sea level. This estimation is necessary after adding global warming sea level rise to the sometimes coincident storm and superstorm surges occurring at the same time as "king" high tide peaks. It also factors in an additional safety margin for crossing more known or unknown global warming tipping points.

"If there's a sustainable job that will create sustainable value, people will hire for it."
— David Cunliffe, New Zealand Member of Parliament

There is also much new construction and reconstruction work that we will have to do for wildfire, drought, and inland lake and river flooding mitigation. For example, the superstorms that will be coming in nontraditional locations and at nontraditional times will require new infrastructure, water storage, and management facilities all over the world.

We will need to create a green *Third Industrial Revolution*[95] that could directly and indirectly create millions more new green energy-related jobs worldwide. This green energy generation revolution will replace the preceding Second Industrial Revolution and the polluting fossil fuel energy generation that has powered it.

Going to green energy generation as rapidly as possible also has an important additional sustainability and resilience-

---

[95] This refers to Jeremy Rifkin's concept of a Third Industrial Revolution. Like the mechanization of the textile industry in the First Industrial Revolution of the 1800s and mass production via assembly lines in the Second Industrial Revolution of the 1900s, a Third Industrial Revolution is occurring as manufacturing goes digital. Paraphrased from Paul Markillie, "A third industrial revolution." *The Economist*. April 21st, 2012. http://www.economist.com/node/21552901

building effect for surviving the growing consequences of escalating global warming. Solar and wind energy generation is often *decentralized,* which allows for it to be put on local homes and businesses. When climate catastrophes occur, power will come back up much faster because of this decentralization, with energy generation located right where the power is most needed and used.

In finally resolving escalating global warming, we will also be forced to create new, better, and more sustainable lifestyles, livelihoods, and community models. They will demonstrate the validity of sustainability principles to further guide us once we end the escalating global warming emergency and then need proven strategies to maintain our success.

> "Sustainable development is the pathway to the future we want for all. It offers a framework to generate economic growth, achieve social justice, exercise environmental stewardship and strengthen governance."
> — Ban Ki-moon, Secretary-General of the United Nations

Working together in these new *sustainable prosperity* lifestyles, livelihoods, and communities, we can also make our lives as good as possible. It is not difficult to envision how these new lifestyles, livelihoods, and communities will play an essential climate restabilization role. They will be a new sustainable prosperity model for the world in that they will also help create a long-term evolutionary future for today's population and for generations to come.

> "In the 21st century, I think the heroes will be the people who will improve the quality of life, fight poverty and introduce more sustainability."
> — Bertrand Piccard, Swiss psychiatrist; pioneering trans-global balloonist

What's next

At this point, it is fair to say that you now know more about the global warming emergency than most any politician or bureaucrat in the world. The next chapter will present the six phases of the Climageddon Scenario model for how escalating global warming will unfold and proceed. In it, you will find a detailed list of *must-know* warning signals for how and when we will enter its endgame phases. And finally, if all of the preceding tough news is getting to you, keep in mind that in Part 2 you will find effective actions to make a difference and help solve this emergency.

Summary

- In the above graphs of this chapter, the predictions for increased carbon ppm levels and temperature unfortunately *does not also include*: the continued likelihood that more carbon ppm will enter the atmosphere each year due to increasing population and fossil fuel use, causing an ever-faster rate of average global temperature increase, or the effects of the additional methane going into the atmosphere because of existing and new natural gas fracking, all of the existing leaks in methane storage and transportation systems, and big agribusiness, or calculations for more climate tipping points that will be crossed as the atmosphere heats up in a vicious self-reinforcing cycle and a positive feedback loop.

- Despite 30 years of warnings from credible scientists and compelling scientific evidence, atmospheric carbon dioxide and methane pollution have only worsened.

- We are already in an unacknowledged global warming State of Emergency.

- Do not be fooled by what you read about global warming reduction progress or fossil fuel reduction commitments in fossil fuel-lobbied and influenced mainstream media. The fossil fuel industry wants to keep making money and polluting our atmosphere without charge.

- In a nutshell, the global warming emergency is due to:

    o today's carbon ppm level of 410 ppm doubling from the carbon 200-270 range it held consistently for hundreds of thousands of years,

    o carbon ppm levels rising exponentially at the greatest levels since the Industrial Revolution, and

    o we are poised to cross more global warming tipping points, moving us ever closer to the extinction phases of the Climageddon Scenario.

b. According to James Hansen, even a carbon 450 ppm level (which will occur in about 10-15 years at present carbon pollution rates) would eventually correspond to an average global temperature increase of 6° Celsius (10.8° Fahrenheit) in this century and the end of human civilization as we've come to know it.[96]

The current global warming emergency marks the end of the climate stability that has allowed humanity and humanity's near ancestors to flourish for hundreds of thousands of years.

---

[96] Hansen, James, et al. "Target atmospheric CO2: Where should humanity aim?" *The Open Atmospheric Science Journal* 2, no. 1 (2008): 217-231. DOI: 10.2174/1874282300802010217

PART 1, CHAPTER 6

HOW THE CLIMAGEDDON SCENARIO WILL HELP YOU PLAN YOUR *NEW* FUTURE

Overview:

- Despite the intense risk factors and negative wild cards of the new Climaggedon Scenario model, there also may be undiscovered positive wild cards that could help significantly slow, lessen, and eventually end global warming.

- At this moment in time, as some Arctic and Antarctic ice sheets have already melted irreversibly, we are most likely either in mid-to-late Phase 1, or the beginning stages of Phase 2 of the Climageddon Scenario.

- In Phase 3, a cascading chain reaction of crossed tipping points and points of no return accelerates the scale, severity, and frequency of global warming consequences—thus creating the ideal end game conditions for Phases 4 through 6.

- By Phase 5, we will have reached extinction-level climate destabilization. Approximately half or more species on Earth, including most or all of humanity, will die.

- With the current levels of carbon going into the atmosphere, we could reach Phase 5 *in far less than* a century.

The Climageddon Scenario is a new global warming process prediction model to help individuals visualize the unfolding 6 phases of the escalating global warming emergency as one interconnected whole as well as one interdependent and continually evolving climate, human, and biological system. In a way never seen before, it sequences and integrates the most important global warming factors from the previous chapters.

Understanding the unfolding progression of the 6 phases of the Climageddon Scenario is life-critical for any individual, organization, or nation that takes planning for their physical security or financial future seriously. It is also crucial to anyone involved in:

a. personal, financial or security mid- to long-range planning,
b. threat, hazard, and insurance risk assessment,
c. city, corporate, or national mid- to long-range planning,
d. planning, financing, or building mid- to long-term infrastructure such as highways, water treatment or sewage plants, power plants, transfer stations, power lines, hospitals, government buildings, manufacturing facilities, military bases, corporate headquarters, real estate developments, and telecommunications facilities.

The Climageddon Scenario will also help you to see and understand the escalating global warming emergency as a *holistic* gestalt. (A gestalt in holism is the idea that the properties of natural *systems* should also be viewed as an interconnected, unified whole and not simply as collections of, or summations of, separate and individual non-interdependent or interconnected parts.)

Please keep in mind that the temperature, carbon ppm, and loss or cost levels described below for each phase of the Climageddon Scenario are not hard and rigid boundaries, but boundary *ranges* designed to help you think about a set of related consequences and their intensities associated with that phase of the scenario. The temperature, carbon, cost, and loss phase boundary levels below may be modified by future research.

The Climageddon Scenario

The Climageddon Scenario is far more than just the sum of the individual global warming consequences and tipping points presented earlier. In the unfolding phases of this scenario, it becomes easier to see these heat-intensified *individual* consequences and tipping points churning into something far more dangerous than just the collective summation of individual consequences or tipping points. *Collectively,* all of these things create and fuel the deadly later stages of the Climageddon Scenario described fully below.

When you begin viewing the Climageddon Scenario model as an integrated climate, human, and biological super system, as well as seeing it from a meta-systemic perspective, you will also discover:

a. new critical *relationships* between the climate, human, and biological systems and processes,

b. new qualifying and conditioning climate, human, and biological *contexts*, and finally,

c. new phase-by-phase catastrophic interactions and magnifying *transformations* of interconnected and interdependent climate, human, and biological system consequences that will dramatically worsen our lives.

Don't worry if you do not see the big picture quite yet. There is a lot to see within it. To help you, there are illustrations throughout this chapter.

One last thing: all temperature amounts in this or any other chapter are always displayed as the Celsius or Fahrenheit increase from preindustrial average global temperatures. All temperature and estimated timetable predictions given below will be updated on the Climageddon Book Support Navigation Center page at JobOneforHumanity.org whenever relevant new research comes out. This book support navigation page will contain other types of updates, options, and action list support information referred to throughout the book.

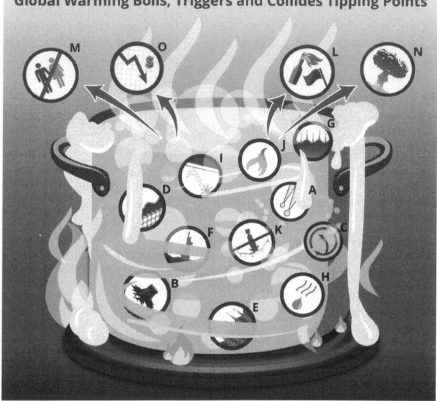

Global Warming Boils, Triggers and Collides Tipping Points

A - Melting Ice	**F** - Weight of Rising Seas	**K** - Plankton Dying
B - Forest Loss	**G** - Soils Overheating	**L** - National Instability
C - Ocean Current Change	**H** - Water Vapor Increase	**M** - Social Instability
D - Permafrost Pandemic	**I** - Albedo Effect	**N** - War & Conflict
E - Ocean Heating	**J** - Methane Release	**O** - Economic Loss & Collapse

Assigning risk levels to the 6 phases of the Climageddon Scenario

To help you put into perspective the serious implications of the consequences unfolding at each of the 6 phases of the Climageddon Scenario, we use three commonly recognized risk, threat, and hazard alert scales. Those three scales are:

a. The DEFCON 5-1 levels used by the U.S. government and military regarding preparedness for nuclear or conventional war. (The DEFCON rating system goes from 5 to 1. DEFCON 5 is normal peacetime military readiness, and 1 is highest military alert, such as imminent nuclear war. As the climate continues to destabilize, at some point the nations of the world will have to declare emergency regulations and martial law to deal with the escalating crisis and the internal and external instability it creates. Using this scale is appropriate because if left unchecked, global warming will parallel and eventually exceed the destructiveness of all non-nuclear world wars.)

b. The current US Homeland Security Advisory System. (The Homeland Security Advisory System is a color-coded terrorism threat advisory scale. The different levels trigger specific actions by federal agencies and state and local governments, and they affect the level of security at some airports and other public facilities. Although this is a terrorist threat risk system, it is also useful for climate crises. In the mid-to-later phases of the Climageddon Scenario, as our political, economic, and social systems break down, the nations of the world will react similarly to how they would react to a high-level terrorist threat or an actual attack. Martial law and other restrictive emergency measures with curfews, new regulations, loss of civil rights, and normal legal protections will be enacted.)

c. The Torino Impact Hazard 0-10 Scale used to quantify the many risks and hazards of asteroids of different sizes hitting the earth. (The Torino Scale goes from 0 to 10, where a 0 rating is no hazard or threat and a 10 is "a collision is certain, capable of causing global climactic catastrophe that may threaten the future of civilization as we know it, whether impacting land or ocean.")

There is good reason to use the Torino Impact Hazard Scale with the Climageddon Scenario. Depending upon what phase of the scenario we enter, how we adapt may be uncannily similar to how we might adapt to survive impacts of various asteroid sizes.

For example, if we knew *well in advance* that a small, survivable asteroid would hit the earth, using the Torino scale advisories could provide enough time to relocate almost everyone from the *local* hazardous area of impact. If a larger but still survivable asteroid were to hit, once again using the Torino scale, we could have time to relocate almost everyone from the larger *regional* area of impact.

Similar to these asteroid impact scenarios, as the escalating global warming emergency continues through the 6 Climageddon Scenario phases, it will also eventually force us to relocate first millions, then billions of people. We will relocate them first locally, then regionally, next nationally, and eventually internationally to the far north or far south.

We may have to move as much of the total human population as can survive even in the poorer soils and shorter growing seasons of the northernmost countries of the world (above the 45th parallel north to Canada, Russia, Scandinavia, Alaska, Iceland, and Greenland), and also potentially below the 45th parallel south to utilize a haven in the south island of New Zealand or the tip of South America.

Assuming you have read the essential information of the previous chapters on global warming consequences and tipping points, you are properly prepared to explore the 6 phases of the Climageddon Scenario described below to see how what we call the *perfect storm of perfect storms* unfolds.

Introducing the 6 phases of the Climageddon Scenario (CS)

The beginning and ending boundaries for each phase of the Climageddon Scenario are *approximate* temperature, time frame, and carbon ppm levels. As such, there will be some inherent overlap in temperature, timetable, and carbon parts per million (ppm) levels between the scenario phases.

While you are reading about the 6 phases below, please keep in mind that as each phase occurs, our ability to control or prevent the subsequent phase drops drastically. This ever-increasing *loss of effective control* helps to facilitate an ever-increasing chain reaction of more and more crossed tipping points, leading eventually to the extinction event described in Phases 5 and 6 below.

CS Phase 1: Temperature continues to rise, catastrophes increase, and carbon hits 400-450 ppm

Phase 1 is the beginning of *catastrophic climate destabilization*. Phase 1 is associated with a measurement of atmospheric carbon in the range of 400-450 ppm. As of August 2016, we were at carbon 407 ppm.

In Phase 1, the atmospheric carbon ppm rate continues to increase each year at *only* 3 ppm per year. The average global temperature continues to go up in a continuous *but linear* degree-by-degree manner.

In this phase, the many global warming consequences described in Chapter 2 continue increasing in frequency and magnitude, but once again in a linear manner. In Phase 1, the cost of significant *single-instance*, global warming-influenced disasters will average in the $30-$100 billion range.

In the early stage of Phase 1 (carbon 407-425 ppm) temperatures will increase beyond the *estimated* current 1.2° Celsius[97] (about 2.2° Fahrenheit) rise. They will increase by about 1.7°-2.2° Celsius (3°-4° Fahrenheit) and millions of people will become climagees and migrate toward the northernmost countries.

---

[97] Other research estimates our current average global temperature is between 1.2°-1.5° Celsius (2.2°-2.7° Fahrenheit) above preindustrial levels.

> "[The] ...atmospheric greenhouse gas levels (~400ppm CO2 and ~485 CO2e [carbon dioxide equivalent]) are likely the highest in the last 15 million years, and never previously experienced by humans. The current conditions, if maintained over centuries/millennia (that is, until the system reaches equilibrium), would likely produce temperature increases of +3-6° Celsius and sea levels 25–40 metres higher, based on evidence of past climates." —David Spratt, "Climate Reality Check"[98]

If the average global temperature in Phase 1 continues to rise degree-by-degree, even without crossing any more points of no return or global warming, climate, human, and biological system tipping points, the bad news is we can still bring about the *end-of-the-world* scenario of the later phases of the Climageddon Scenario.

In the later stages of Phase 1, if we continue *only* up to carbon 450 ppm, in 16 years or less (about 2022-2032) we can expect an eventual increase in average global temperature of 2.2°-2.7° Celsius (4°-4.9° Fahrenheit), and many more people will either migrate or die. When we cross the carbon 425-450 ppm mark and possibly enter Phase 2, we are *highly likely* to continue rapidly toward the 3°, 4°, 5°, and 6° Celsius increases (5.4°, 7.2°, 9°, and 10.8° Fahrenheit).

The steadily rising temperatures of Phase 1 will unfortunately also feed and accelerate the processes of crossing more *points of no return* and global warming, climate, human, and biological system tipping points. The possibility of maintaining only a gradually increasing average global temperature is highly unlikely (less than 10-20%) because of the higher probability of crossing more tipping points.

In 2016, we added *4 ppm* of new carbon to the atmosphere as our per year average. In Phase 1, *as well as all of the other 5 phases below*, it is highly unlikely that we will be able to

---

[98] David Spratt. "Climate Reality Check." *Breakthrough - National Centre for Climate Restoration*. March 2016.
http://media.wix.com/ugd/148cb0_4868352168ba49d89358a8a01bc5f80f.pdf

maintain the previous average annual increase of only carbon 3 ppm. This is due *in part* to the Earth's population soaring to 9 billion, causing our estimated energy needs to skyrocket by 40% as more of the world's population enters into the middle class.

As described earlier, for each Climageddon phase, three different risk ratings are provided.

Phase 1 US military DEFCON rating:

DEFCON 4, described as *increased intelligence gathering and security measures.*

Phase 1 US Homeland Security risk rating:

Orange: *High risk.*

Phase 1 Torino impact rating:

Torino rating 8: *The threat is highly certain for localized and regional destruction. Attention by public and governmental contingency planning is merited if the events are less than 3 decades away.*

CS Phase 2: We have crossed significant *points of no return* and more tipping points. Normal life begins changing significantly, carbon hits 450-500 ppm

Phase 2, the beginning of *irreversible climate destabilization*, is associated with a measurement of atmospheric carbon in the range of 450-500 ppm. Phase 2 *could begin* as early as carbon 425 ppm if the annual carbon ppm per year average does not return to the annual carbon 3 ppm or lower range, or we cross more tipping points.

If the carbon ppm increase averages *only* around 3 ppm per year in Phase 2, the average global temperature rises faster *and in a less gradual* (i.e., less linear) manner. In Phase 2, the global warming consequences described in Chapter 2 continue to increase magnitude and frequency, but also in a *less gradual, faster* manner. It is important to understand the accelerating effect of interacting global warming consequence processes and relationships as the phases unfold. As global warming continues, its consequences will not just become more frequent; they will also keep expanding and intensifying in the other two dimensions of scale and severity.

Phase 2 begins the process of *irreversible climate destabilization*. It is considered irreversible because the time scale to repair the damage goes far beyond human lifespans. In this phase, the cost of single instance, global warming-related disasters may average in the $100-$300 billion range.

Because of melting ice and permafrost and crossed tipping points in the Arctic, in the beginning of Phase 2 we are highly likely to cross more points of no return and tipping points in climate human and biological systems. Evidence we could soon enter Phase 2 is already found in the North and South polar regions as they are warming at about twice the speed as the rest of the world.

Rapidly increasing temperatures and changing polar currents have already demonstrated major effects on weather all over the world. The significantly higher temperature range in the polar regions is a likely "hot spot" to trigger crossing many known and unknown points of no return in these regions.

In addition to our rapidly rising carbon ppm level, another powerful indicator that we are rapidly approaching Phase 2 is the melting and breaking off of the West Antarctic ice sheet. Scientists are now saying the ice sheet has passed its *point of irreversibility*, meaning it will not return within a time frame that would enable us to solve our situation.

The loss of the West Antarctic ice sheet is *extremely* dangerous because it has held back much more massive Antarctic ice fields from plunging into the sea. If this happens, sea levels will quickly rise 10-20 feet (3-6 meters) over a time frame that we will not be able to adapt to without massive financial losses and casualties.

If we are lucky and maintain an average carbon increase of 3 ppm per year and we *do not* cross more points of no return or tipping points, it will take about 16 to 33 years (about 2032-2050) to reach carbon 450 or 500 ppm. The eventual average global temperature increase range commonly associated with Phase 2's climate destabilization is about 2.5° to 3.2° Celsius or 4.5° to 5.8° Fahrenheit.

In Phase 2, when more global warming points of no return and tipping points are crossed, the progression resembles what occurs when one changes from careening down a gradual slope into a steeper one. You are not yet rolling uncontrollably. You still have time left to think about what is coming before you crash, but the steeper the hill's incline, the less chance you have of stopping or controlling your momentum.

In Phase 2, hundreds of millions of people will become climagees and migrate toward the northernmost countries. Hundreds of millions will die. If we are not already in Phase 2, we could reach it as early as 2022-2026 if we continue at 2016's carbon increase of 4 ppm per year and we cross more tipping points. The probability of crossing from Phase 2 into Phase 3 is more likely than not, 50% or more.

Phase 2 US military DEFCON rating:

DEFCON 3: *Armed forces readiness increased above normal levels; Air Force ready to mobilize in 15 minutes.*

Phase 2 US Homeland Security risk rating:

Severe risk.

Phase 2 Torino impact rating:

Torino rating 9: *The threat is highly certain for unprecedented localized regional and national destruction. Attention by public and both national and*

*international governments to contingency planning is
critical if the event is less than 3 decades away.*

The hidden danger of Phase 2 is that it is a *key* transition phase
within the scenario. From there on, with each new tipping
point and point of no return crossed, the effects collide across
climate, human, and biological systems, and we radically lose
so much additional control so much faster. So much so that, for
all intents and purposes, we face more than irreversible climate
destabilization. In this phase, the global warming process itself
begins to become irreversible.

When global warming becomes irreversible, it is important to
understand that it will remain irreversible beyond any
meaningful time frame compared to a human lifespan. It will
persist for hundreds or thousands of years. This phase-by-
phase loss of meaningful and effective control is also not
gradual or linear—it *accelerates and steepens as* each
subsequent phase of the Climageddon Scenario is entered.

CS Phase 3: We continue crossing more global warming tipping points, life becomes unbearable for many areas of the world, and carbon hits 500-550 ppm

Phase 3 is associated with a measurement of carbon parts per
million (ppm) in the range of 500-550 ppm. The eventual
temperature range increase commonly associated with Phase 3
will be 2.7°-3.5° Celsius, or 4.9°-6.3 ° Fahrenheit. In Phase 3, the
cost of a single significant global warming-related disaster may
average in the $300-billion to $500-billion range.

*More global warming tipping points and points of no return
are crossed.* The average global temperature continues to rise
at an even faster rate. In this phase, the global warming,
climate, human, and biological systems consequences
described in Chapter 2 (shown further below in the illustration
called *Global Warming and the Climageddon Scenario*)

continue to increase in frequency and magnitude, but *at a significantly steeper and faster* rate.

When crossed, the related multiple *global warming* tipping points of Phase 3 will also collide back and forth into *each other*, amplifying and multiplying global warming consequences across climate, human, and biological systems, setting the stage for a cascading chain reaction. (*See boiling pot illustration above.*) This creates a self-reinforcing cycle (positive feedback loop) as tipping points trigger each other, which once agains accelerates the scale, severity, and frequency of global warming consequences.

These cascading and colliding global warming tipping points foster the ideal conditions for Phases 4, 5, and 6 of the Climageddon Scenario and lead into the *perfect storm of perfect storms*. As Phase 3 unfolds, it will eventually destabilize the global economy because of the *ever-rising infrastructure repair and replacement* costs and the increasing damage to the world's other climate, human, and biological systems.

These costs will eventually become unbearable for even the economically strongest nations. In Phase 3, the world economy will likely fall into a deep recession. Politically this will destabilize first the weaker nations, then the higher functioning nations. As the climate, the global economy, and functioning nations destabilize, this cascading consequence effect will lead to chaos in the social systems and the smaller subsystems within our individual lives, businesses, and organizations.

This phase is *irreversible* climate destabilization *passing its early stages*. In this phase, unpredictable global warming-related disasters and consequences will continue to increase in magnitude, frequency and scale, but now in an *exponential progression*.

Billions of people will die and others will become climagees and migrate toward the northernmost countries. Phase 3 should also be seen as the most likely tipping point for the Climageddon Scenario *itself* when viewed as a *whole system* and set of interconnected and interrelated systems and *processes*.

At the current rate, we could be in Phase 3 *in 33 years* (about 2050) if the average annual increase in carbon dioxide and methane pollution does not rise any higher than the current average of 3 ppm and we do not cross any more points of no return and tipping points in Phase 2 of the Climageddon Scenario. Unfortunately, it is *more likely* we will hit the predicted higher average global temperatures sooner (2030-2040) due to crossing many colliding tipping points and higher annual carbon levels in the atmosphere.

In this phase, the percentage probability that we will cross many new global warming tipping points could be as high as 60 to 70%. The climate chaos, risk, and loss will rise exponentially. The probability of entering Phase 4 once Phase 3 has been entered and maintained for a considerable period of time (5-20 years) is high (60% or more).

Phase 3 US military DEFCON rating:

DEFCON 2: *High readiness; armed forces ready to deploy in six hours.*

Phase 3 US Homeland Security risk rating:

Severe risk.

Phase 3 Torino impact rating:

Torino rating 10: *The threat is highly certain for unprecedented localized regional, national, and international destruction. The threat is capable of causing global climactic catastrophes that may threaten the future of civilization as we know it. Attention by the public and both national and international governments to contingency planning is <u>mandatory</u> if the event is less than 3 decades away.*

CS Phase 4: The cascading tipping point meltdown continues; new crossed tipping points collide into global warming, climate, human, and biological systems; carbon hits 550-600 ppm

Phase 4 is associated with a measurement of carbon parts per million in the atmosphere in the range of 550-600 ppm. The eventual average global temperature range increase associated with irreversible climate destabilization is 4°-4.5° Celsius or 7.2°-8° Fahrenheit.

In Phase 4, average global temperature continues to rise even faster. In this phase, the global warming consequences described in Chapter 2 continue to increase in scope, frequency and magnitude, and at a *steep, exponential* rate.

Phase 4 of the Climageddon Scenario expands the perfect storm of perfect storms. Crossed global warming tipping points collide into each other at such a fever pitch that they *initiate* a cascading global warming system and subsystem tipping point *meltdown*. This intensifying meltdown of colliding global warming, climate, human system and biological tipping points acts to amplify, accelerate, and multiply all other *non-global-warming* related challenges such as overpopulation and poverty, pre-existing national and regional conflicts, and our pre-existing economic instabilities.

This tipping point cascading meltdown process across numerous global warming, climate, human and biological systems at one time creates ever more deadly *positive feedback loops*. This makes almost everything much harder, if not impossible, to resolve in such a chaotic environment as the world deteriorates simultaneously on many system and subsystem fronts.

Phase 4 is a deeper phase of irreversible climate destabilization. This deeper level occurs when we have moved farther away from the relatively stable dynamic equilibrium of temperature and other key weather conditions we were experiencing in our normal cyclical Ice Ages. Once we reach this stage, we will face crossing from irreversible climate destabilization into *near extinction-level* climate destabilization.

Irreversible climate destabilization defines a new average global temperature range and a set of climate destabilization consequences we might never recover from, or that could take hundreds or even many thousands of years to correct. In Phase 4, if we also hit a keystone tipping point or have a full-on cascading meltdown of many more tipping points, we will cross over into *irreversible global warming*, which is the entrance point to Phase 5. In Phase 4, the cost of a single significant global warming-related disaster may average in the $500-billion to $900-billion range.

We could reach Phase 4 in less than 58 years (about 2074) if the rate at which we are polluting the atmosphere with carbon dioxide and methane does not go up any higher than it is already (about carbon 3 ppm per year) and we do not cross many more additional tipping points in Phase 2 or Phase 3 of the Climageddon Scenario. Unfortunately, once again it is *far more likely* that we will hit the predicted higher average global temperatures *much sooner* (2045-2060) due to many more cascading crossed points of no return, tipping points, and the higher carbon levels in the atmosphere.

In late-stage Phase 4, we will be lucky if there are several billion survivors left of our current almost eight billion in the northernmost countries. Late Phase 4 is also the beginning of a global financial depression.

The probability of entering Phase 5 after being in Phase 4 for a considerable length of time (10-30 or more years) is extremely high (70% or more) because with each new phase entered, society has less and less meaningful control over the collapsing climate, human, and biological systems as more and more tipping points are crossed. These systems also collapse faster and faster with critically fewer resources available to deal with all of their unpredictable new problems.

In Phase 4 we reach the top of the risk, threat, and hazard scales as seen here. These same levels will apply to Phases 5 and 6 as well (though they are essentially inadequate to describe what has never happened before in our geologic history).

Phase 4 US military DEFCON rating:

DEFCON 1: *Maximum readiness; all forces ready for combat; nuclear war imminent or likely.*

Phase 4 US Homeland Security risk rating:

Severe risk.

Phase 4 Torino impact rating:

Torino rating 10: *The threat is highly certain for unprecedented localized regional, national, and international destruction. The threat is capable of causing global climatic catastrophes that may threaten the future of civilization as we know it Attention by the public and both national and international governments to contingency planning is* <u>*mandatory*</u> *if the event is less than 3 decades away.*

CS Phase 5: Extinction looms for the human race, we hit carbon 600-750+ ppm

The longer Phase 4 continues, the more likely we are to enter Phase 5. In Phase 5, *more global warming tipping points and points of no return are crossed in all of the systems previously mentioned.* These additional crossed tipping points will further accelerate the colliding into other global warming, climate, human and biological systems and subsystems, which will trigger more of their tipping points as well. As this meltdown continues, almost all previously mentioned systems will be thrown into utter chaos.

In Phase 5, the average global temperature continues to rise at an even faster rate than previous phases and in a *fully exponential manner*. In this phase, the global warming consequences described in Chapter 2 continue to increase in frequency and magnitude, also in *a fully exponential manner*.

This is what is called *near-extinction or extinction-level climate destabilization*. It is the near to last stage of the Climageddon Scenario.

Environmental collapse, failing economies, and failing nations will begin to collectively collide into each other and into collapsing biological systems, causing unpredictable negative consequences due to the unseen interconnections and interdependencies between climate, human, and biological systems interacting within today's complex and globalized societies. This *perfect storm of perfect storms* phase has the potential to wreak havoc upon humanity at a level never seen before in human history.

This extinction-level climate destabilization is also defined as the projected potential and eventual extinction of approximately half or more of the biological species on earth and most, if not all, of humanity. Extinction-level climate destabilization will cost billions of lives, possibly the survival of the human species itself.

This extinction-level climate destabilization is associated with the measurement of carbon parts per million in the atmosphere in the range of 600-750+ ppm. The eventual average global temperature increase range associated with Phase 5 is 5°-6° Celsius or about 9°-10.8° Fahrenheit. (This 5°-6° Celsius range is historically significant because scientists have estimated the previous global PETM mass extinction event occurred when the world was only about 5-6° Celsius warmer than it is today.)

There also is a real possibility that extinction-level climate destabilization may never correct or re-balance itself to some new climate equilibrium level, but simply move to Phase 6. And even if the climate were able to correct or re-balance itself, it could take thousands or hundreds of thousands of years. In this phase, the cost of such cascading chains of global warming-related disasters and consequences across *all of the interconnected systems* is likely to be in the $200-$600 trillion range.

At the current rate, we could be in Phase 5 in *less than 83 years* (about 2099) if the carbon 3 ppm annual increase does not go up any higher *and we do not cross* additional tipping points in Phase 2, 3, or 4 of the Climageddon Scenario. Once again, it is *far more likely* we will hit the predicted higher average global temperatures *much sooner* (2050-2070) due to crossing many global warming tipping points and the higher average annual carbon ppm levels going into the atmosphere. In Phase 5, there may be a possibility that several hundred million humans will still be able to survive in the poorer growing soils of the northernmost countries.

When all or most of the previously mentioned five phases have occurred, it is the second last step to the end game of the Climageddon Scenario. The probability of entering Phase 6 once Phase 5 has been entered and maintained for a considerable length of time (25-100+ years) is unknown. Currently, there is not enough research to know at what level of carbon ppm we will enter into Phase 6. It could be somewhere near carbon 750 ppm, or it could occur considerably above that level.

Phase 5 US military DEFCON rating: DEFCON 1.
Phase 5 US Homeland Security risk rating: *Severe risk.*
Phase 5 Torino impact rating: 10

CS Phase 6: We eventually lose our overheated atmosphere into space, we pass beyond carbon 750 ppm, and all life on Earth ends

At the current rate, we could move into Phase 6 at some unknown point as atmospheric carbon pollution continues to rise and as cascading crossed global warming points of no return and tipping points in all climate, human, and biological systems go into a *total meltdown* as well as an *endless* positive feedback loop.

In Phase 6, humanity will not have been able to control or slow escalating global warming to create a stabilized climate at any previous phase of the Climageddon Scenario. Average global temperature continues to rise with no end in sight or any way to slow it.

This is what is also known as *runaway global warming* and leads to the Venus effect. This is where our climate changes permanently in an endless and runaway *positive feedback loop*.

The Venus effect is what is believed to have happened to the atmosphere that once existed around the planet Venus. At some point, the atmosphere of Venus became so hot that the conditions that kept its water and the atmosphere from being stripped off into space were lost.

In Phase 6, all planetary life dependent upon the atmosphere will be lost. We do not know what level of greenhouse gases have to be present in our atmosphere before Earth could suffer the same loss of water and atmosphere the way Venus did. It is probably many times above our current carbon ppm level.

Because of the previous mentioned factors, it is impossible to predict when humanity could face Phase 6 of the Climageddon Scenario. In this phase, the costs will be incalculable in terms of human life, suffering, and property. It will cost us everything we know and love.

>**Phase 6 US military DEFCON rating:** DEFCON 1.
>**Phase 6 US Homeland Security risk rating:** *Severe risk.*
>**Phase 6 Torino impact rating:** 10

Overviewing Climageddon Scenario phase temperatures

There was a lot of information presented in the above description of the 6 phases of the Climageddon Scenario. To help make key areas of it easier to remember and use for future planning, the following illustrated sections have been provided.

The table below illustrates the temperature increases associated with each of the 6 phases. All the temperatures are increases over the average global temperature just before the Industrial Revolution.

Temperatures & Times of Climageddon Scenario Phases			
CS Phase	Celsius	Fahrenheit	Timeframe
1	1.7°-2.2°	3°-4°	Now
2	2.5°-3.2°	4.5°-5.8°	As soon as 2022-2026
3	2.7°-3.5°	4.9°-6.3°	As soon as 2030-2040
4	4°-4.5°	7.2°-8°	As soon as 2044-2060
5	5°-6°	9°-10.8°	As soon as 2050-2070
6	Unknown	Unknown	Unknown

Overviewing mass extinction events in a historical perspective

The possibility of a massive extinction due to entering the later phases of the Climageddon Scenario should also be seen within the context of the history of extinction events and how the species population living at the time died off in each one of these events. The following illustration shows the five known previous mass extinction events.

Mass Extinctions of Past & Climageddon Scenario

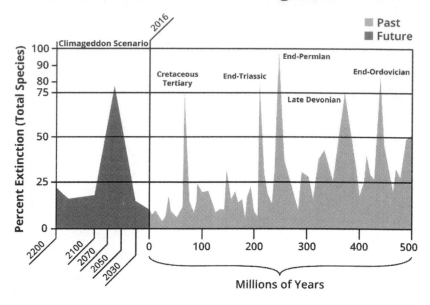

To the left in the illustration above are projections for future species losses (including humanity) if we reach the later phases of the Climageddon Scenario. Some scientists are already calling the 21st century the beginning of the Sixth Great Extinction because of the high level of species die-offs already occurring.

Overviewing the Climageddon Scenario carbon levels and rising temperatures by phase

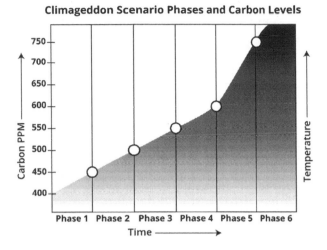

Overviewing the Climageddon Scenario financial costs

The following illustration shows how total related costs will rise dramatically at each Scenario phase for single-incident global warming disasters. In Phases 5 and 6, you will notice that the financial costs increase radically. In Phases 5 and 6, there will be many related and interconnected disasters occurring simultaneously all over the world, which collectively cause the skyrocketing amounts.

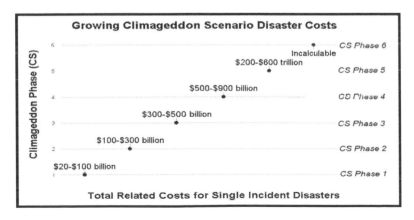

Overviewing the Climageddon Scenario as a complex adaptive system

At a meta-systemic level, the full-page illustration called *Global Warming and the Climageddon Scenario* further below makes it easier to visualize many of the Climageddon Scenario cross-system factors such as global warming consequences (Chapter 3) and tipping points in climate, human, and biological systems (Chapters 4 and 5) interacting with each other in all possible directions toward the cascading meltdown of the later Climageddon Scenario phases.

If it were possible to draw every complex interaction of the climate system within the three large boxes in the full-page illustration farther below, it would look much like a plate of tangled spaghetti noodles, slithering every possible way between each of the items within each box and between each larger horizontal box.

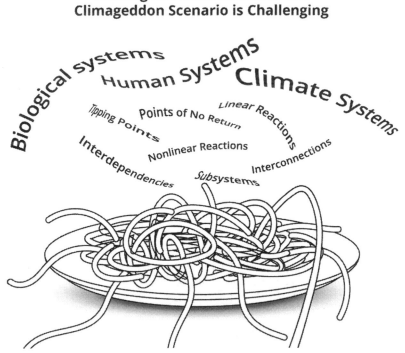

Viewing the Interactions of the Climageddon Scenario is Challenging

Many of the factors listed *within* each horizontal box in the illustration below not only react and collide amongst themselves, but each of the three large horizontal boxes *also collectively* interact with and collide into *the other* large horizontal boxes as <u>*collections*</u> of consequences and tipping points in highly unpredictable, *linear, and nonlinear* ways.

How to view the Climageddon Scenario flowchart illustration

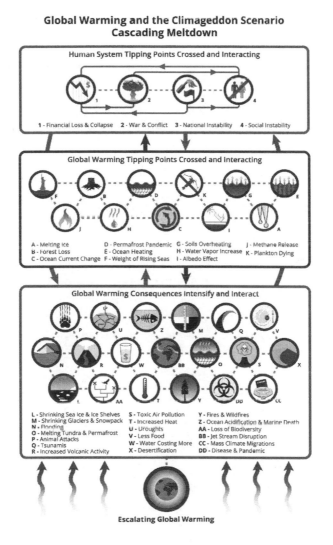

To see how one global warming factor builds upon and contributes to another it is best to review this *Global Warming and the Climageddon Scenario* illustration below starting at the bottom and then moving up to the next level. This flowchart type illustration shows the key processes, relationships, contexts, and transformations creating and fueling the full Climageddon Scenario.

Box 1 at the bottom shows how global warming creates a number of significant consequences. Below that box, increasing heat continues to increase the scale, frequency, and severity of the consequences. Moving up to Box 2, we see how increasing global warming also triggers more climate and biological tipping points. And finally, Box 3 at the top shows how global warming consequences and tipping points then spill over and trigger human system tipping points.

Unfortunately, reproducing all this global warming information in a linear flow chart does not do justice to the full complexity of either the climate system or the Climageddon Scenario's phased interactions. It does, however, help many individuals visually grasp the many layers of interactions.

From your understanding of the preceding illustration and the preceding materials, by this time it should become abundantly clear why we cannot ever let the Climageddon Scenario monster reach carbon 425-450 ppm (Phase 2). (After you have reviewed the illustration below for more on complex adaptive systems, see the "deeper dive" section of Part 1, Chapter 4.)

The Climageddon Scenario phase boundaries

It is best to think about the phases of the Climageddon Scenario as sequential stages of a logical analytical model and description of what will happen phase-by-phase as global warming unfolds and grows progressively worse. But, the Climageddon Scenario is not a rigid model cast in stone.

The 6 phases of the Climageddon Scenario *are not* separated by rigid carbon ppm levels. They are fluid. The ppm demarcation levels may evolve up or down as new research is released. For example, Phase 2 could begin as early as carbon 425 ppm, as late as carbon 475 ppm; within Phase 2 more tipping points and points of no return could be crossed sooner or later than described previously.

Other critical Climageddon Scenario risk factors: 3 wild cards

There are additional *critical* risk variables or wild cards to consider in relating to how fast the unfolding Climageddon Scenario will be. A wild card is another kind of unpredictable positive or negative factor that can drastically influence the outcome of a situation. The following negative global warming wild cards can radically spike average global temperatures and/or radically shorten or lengthen the time frames for the predicted temperatures of the 6 phases of the Climageddon Scenario.

Wild card 1: Atmospheric carbon ppm rises faster than its current average pace of about 3 ppm per year

In this wild card, we are unable to hold to the already *dangerously high* pace of adding 3 ppm of carbon per year. This causes average global temperature to increase faster than is currently predicted in the Climageddon Scenario phases. This wild card alone could *significantly* change an individual, business, or nation's long-term planning or their emergency preparedness schedules.

In the graph below, you can see our current atmospheric carbon ppm levels are not rising in a simple linear gradual line, but on a steepening exponential curve. This steep carbon ppm curve also implies that temperatures *will not* rise gradually. (This will be described in the four decade-by-decade IPCC temperature and consequence prediction scenarios in the next chapter.)

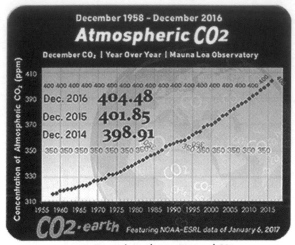

Image via Show.earth[99]

Due to the inertia factor in human systems (discussed at the end of Chapter 5 and in more detail in Chapter 7) as well as the well-financed fossil fuel industry counter forces, it is highly likely we will continue for some time to fail to pass laws that effectively limit atmospheric pollution from fossil fuel use. This strongly implies that with our skyrocketing global population, and with as many as a billion or more individuals coming into the middle class with higher energy needs, atmospheric fossil fuel levels and pollution will steadily and dramatically increase for the foreseeable future.

Therefore, it is also not unreasonable to project we will reach the new levels of 4, 5, or even 6 carbon ppm average increases per year within as little as 10-30 years. When looking at the higher carbon ppm calculations below, keep in mind that all projections are for temperatures above pre-industrial levels. It is also important to know that once *carbon* reaches the atmosphere, 75% of that carbon will not disappear for thousands of years. The other 25% stays forever. This means that we will be living with radically higher average global temperature ranges for a long, long time even after *we* finally get serious about ending the global warming emergency.

[99] Show.earth. "Keeling Curve Monthly CO2 Widget." *ProOxygen*. Accessed January 17, 2017 from https://www.show.earth/kc-monthly-co2-widget

If the annual average carbon increases of *only* 4, 5, or 6 ppm happen, *and everything goes perfectly, and we do not cross more points of no return and global warming tipping points*, the following is an approximation of what the accelerated time frames and temperatures would look like. Of course, if any of the annual carbon increases of 4, 5, or 6 ppm occur earlier than these projections or we cross more points of no return and tipping points, it will get much warmer *much faster*. Please note: None of the 3 carbon ppm variation graphs below have included *any* calculations for crossing tipping points.

If we stay at a carbon 4 ppm increase per year (like we did in 2016), we would reach:

a. carbon 450 (increase of 2.2°-2.7° Celsius or 4°-4.9° Fahrenheit) in about 15 years (2031). (This is the critical transition from Phase 1 to Phase 2 in the Climageddon Scenario, as well as the strong probability of crossing more global warming, climate, human, and biological system tipping points.)

b. carbon 500 ppm (increase of 2.5° 3.2° Celsius, or about 4.5°-5.7° Fahrenheit) in about 26 years (2042). (Phase 2).

c. carbon 550 (increase of 2.7°-3.5° Celsius, or 4.9°-6.3° Fahrenheit) in about 38 years (2054). (Phase 3).

If We Average Carbon 4 PPM Per Year

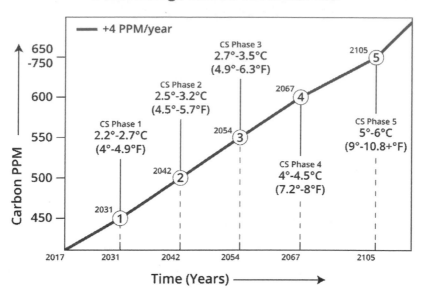

d. carbon 600 (increase of 4°-4.5° Celsius, or 7.2°-8° Fahrenheit) in about 51 years (2067). (Phase 4).

e. carbon 650-750 (increase of 5°-6° Celsius, or 9°-10.8°+ Fahrenheit) in about 89 years (2105). (Phase 5).

If we increase carbon at 4 ppm per year *at 2026* and then go to a carbon increase of 5 ppm per year *by the year 2036*, we would reach:

f. carbon 450 (increase of 2.2°-2.7° degrees Celsius or 4°-4.9° Fahrenheit) in about 15 years (2031). (This is the critical transition from Phase 1 to Phase 2 in the Climageddon Scenario, as well as the strong probability of crossing more global warming, climate, human, and biological system tipping points.)

g. carbon 500 ppm (increase of 2.5°-3.2° Celsius or 4.5°-5.7°° Fahrenheit) in about 25 years (2041). (Phase 2).

h. carbon 550 (increase of 2.7°-3.5° Celsius or 4.9° to 6.3° Fahrenheit) in about 35 years (2051). (Phase 3).

If We Average Carbon 4 and 5 PPM Per Year

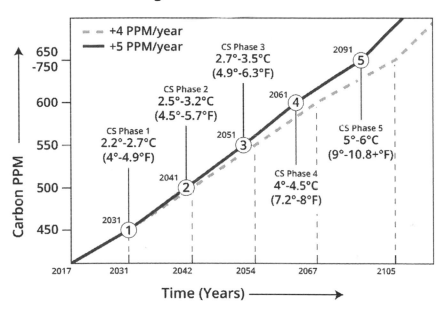

i. carbon 600 (increase of 4°-4.5° Celsius or 7.2°-8° Fahrenheit) in about 45 years (2061). (Phase 4).

j. carbon 650-750 (increase of 5°-6° Celsius, or 9°-10.8° Fahrenheit) in about 75 years (2091). (Phase 5).

If we increase carbon at 4 ppm per year *starting in 2026*, then go to a carbon increase 5 ppm per year *in the year 2036*, and finally reach carbon increase of 6 ppm per year *by the year 2046*, we would reach:

k. carbon 450 (increase of 2.2°-2.7° Celsius or 4°-4.9° Fahrenheit) in about 15 years (2031). (This is the critical transition from Phase 1 to Phase 2 in the Climageddon Scenario, as well as the strong probability of crossing more global warming, climate, human, and biological system tipping points.)

l. carbon 500 ppm (increase of 2.5°-3.2° Celsius or 4.5°-5.7° Fahrenheit) in about 25 years (2041). (Phase 2).

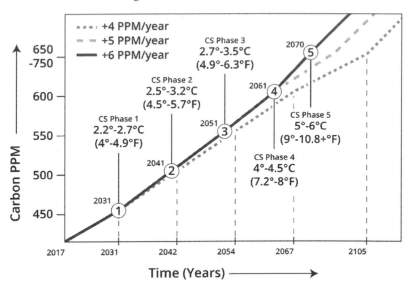

If We Average Carbon 4, 5 AND 6 PPM Per Year

m. carbon 550 (increase of 2.7°-3.5° Celsius or 4.9°-6.3° Fahrenheit) in about 35 years (2051.) (Phase 3).

n. carbon 600 (increase of 4°-4.5° Celsius or about 7.2°-8° Fahrenheit) in about 45 years (2061). (Phase 4)

o. carbon 650-750 (increase of 5°-6° Celsius or 9°-10.8° Fahrenheit) in about 54 years (2070). (Phase 5).

Wild card 2: Crossed global warming tipping points can unexpectedly spike up global temperatures and accelerate timetables

As we cross more global warming tipping points, there is currently no method of *precisely calculating* either how suddenly or how high average global temperatures might spike beyond our current temperature increases. What we do know is that crossing almost *any global warming tipping point* will eventually raise average global temperature and presents the probability of suddenly and unpredictably spiking average global temperatures.

How long it will take to get to a new and significantly higher average global temperature level after crossing a tipping point is unknown, but is almost certainly going to occur sooner than what we are currently preparing for. This high level of unpredictability will make the suddenly occurring and radical adjustments that will be needed nearly impossible for all but those with nearly unlimited resources.

Additionally, not all tipping points are alike in impact. Once a *keystone* global warming tipping point is crossed, many other global warming tipping points can also begin rapidly and simultaneously collapsing into their own respective tipping points. If we cross a keystone tipping point, every current projected time frame relating to global warming consequences and the Climageddon Scenario will rapidly change for the worse. Consequences predicted to be *many* decades away could be upon us in a decade or two—or even sooner.

Wild card 3: The methane time bomb

What could eventually become the determinant wild card in the Climageddon Scenario is the growing role of methane pollution in our atmosphere. Even though methane lasts (3 years to decades) in the atmosphere and far less time than carbon, methane is 20 to 100 times more potent than carbon in producing increased heat by way of the greenhouse gas effect.

Increasing methane pollution is a hidden global warming crisis waiting to happen. The only way that increasing atmospheric methane pollution is indirectly measured is by what's called the *carbon equivalent* score, or CE score. The CE score includes other greenhouse gases besides methane, so we can never be quite certain just how much methane is contributing to the overall CE score.

Currently, the carbon dioxide ppm-only score is about 407, but our carbon equivalent (CE) score is around 485 CE ppm. As you can see, with the higher 485 CE ppm measurement, carbon dioxide ppm is not the only measurement to be concerned about. One could easily wonder if this seldom seen or publicly discussed higher carbon CE score is also part of the reason temperatures are rising so much higher and faster than predicted by those in authority.

Some research suggests that total atmospheric methane pollution from *all its sources* may be responsible for up to 30% of all global warming. The expansion of methane energy generation is being extolled by the fossil fuel industry as a safer, less polluting, less costly alternative to oil and coal energy generation. The U.S. and other countries with abundant methane have gone on *huge* methane fracking energy generation binges, supplying more and more of their energy needs through this abundant fossil fuel that is extremely dangerous to our *already* overheating atmosphere.

As research continues to show how much methane is leaking from the fracking process, as well as methane leaking in the distribution from the wellhead to the end user, the data looks bad for the future. As new studies come out that *aren't* directly or indirectly funded by the fossil fuel industry, it shows we appear to have significantly underestimated how much methane is leaking into the atmosphere from both the ongoing melting of the tundra permafrost (which is rapidly accelerating as well) and the methane release from fracking. (See this link[100] to learn more about underestimated methane pollution.) This additional unknown amount of leaked methane could be the ultimate Climageddon Scenario wild card and the last straw because:

---

[100] Phil Mckenna. "Environmental group alleges scientific fraud in disputed methane studies." *InsideClimate News*. June 9, 2016.
https://insideclimatenews.org/news/09062016/environmental-alleges-scientific-fraud-disputed-methane-studies-nc-warn-david-allen-EDF

1. Initial studies indicate we are seriously underestimating the total amount of methane now leaking into the global atmosphere from fracking.

2. The underestimated amount of total leaked methane might turn out to be just enough additional *heat leverage* (when it exercises its 20 to 100 times greater heat producing greenhouse gas effect) to spike average global temperature fast enough and high enough to trigger more global warming tipping points or a keystone tipping point, pushing us quickly from Phase 2 to 3 of the Climageddon Scenario.

3. This fracking-related heat leverage is in addition to *any other* increases in methane going into the atmosphere from tundra permafrost thaw or big agribusiness. And finally because,

4. All of the increased methane releases sit on top of the already existing prior and escalating atmospheric *carbon pollution*.

This impending methane time bomb can get much worse. Methane going into the atmosphere from any and all sources (fracking, methane leaks, melting permafrost, and big agribusiness) warms the oceans *even more*. Starting around 5°C, it will begin to thaw and release gigatons of frozen methane hydrate crystals trapped along the continental shelves of our oceans. Ironically, if the additional leaking methane produced by today's fracking boom becomes the "straw that breaks the camel's back," then our short-sighted drive for cheaper, easier-to-reach energy will become our ultimate undoing. (For more on methane and a massive methane hydrate crystals release leading to the Paleocene–Eocene Thermal Maximum and Extinction, see Part 1, Chapter 3.)

Other risk factors within the 6 phases of the Climageddon Scenario and its wild cards

Seeing the risk probabilities and wild card risk factors of the 6 phases of the Climageddon Scenario as a collection or whole is useful in evaluating what the previously mentioned phase-by-phase threat levels could mean for *your* future. Reviewing the additional estimated risk probabilities below will help prepare you for deciding which of the 4 options of inaction or action you might choose in Part 1, Chapter 9.

The risk probabilities and wild card risk factors for the 6 phases of the Climageddon Scenario are:

a. There is a 100% certainty we are already in Phase 1 of the Climageddon Scenario and are in a state of climate destabilization that will be irreversible within anything close to human time frames.

b. Climatologist Michael Mann believes we currently have a 10% probability of crossing more global warming system tipping points as we have already crossed numerous tipping points in the Arctic regions.

c. At carbon 407 ppm now, we are quickly moving toward Phase 2 of the Climageddon Scenario (carbon 450 ppm) which could potentially begin as early as carbon 425 ppm. If we reach Phase 2, tumbling into Phase 3 is more likely than not (greater than a 50% probability) because of tipping point crossing momentum, our ever-diminishing control over global warming processes, and the total carbon added within 6-10 years to the atmosphere.

d. There is a very high probability we will soon be *averaging* an increase in carbon of 4 ppm per year and not carbon 3 ppm as we were previously doing before

2015. From 2015-2016, according to measurements at Mauna Loa, Hawaii, we came close to that 4 ppm mark.

e. There is also a possibility we may have already unknowingly crossed more points of no return and "baked in" irreversible global warming as well as the mid to later stages of the Climageddon Scenario.

f. There is a very high probability we will cross more points of no return and global warming tipping points, but we will not be able to accurately predict when, how much, or how fast they will increase average global temperature.

g. If we reach Phase 3, tumbling into Phase 4 is highly likely (probability greater than 65%) due to both tipping point momentum and our diminishing control.

h. The probability that we have *seriously* underestimated the total global warming effect of fracking for methane and the effects of the other key methane pollution sources is high.

i. Somewhere in late Phase 3 or early Phase 4, there is a good probability we will cross a keystone tipping point for the Climageddon Scenario itself. This is where crossing global warming, climate, human, and biological system tipping points begins a self-reinforcing endless positive feedback loop.

j. The probability of reaching the mid-to-later Climageddon Scenario Phases 3-5 is also high because of human system inertia and momentum factors. (This is discussed in Chapters 5 and 7.)

k. If we reach Phase 4, tumbling into Phase 5 is very likely (a probability greater than 85%) because of both growing tipping point momentum and our diminishing control.

l. Recent research from 2015 has estimated we now have a 10% chance of reaching an average global temperature increase of 6° Celsius (10.8° Fahrenheit)— which is Phase 5 of the Climageddon Scenario. Other research in a new book called *Climate Shock* estimates the current risk of reaching 6° Celsius may be as high as 30%. If we do not act immediately as described in Part 2, the materials within the book you are reading suggest the risk of reaching 6° Celsius could be *considerably higher* than the 30% suggested by the authors of *Climate Shock*.

m. Because of insufficient research on prior temperatures and processes of the Venus effect (where the atmosphere of Venus was stripped off because of rising temperatures), it is impossible at this time to assign a risk probability to Phase 6 of the Climageddon Scenario, other than to say that if we reach Phase 5 and our temperature keeps going up without pause, we are at a high risk of entering Phase 6.

If or when we reach 4°-6° Celsius (7.2°-10.8° Fahrenheit) of average global temperature increase, we will face a threat comparable in scope, scale, and severity to a global nuclear war. So what does this dire comparison imply?

It asks us to consider how we should be handling the escalated global warming risk if the nations of the world would not allow even a 1 percent risk level for global thermonuclear war to remain unmanaged. How can we continue to allow even a 10% risk level of crossing global warming tipping points when it can directly lead to irreversible global warming, 4°-6° Celsius average global temperature increases, and the eventual extinction of humanity?

Overviewing the estimated time frames and consequence intensity of the Climageddon Scenario

Estimated Timetable for Climageddon Scenario

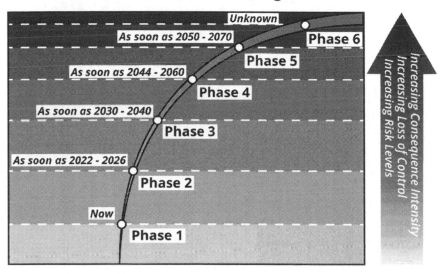

In the above estimated timetable, it is important to keep in mind that these estimates are based on our current path of continuing to cross more and more climate, human and biological system tipping points which *have not* been previously factored into currently accepted global warming consequence timetables by authorities such as the IPCC.

The Climageddon Scenario will multiply the many threats we face through its endless chain of cascading consequences and crossed tipping points, and it will also expose and attack the weaknesses in every climate, human, and biological system directly or indirectly connected. This is also why the Climageddon Scenario is today's most imminent security threat, comparable only to the threat of thermonuclear war and currently more urgent due to the absence of adequate management and preventive measures.

Quick Summary of the Climageddon Scenario Risk levels

Climageddon Scenario Risk Levels

CS Phase	Torino	Homeland Security	DEFCON
CS Phase 1 Carbon 400-450ppm	8	HIGH RISK	DEFCON 4
CS Phase 2 Carbon 450-500ppm	9	SEVERE RISK	DEFCON 3
CS Phase 3 Carbon 500-550ppm	10	SEVERE RISK	DEFCON 2
CS Phase 4 Carbon 550-600ppm	10	SEVERE RISK	DEFCON 1
CS Phase 5 Carbon 600-750+ppm	10	SEVERE RISK	DEFCON 1
CS Phase 6 Carbon 750+ppm	10	SEVERE RISK	DEFCON 1

In the above illustration, you will notice that the mid-to-later phases of the Climageddon Scenario soon reach the highest levels of the 3 previously mentioned risk scales.

Your next vaccination

There may be undiscovered *positive* wild cards that could help significantly slow, lessen, and *eventually* end global warming

The climate future is uncertain and full of both unpredictable negative and positive wild cards. We must remain open to exploring all possible *natural* decarbonization practices. We also need to be open to appropriate technological climate restabilization procedures, as well as all new green energy generation technologies that could be positive wild cards for our global warming future.

Technology's greatest hope for helping to resolve this emergency lies mainly in its ability to more efficiently tap into the abundant sources of clean, green energy all around us (solar, wind, geothermal, etc). Right now, solar panel efficiency is doubling about every three years while at the same time, solar panel cost is rapidly and dramatically dropping.

This, coupled with new technologies for storage batteries, is helping us to resolve green energy battery storage and cost problems that could have significantly slowed our transition away from fossil fuel energy generation. The entrepreneur Elon Musk has stated that with 100 more new battery factories like his new Tesla Giga Factory,[101] green energy generation should have all the battery storage capacity it needs to be able to meet all of the world's energy needs.

There also could be a survival-critical point where we will have to be open to the possibilities of any existing or new technology, even if that technology seems improbable or far-fetched. Stating that we may have to use wise and appropriate technology solutions does not negate the serious warnings (Part 2, Chapter 2) about an overly-optimistic or distorted over-reliance on new technology solutions as the *main way* we end the global warming emergency *without first and also* changing our polluting and destructive fossil fuel-consuming ways.

Among many new technology possibilities, we may even have to use distasteful or disruptive stopgap measures on the way to restabilizing the climate, provided that we have a high certainty these temporary measures will not have *even worse* side effects! For example, fourth generation nuclear breeder reactors, if perfected, are supposed to use and burn the spent

---

[101] Tesla. "Tesla Gigafactory." *Tesla.com*. Accessed January 8, 2017. http://www.tesla.com/gigafactory

existing nuclear waste now being stored at great expense and risk. They will turn stored nuclear waste into a byproduct with a radioactive half-life of just 300 years instead of the average ~10,000 years for many kinds of existing nuclear reactor waste.

What's next

In the next chapter, you will learn how and why we have squandered 30 plus years of warnings about the dangers of global warming. It will also explain what hasn't worked, what isn't working, and what existing authorities and educational structures on global warming must now be bypassed or we will not survive.

Summary

- In Phase 2 of the Climageddon Scenario, with each new tipping point and point of no return crossed, we progressively lose more and more control over the global warming emergency.

- It is not only unconscionable, it is insane to allow the conditions of Phase 2 of the Climageddon Scenario to persist one second longer than is necessary. These conditions must be reversed.

- In Phase 3 of the Climageddon Scenario, should we be unfortunate enough to enter it, we are at the beginning of the perfect storm of perfect storms. Here, unpredictable and colliding crossed tipping points cascade into and within climate, human, and biological systems, creating unmanageable chaos.

- Phase 3 of the Climageddon Scenario is also like entering a race car with no driver and its accelerator pedal pressed to the floor. We rapidly become *passive* rear seat passengers, racing faster and faster toward the cliffs of oblivion.

- Endless global warming catastrophes will find and multiply weaknesses within the world's political, economic, social, and ecological systems. Long before we reach the last phases of the Climageddon Scenario, the world will face global chaos.

- Our current level of global warming places us at the edge of a disastrous chain reaction: crossing more tipping points will lead eventually to crossing keystone tipping points, then irreversible global warming, and finally Phases 4 and 5 of the Climageddon Scenario.

- Once carbon reaches the atmosphere, 75% of that carbon will not disappear for thousands of years. The other 25% stays forever. This means that even after we finally get serious about ending the global warming emergency, we will be living with radically higher average global temperature ranges for a long, long time.

- Endgame global warming consequences will rapidly propagate through climate, human, and biological systems in the later phases (4-6) of the Climageddon Scenario.

- Any global warming wild card can significantly increase the average global temperature and radically shorten the time frames for the predicted temperatures increases of the Climageddon Scenario to occur.

- If we don't work together successfully to resolve the global warming emergency, we may experience a second great evolutionary bottleneck and die off to a few thousand remaining mating pairs. This means that most of us living today may witness, in as little as 30 years, the greatest mass die-off in human history.

- The Climageddon Scenario later phases will kill us all far faster and more efficiently than we ever have been able to kill each other. It ultimately leads us into the *Great Culling* of humanity.

- The Climageddon Scenario is the ultimate unbearable truth of the 21st century.

- In the next several chapters you will learn more about why this is true.

PART 1, CHAPTER 7

HOW DID WE WASTE 30 YEARS OF WARNINGS ABOUT ESCALATING GLOBAL WARMING?

Overview:

- Despite being the world's most recognized authority on global warming, the United Nations Intergovernmental Panel On Climate Change (IPCC) has consistently understated the intensity and timeframes of global warming, as well as the danger that it represents.

- The IPCC's global warming prediction scenarios fail to include going over more global warming tipping points—or, in the IPCC's nomenclature, "high-impact events" or fat tails—in the climate's major or minor systems or subsystems.

- The greatest loss caused by IPCC's underestimation problem is that it quells, if not removes, the appropriate sense of urgency essential to motivating the world to deal with the escalating global warming emergency's present and future threats.

Before moving on to the last two chapters of Part 1 or exploring the global warming solutions found in Part 2, it is wise to examine how we have wasted so much valuable time and put ourselves into this untenable State of Emergency. This way, we have a better opportunity to resolve the issue and avoid the same mistakes.

There are many reasons why we have ignored over 30 years of valid warnings about the consequences of escalating global warming. A key reason is because the recognized world authority on global warming, the IPCC, has failed to adequately inform us as to the *real* risk and urgency of our crisis.[102]

Before discussing the numerous problems with the IPCC's global warming information and predictions, it is necessary to frame the challenge to the IPCC's reports appropriately. In the criticisms below, we are not in any way criticizing the thousands of climate scientists, many of whom at their own expense provide uncensored, accurate, and up-to-date global warming research to the IPCC's bureaucrats.

However, those IPCC bureaucrats are the individuals who, through a highly constrained administrative process, create the final reports and predictions. What follows also does not question the good intentions of the constrained IPCC bureaucrats caught in the slow and conservative bureaucracy of an international entity, which must not only seek member consensus and funding, but also avoid panicking the public.

Additionally, do not misconstrue the following criticism of the IPCC's bureaucratic process results in any way as a criticism of the underlying valid science of global warming being presented by the thousands of climate scientists contributing their research to the IPCC reports or the vast <u>97 percent</u>[103] consensus of climate scientists who, as a whole, agree that global warming has human causation and one of the largest human causes is the burning of fossil fuels.

Now that you have this background, let's look at the IPCC problems.

---

[102] Glenn Scherer. "How the IPCC Underestimated Climate Change." *Scientific American.* December 6, 2012. https://www.scientificamerican.com/article/climate-science-predictions-prove-too-conservative/

[103] "Scientific consensus: Earth's climate is warming." *Climate.Nasa.Gov.* Last modified January 24, 2017. http://climate.nasa.gov/scientific-consensus/

In their 5-7 year climate update reports and predictions for politicians and policymakers, the IPCC has a repeated history of significantly underestimating how much of a problem global warming could become, as well as its time frames.[104] Before expanding upon the IPCC's climate data underestimation problem, it is essential to understand how they create their 5-7 year global warming and prediction scenario updates for the world's politicians and policymakers.

What surprises many individuals is that the IPCC itself does not do original global warming research. Working as unpaid volunteers, thousands of scientists from around the globe sift through the most current scientific literature on global warming and the climate. After completing this review, these unpaid scientists identify trends, write a draft report, and submit it to the IPCC.

Next, the IPCC reviews the submitted research from these scientists. This typically takes five to seven years to complete. Then, in a tediously slow and bureaucratic process, the IPCC creates comprehensive reports and assessments, including global warming prediction scenarios. Then, in the *near to last step*, other scientists once again take the assembled draft and review and revise it as needed.

Finally, a summary for national politicians and policymakers is written. This condenses the science even further. This new and final summary report is then subjected to a line-by-line review and possible revision by *non-scientist* national representatives from more than 100 world governments—*all* of whom *must approve* the final summary document before it is signed and presented to the public.

Now that you understand the process for how the IPCC creates its reports, the following will not seem so surprising. A growing number of studies (referenced elsewhere) claim that across

---

[104] Dana Nuccitelli. "Vision Prize: scientists are worried the IPCC is underestimating sea level rise." *The Guardian*. February 18, 2014.
https://www.theguardian.com/environment/climate-consensus-97-per-cent/2014/feb/18/scientists-worried-ipcc-underestimate-sea-level-rise

two decades and thousands of pages of IPCC climate reports, the IPCC has consistently understated the rate and intensity of global warming, *as well as* the danger that it represents.[105]

Since the IPCC 2007 assessment, these studies have shown that the speed and ferocity at which the climate is destabilizing are *at the extreme edge of*, or are outpacing, IPCC projections on many fronts, including temperature rise, carbon emissions, sea level rise, continental ice-sheet melt, Arctic sea ice decline, ocean acidification, and thawing tundra.

One glaring example of IPCC underestimation can be found in the IPCC's previous 2007 report[106] that concluded the Arctic would not lose its summer ice before 2070 at the earliest. But the ice pack has shrunk far faster than *any scenario* IPCC scientists felt politicians and policymakers should consider.

Just a few years after that report, a new study predicted that by 2016-2020, the Arctic's Northwest Passage will be completely ice-free during the summers. This means that in 2007, the IPCC was off by an incredible 50-54 years on a key climate prediction over an estimation prediction period of *only* 63 years!

Another glaring example of the dangerous IPCC underestimation problem surfaced from James Hansen, the former NASA scientist who originally warned the world about global warming nearly 30 years ago. Hansen's new study says sea levels could rise by as much as 10 feet (3 meters) by 2050.

The IPCC has repeatedly and consistently predicted that sea levels should rise *only 3 feet* (0.9 meters) by 2100. That's a 60-70% underestimation by the IPCC occurring *50 years earlier!*

---

[105] Bill McKibben. "The IPCC is stern on climate change - but it still underestimates the situation." *The Guardian.* November 2, 2014.
https://www.theguardian.com/environment/2014/nov/02/ipcc-climate-change-carbon-emissions-underestimates-situation-fossil-fuels

[106] Solomon, S., D. Qin, M. Manning, Z. Chen, M. Marquis, K.B. Averyt, M. Tignor and H.L. Miller, eds., "Contribution of Working Group I to the Fourth Assessment Report of the Intergovernmental Panel on Climate Change," (Cambridge: Cambridge University Press), http://www.ipcc.ch/report/ar4/wg1/

Over its history, the IPCC's global warming consequence and timetable scenario predictions are regularly underestimated by anywhere from 25 to 40%.

Why the IPCC's global warming underestimation problem is critical to you, your business, and your nation's future

All underestimation by the IPCC is dangerous. First, because the organization is treated as the most recognized authority on global warming and is charged with advising national politicians and policymakers on the most relevant and accurate climate science so they can make the necessary laws and policy changes to keep us safe.

Next, the IPCC's overly conservative reading and underestimation problems means that national governments, businesses, and the public will be *grossly* unprepared and blindsided by the more rapid onset of higher flooding, extreme storms, drought, and other global warming impacts and consequences far beyond what they are currently prepared for.[107] Worse yet, a society blind to the full *range and speed* of potential global warming outcomes can remain unconscious of or apathetic to the growing emergency, causing them to push the hard but necessary global warming reduction decisions farther and farther off into the future.

Probably the greatest loss caused by IPCC's underestimation problem is that it quells, if not removes, the appropriate sense of urgency essential to motivating the world and its nations to deal with escalating global warming's present and future threats. For example, what if the global warming disasters projected by the IPCC to start arriving in 2060-2080 begin in 2030-2040? If that happens, we won't be prepared for the true scale, severity, and frequency of the disasters to come. (Graphs

---

[107] Chris Mooney. "The world's climate change watchdog may be underestimating global warming." *The Washington Post.* October 30, 2014. https://www.washingtonpost.com/news/wonk/wp/2014/10/30/climate-scientists-arent-too-alarmist-theyre-too-conservative/?utm_term=.8e8e665ddf76

shown below in the underestimation correction section will help you visualize what this means in shortened time frames.)

Conflicts of interest and the IPCC's underestimation problem

Because the IPCC's final summary report is subjected to a *line-by-line* review/revision by representatives from more than 100 world governments, all of whom must *individually approve* and sign off on the final summary document before it is presented to the public, it is only reasonable to consider that inherent national *conflicts of interest* will also act to water down, delay, or delete those sections of each global warming report that directly and significantly impact the overall military, security, economics, or other key well-being factors of the sign-off nation.

For example, countries like Venezuela, Saudi Arabia, Iraq, Russia, the United States, United Arab Emirates, Kuwait, and Iran have huge portions of their annual gross domestic product (GDP) dependent upon producing and/or exporting fossil fuels. If there were a sudden and significant mandated reduction in use of global fossil fuel, some of these countries, particularly the ones with large national debts or without large financial reserves like Russia, Venezuela, the United States, Iraq, and Iran, could plunge into rapid economic decline and in some cases, possibly even social and political unrest or collapse.[108] Unless something shifts radically, these serious conflicts of interest in sign-off nations will be a continuous source of watered-down or missing key facts.

The IPCC's most fatal flaw and shocker

The previously mentioned underestimation problems with the IPCC are not even its worst global warming data integrity problem. It also has a problem with its global warming tipping point education and disclosure scenarios.

---

[108] Nicholas Stern. "Economics: Current climate models are grossly misleading." *Nature.com*. February 24, 2016. http://www.nature.com/news/economics-current-climate-models-are-grossly-misleading-1.19416

To fully appreciate how important that fatal flaw is, it is necessary to review a bit of basic logic. There is a principle in logic that if all or a significant part of the foundational premise upon which you build a theory or solution is insufficient or false, the consequent theory or solution created will also be insufficient or false either in total or to a significant degree.

Keep this principle of logic in mind as there is a giant data analysis fatal flaw in the premise upon which the IPCC builds its global warming risk analysis for its global warming consequence prediction scenarios and timetables. To many individuals who are well-informed about global warming, this lack of cognizance by the IPCC about this second tipping point issue is seen as the one fatal flaw that will most quickly force us unknowingly into the later phases of the Climageddon Scenario.

Let's review the four newest global warming prediction scenarios provided in 2014 by the IPCC to the world's politicians and policymakers. It will provide foundational evidence for the biggest flaw in the IPCC's global warming risk analysis process and consequence prediction scenarios.

The following four global warming prediction scenarios of the IPCC are based on the assumption that we have no major climate system surprises such as going over more global warming tipping points. Those predictions are:

> Scenario One: Global warming is, at the most optimistic of projections, only a 2° Celsius increase by 2100 (3.6° degrees Fahrenheit).

> Scenario Two: Global warming is, at a more likely projection, a 3° Celsius increase by 2100 (5.4° degrees Fahrenheit).

> Scenario Three: Global warming is, at the less optimistic of IPCC projections, only a 4° Celsius increase by 2100 (7.2° degrees Fahrenheit).

Scenario Four: Global warming is, at the least optimistic of IPCC projections, a 6° or more Celsius increase by 2100 (10.8°+ degrees Fahrenheit).

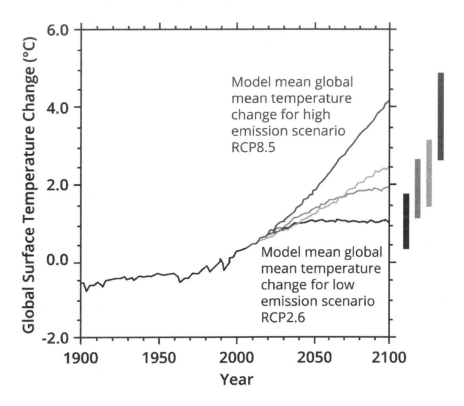

This graph shows four different trajectories for greenhouse gas concentrations. These representative concentration pathways (RCPs) show four potential climate futures. The lowest pathway, RCP2.6 (the bold blue line) shows an average global temperature increase of 1° Celsius. The highest pathway, RCP8.5, shows an average increase of 2.0° to 3.7° Celsius. Source: IPCC, 2013, FAQ 12.1, Figure 1.[109]

---

[109] FAQ 12.1, Figure 1, from Collins, M., R. Knutti, J. Arblaster, J.-L. Dufresne, T. Fichefet, P. Friedlingstein, X. Gao, W.J. Gutowski, T. Johns, G. Krinner, M. Shongwe, C. Tebaldi, A.J. Weaver and M. Wehner, 2013: Long-term Climate Change: Projections, Commitments and Irreversibility. In: *Climate Change 2013: The Physical Science Basis. Contribution of Working Group I to the Fifth Assessment Report of the Intergovernmental Panel on Climate Change* [Stocker, T.F., D. Qin, G.-K. Plattner, M. Tignor, S.K. Allen, J. Boschung, A. Nauels, Y. Xia, V. Bex and P.M. Midgley (eds.)]. Cambridge University Press, Cambridge, United Kingdom and New York, NY, USA.

From each of the four IPCC prediction scenarios, what is missing and what has been unwisely omitted is the essential inclusion of tipping point calculations. The IPCC's four prediction scenarios rest on the assumption that we will never go over any global warming tipping points in any of the climate's major or minor systems or subsystems.

Planning for everything going perfectly is the perfect plan for failure!

In effect, what the IPCC has done is to all but *remove or ignore* high-impact, often unrecoverable global warming, climate, human, and biological system tipping point variables that should have been included in an accurate and complete risk spectrum analysis. Without including and considering these critical high-impact tipping point *consequence events* in their master risk analysis, the IPCC has not met the *minimum essential data inclusion* threshold necessary to create a valid *and complete* global warming risk analysis that could be used to properly inform our politicians and policymakers, as well as the general public, of *all* real and significant current and future risks and timetables their nations and people face.

IPCC Prediction Scenario Inaccuracy Issues

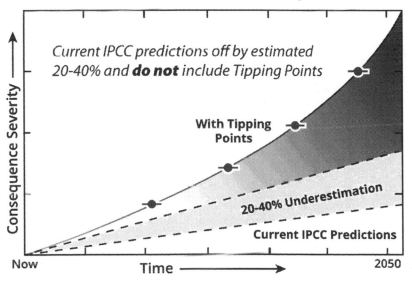

Correcting for the underestimation in the current IPCC temperature projections

It is useful to now update the IPCC's four most recent 2014 average global temperature and time frame predictions (listed previously) while *compensating for* their regular underestimations of about 25-40%. Please keep in mind the IPCC's 2014 prediction scenarios also *do not* include any calculations or adjustments for crossing more global warming tipping points during their prediction scenario periods.

Here is what the IPCC's temperature and arrival date estimates might look like if their underestimation bias were corrected:

In IPCC Scenario 1, *their most optimistic projection,* they say we will have only a 2° Celsius increase by 2100 (3.6° Fahrenheit). (Please note that in all 4 graphs below, CS stands for Climageddon Scenario and the 25% and 40% are underestimation correction levels for the 4 IPCC prediction levels.)

> At the 25% underestimation level, this means that we will reach 2.5° Celsius (4.5° Fahrenheit) *about 21 years* sooner than they predict will occur—at about 2079. This puts us in the later part of Phase 1 of the Climageddon Scenario, or more likely, in the beginning of Phase 2.
>
> At the 40% underestimation level, we will reach 2.9° Celsius (5.2°+ Fahrenheit) *roughly 34 years sooner* than they predict—at about 2066. This puts us somewhere within Phase 2 of the Climageddon Scenario.

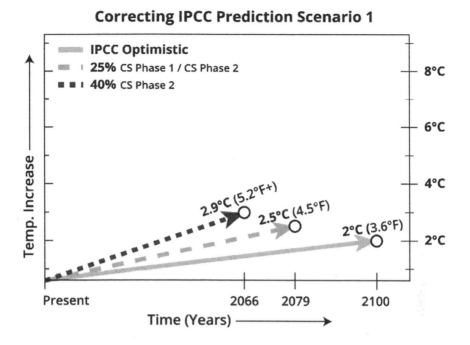

In IPCC Scenario 2, *their more likely projection*, they say we will have only a 3° Celsius increase by 2100 (5.4° Fahrenheit).

> At the 25% underestimation level, this means we will reach 3.5° Celsius (6.9° Fahrenheit) *about 21 years sooner* than they predict—at about 2079. This puts us in or near Phase 3 of the Climageddon Scenario.

> At the 40% underestimation level, we will reach 4.2° Celsius (7.5° Fahrenheit) *about 34 years sooner* than they predict—at about 2066. This puts us in or near Phase 4 of the Climageddon Scenario.

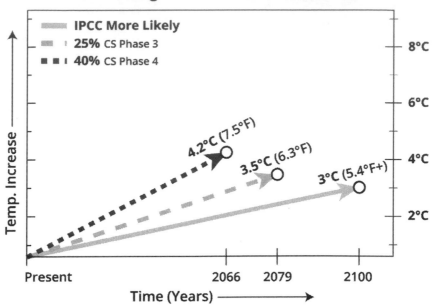

Correcting IPCC Prediction Scenario 2

In IPCC Scenario 3, *their less optimistic projection*, they say we will have only a 4° Celsius increase by 2100 (7.2°+ Fahrenheit).

> At the 25% underestimation level, this means we will reach 5° Celsius (about 9° Fahrenheit) *21 years sooner* than they predict—at about 2079. This puts us in or near the chaos and collapse of Phase 5 of the Climageddon Scenario.

> At the 40% underestimation level, we will reach 5.6° Celsius (10° Fahrenheit) *34 years sooner* than they predict—at about 2066. This also puts us in or closer to phase 5 of the Climageddon Scenario.

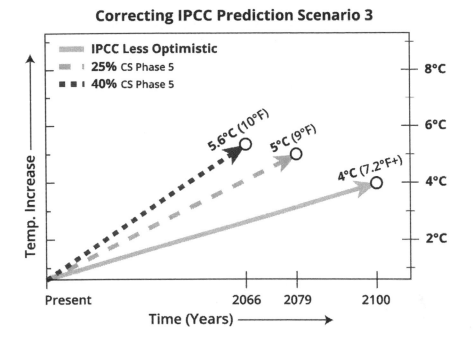

In IPCC Scenario 4, *their least optimistic projection*, they say we will have only a 6° or more Celsius increase by 2100 (10.8°+ Fahrenheit). A 6° Celsius increase in average global temperature is the end of most human life as we know it.

At the 25% underestimation level, this means that we will reach 7.8° Celsius (about 13.5° Fahrenheit) at about 2079. This will put us well into Phase 5 of the Climageddon Scenario.

At the 40% underestimation level, we will reach 8.4° Celsius (about 15° Fahrenheit)—at about 2066. This could put us in Phase 5 of the Climageddon Scenario faster than anyone is ready for.

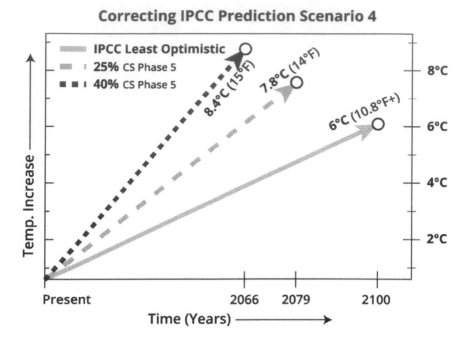

Correcting IPCC Prediction Scenario 4

(Please note: In the four corrected IPCC graphs above, we are using recalculated temperature estimates to extrapolate approximate placement positions for the graph's new projected time lines. Rather than show the precise new time frames of a particular recalculated temperature, these four graphs illustrate relative differences from the IPCC's predicted temperatures and time frames. These four graphs additionally point toward how *unanticipated* higher temperatures will also drastically accelerate consequence arrival times and increase consequence severity. It is difficult to precisely recalculate new timeframes with temperature calculations only, and because there is always a delay in the actual time that it takes to get to higher temperatures because of inertia and momentum factors in climate systems and subsystems.)

What can we do

The IPCC's underestimation presents an absolute nightmare for anyone trying to do long-term planning, whether it be personal, business, local, regional, or national. When we take into account the IPCC underestimations and come up with new temperature and timetable predictions, it appears any mid-term to long-term future planning based on the IPCC's predictions will put us in a world of hurt.

When we reach 5 to 6° Celsius (9-10.8° Fahrenheit) it will be the end of the world as we know it and, as you can see from the above data, it is not far off in the future. When you factor in crossing more global warming tipping points (which is highly probable and which was completely absent from the IPCC predictions and is also _not included_ in the graph calculations above), our world is in serious peril, not 40 or 80 years from now, _but right now and over the next 20-40 years._

It is illogical beyond all comprehension to assign full responsibility for evaluating and predicting the single greatest security threat of the 21st-century to a group of volunteer and underfunded climate scientists who submit their research to an bureaucratic and underfunded United Nations agency. But who should be doing this work?

If not the IPCC, who _is_ most qualified to do needed tipping point research and prediction?

It is clear the IPCC is not doing its job. The world's current leading authority on global warming is _no longer_ the appropriate agent we can trust to manage the research, analysis, and planning necessary to save us from the escalating global warming emergency. The danger is so great and imminent that we can't keep doing the same thing over and over, expecting a different result.

We have no other rational choice but to _bypass_ any existing failed authorities, structures, and processes that have not worked and are not working. That is the only way we will have any honest hope of handling the global warming emergency. Part 2 of this book will tell you who should be doing this research and prediction work.

Other reasons for 30 years of failure

There are many other *contributing* reasons for why we have failed to resolve the global warming crisis over the last 30 years, but a major reason lies within the data we've been given and the organization trusted to give us that data. More of these other contributing reasons will be revealed in later chapters.

A deeper dive into the science of the IPCC's prediction underestimation issues

For those who want to go into more detail, Climate Interactive's scoreboard[110] provides a helpful visualization of the mess the IPCC has created. Not including any tipping point scenarios, this scoreboard will further illustrate where average global temperature is headed using the IPCC's current underestimated and uncorrected calculations.

What's next

The next chapter contains some of the most challenging information of this book. It discusses other problems and dilemmas we must overcome to be successful in preventing the later extinction level stages of the Climageddon Scenario.

Unfortunately, there is another serious IPCC error that significantly reduces the reliability of the predicted times, temperatures, and results of the IPCC's four prediction scenarios listed earlier. A professor of atmospheric sciences discovered this while developing a predictive formula for how either maintaining or growing the world's economy directly relates to atmospheric carbon levels.

This formula and the unsettling research behind it is better described within the context of the next chapter. In case you are wondering: if not the IPCC, who will do this work correctly?

---

[110] Climate Scoreboard. http://www.climateinteractive.org/programs/scoreboard/ *Climate Interactive.* Accessed December 13, 2016.

The best answer for that question will be disclosed in Part 2 of this book.

Summary

- Over its history, the IPCC's global warming consequence and timetable scenario predictions are believed to be regularly underestimated by anywhere from 25 to 40%.

- Not only does the IPCC have a serious data underestimation problem, but it also has a problem with its global warming tipping point education and disclosure scenarios.

- The recognized world authority on global warming has failed us. Continuing to use the IPCC's inadequate global warming data *and the ever-increasing fossil fuel pollution of our atmosphere* will *inevitably* lead to crossing more global warming tipping points.

- The IPCC's 25-40% underestimations will create an absolute nightmare for anyone trying to do mid-term or long-term planning, whether it be personal, business, city, or national, because the wrong facts will lead them to wrong actions and failure.

- When you factor in crossing more global warming tipping points (which is highly probable and which was completely absent from the IPCC predictions), our world is in serious peril, not 40 or 80 years from now, *but now and over the next 20-40 years.*

- It is illogical beyond all comprehension to assign full responsibility for evaluating and predicting the single greatest security threat of the 21st-century to a group of volunteer and underfunded climate scientists who submit their research to an bureaucratic and underfunded United Nations agency.

- The unresolved global warming danger is so great and imminent, we have no other rational choice but to *bypass* any existing failed structures or processes that have not worked or are not working effectively.

- At best we had about 40 years to make the necessary changes when we were warned 30 years ago by climate scientists. If we are very, very lucky, we have about 10 years left to make the radical, costly, and painful changes that would've been far easier, cheaper, and less painful had we begun them 30 years ago.

Part 1, Chapter 8

Dilemmas, Shockers, and Our Last Battle Line for Survival

Overview:

- At best, we have about 6 to 10 years remaining to prevent the acceleration of global warming processes that will cross the critical carbon 425-450 ppm battle line. All efforts must be made now to prevent this or we will quickly descend into the no-win endgame.

- To secure a prosperous economy and a safe future, we need to persuade our economy-sensitive politicians to realize there will be no possible long-term economic prosperity (or even livable conditions) without immediate and complete transition to global green energy generation for all of our energy needs.

- If we can't scale up a full global green energy generation replacement in time, while we are also making all of the required global fossil fuel reductions, the steep crash of the global economy will financially destroy us. If we continue as we are now, carbon dioxide levels will likely exceed carbon 1,000 parts per million by volume (ppmv) and civilization will collapse. (Note: ppmv is different from carbon parts per million [ppm and carbon equivalent, CO2e]. The distinction is that ppmv is used to describe *all* trace gases found in the atmosphere such as sulphur dioxide, carbon dioxide, nitrogen, and other pollutants by *volume*.)

Prepare yourself for additional difficult news about global warming. This chapter discloses new, nearly intractable problems and dilemmas that we will need to overcome if we are going to prevent irreversible global warming and the later extinction stages of the Climageddon Scenario.

By the end of this chapter, you will be able to *feel* the complete seriousness and immediacy of the predicament we have created for ourselves. Hopefully, these shocking new perspectives will be the final factors necessary to motivate you to become active in resolving the global warming emergency, or, at the least, not give up all hope and protect *only* yourself.

It is time to look at some of significant remaining problems and dilemmas that could prevent us from being successful.

The delayed momentum and inertia problems in human systems and subsystems

Momentum and inertia factors within our global warming and climate related systems and subsystems were described in Part 1, Chapters 3-6. Even if we stop *all* fossil fuel-related pollution of our atmosphere today, those previously mentioned momentum and inertia factors alone necessitate continuous, diligent action for at least another 3 to 5 decades to get this emergency under control. Unfortunately, there are other more troubling momentum and inertia factors that will challenge us from within other *human* system and subsystems.

Some of these problems are as follows:

a. *The fossil fuel industry has financial momentum.* The high-profit fossil fuel related industries generate approximately ⅓ of the world's gross domestic product (GDP). It is the largest multinational corporate conglomerate in existence! It is so powerful that it manages to secure $5.3 trillion a year in subsidies from the world governments even as it continues polluting our atmosphere, ruining our health, and raising our average global temperature. It has *gigantic* financial momentum and resources beyond any other single industry on Earth. Without a doubt, the fossil fuel industry will use that enormous financial momentum and power to slow or stop all actions to reduce or end fossil fuel use.

Fossil Fuel Industry Mechanical Inertia

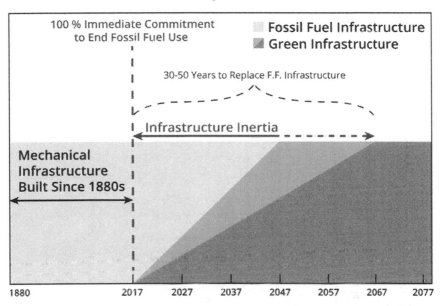

b. *The fossil fuel industry has mechanical inertia.* Since the beginning of the Industrial Revolution in the 1880s, the fossil fuel industry has been steadily expanding the mechanical infrastructure to find, transport, refine, and deliver *almost all* of the world's energy needs. If all the governments of the world were to commit *today* to immediately end all fossil fuel use, it is estimated that *at our current unworkable pace*, it will take another 30 to 50 years to replace all existing fossil fuel energy generation infrastructure with green energy generation infrastructure. (In the mechanical inertia illustration below, if we were 100% committed to end all fossil fuel use today *and* replace all of its infrastructure, and we continue reducing fossil fuel use at our current pace, it will take us another 30 to 50 years or more to replace most fossil fuel infrastructure with green energy generation.)

c. The fossil *fuel industry has created highly resistant legal inertia by using every legal means to defuse, delay, and/or diminish any new global warming restrictions, treaties, or laws that might be passed.* It is fully possible for the fossil fuel industry to delay the enactment of any new effective laws or treaties by up to another 20 to 30 years. By challenging any and all new global warming laws or treaties and then repeatedly appealing every court action it loses, the fossil fuel industry can and will exhaust all national and international courts with decades of delay while *simultaneously* lobbying politicians for new laws to overturn, water down, or counteract any previous global warming remedial laws passed and upheld by national or international courts. Between these two tactics, it is also not unreasonable to estimate significant fossil fuel reduction actions will be delayed, if not totally stopped, for another 20 to 30+ years unless we anticipate this tactic and counter it brilliantly. For more information on how Big Oil blocks climate laws, see this recent article.[111]

d. *Human system educational inertia.* Sufficiently educating a large enough group of individuals on a complex topic like global warming and all it entails is

---

[111] Larry Buhl. "Big Oil renewing effort to kill California's landmark climate law." *Desmog.* August 4, 2016. https://www.desmogblog.com/2016/08/04/big-oil-renewing-effort-kill-california-s-landmark-climate-law

inherently full of change-resistant educational inertia. It will be very difficult to get a large portion of the population to understand the complex issues of global warming well enough to become activists, as well as to organize enough mass public demand for change *from the bottom up* to sway politicians away from fossil fuel lobbyists wielding financial clout. The task is made exponentially more difficult because of ongoing fossil fuel industry-financed media campaigns designed to intentionally confuse global warming issues with false doubts and bad science so that the general population goes into an intentionally-created *"analysis paralysis."* Using their vast wealth and stockholder positions in the world's media, as well as employing the same successful tactics as tobacco companies to cast doubt on legitimate science, the fossil fuel industry continues to be able to cash in, pollute our atmosphere, destroy our health and ultimately pass the costs onto the unsuspecting individual taxpayers of every nation of the world.

e. *Human reproduction and population momentum.* We will continue adding more carbon into the atmosphere as the population soars another 40% for the next 30 to 50 years, and more of that increased population will be rising into the middle class, demanding the same energy-using comforts enjoyed by the developed world today. By 2040, world energy use is estimated to rise by 48%. See more information at this article.[112]

---

[112] Linda Doman. "EIA projects 48% increase in world energy consumption by 2040." *U.S. Energy Information Administration.* May 12, 2016.
http://www.eia.gov/todayinenergy/detail.php?id=26212

Human Reproduction & Population Momentum

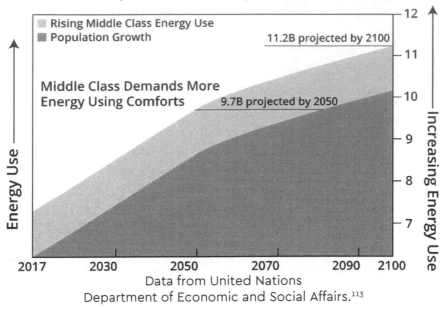

Data from United Nations
Department of Economic and Social Affairs.[113]

f. *Political inertia.* It will be very difficult to get politicians of the world to go against the wealthy fossil fuel donors and lobbyists. Mass public will coming from the bottom up is nowhere near as powerful as it once was. To make matters worse, politicians have developed great skills in ignoring and resisting mass public will even when it does surface and it goes against powerful and abundant funding received from special interest lobbyists.

g. *Global government inertia.* Even though the absence of a functioning international government was mentioned in a different context earlier, it is critical to discuss it further in a slightly new form. First, the idea of *global government inertia* is a misnomer as there is no current global government to demonstrate inertia, or that could

---

[113] Data from United Nations Department of Economic and Social Affairs. "The World Population Prospects: 2015 Revision." *UN.org.* July 29, 2015.
http://www.un.org/en/development/desa/publications/world-population-prospects-2015-revision.html

resolve global warming, or that could create enforceable and verifiable climate law to effectively and efficiently end global warming. The second problem is that today's nations, even newly evolving nations, recognize only other national governments. No major nation today appears willing to relinquish its sovereignty *to the degree needed* for an international or global government to be formed. At this stage in our human political evolution, we have not broken through this global governance inertia to create a truly effective global government. Without some form of effective global government with the powers of enforcement and verification, we will continue to have nothing but toothless international treaties. Another sign of this seemingly intractable inertia is the endless climate treaty negotiations between "have and have-not" nations jockeying for the slightest economic advantage. True climate justice between nations cannot be enacted because we have no true global law, empowered global governance, or global court system whose rulings can be equally and fairly enforced upon *all* existing nations. It will take many more decades, if not centuries, before anything resembling an effective global government emerges. Until then, all we can do is enact the creative, radical, and difficult bypass and work-around solutions of the Job One Plan.

As you can see, we may be facing another 30 to 50 years before our actions to slow and end global warming may be fully effective (if we are not successful executing the Job One Plan steps found in Part 2).

"Anyone wishing to see what is to come should examine what has been." —Machiavelli

The preceding human system momentum and/or inertia factors *by themselves* strongly indicate that any *small or gradual* changes we make to reduce atmospheric carbon and methane pollution will not have enough effect to save us in time. The combination of global warming (described in Part 1, Chapters 3-6) and human system and subsystem momentum and inertia factors means that if our governments take any significant amount of time to agree to pass effective, verifiable, and enforceable laws, it may be too late.

When we were warned 30 years ago, we had about 40 years to reduce escalating global warming and keep ourselves out of the extreme danger zone. Now, if we are very lucky, and we manage to radically reduce fossil fuel use to the targets mentioned in Part 2, Chapter 2, we should be able to successfully utilize the remaining 6-10 years we have left in which we can still exert meaningful control over our fate.

Unfortunately, in addition to everything you have read thus far, there are still some final shocks to deal with.

Which do you prefer: partial economic collapse now, or total economic collapse later, with the bonus collapse of civilization

Tim Garrett, professor of Atmospheric Sciences at the University of Utah, has researched the physics of atmospheric thermodynamic change (changing air temperatures) over the history of human civilization. His unsettling research indicates the only workable way left in which to avoid irreversible global warming will involve allowing our fossil fuel-driven global economy to collapse.

It appears from his research that the laws of physics predict that we will have to go into an immediate economic recession or depression to save the future from irreversible global warming and ourselves from extinction. Most of us are not economists, physicists, or climatologists, so this lesson may seem a little difficult to understand. The following summary of Garrett's research should help:

a. The core finding of his research is that maintaining *only* our current levels of economic production and wealth requires *continual* energy sustenance and supply. Like a living organism, civilization requires energy *to not only grow*, but also to continue to sustain and maintain its current size or wealth.

b. In today's terms, this also means that *additional* economic production (wealth) equals *more* carbon emissions from burning fossil fuels. *Less* carbon emissions from less fossil fuel burning equals *less* economic production (wealth).

c. The fixed and direct link between energy sustenance and the additional production of more wealth means that the existence of a financially measurable economy cannot be *decoupled* from a continuing rise in its energy consumption.

d. This means contrary to current popular global warming prediction theories, neither population size nor the population's standard of living *has to be included* in the computer modelling for predictions on what will happen in the future with a growing or shrinking economy and the amount of carbon dioxide that will go into the atmosphere affecting global warming. Global warming is linked closer to the increased or decreased carbon levels of increased or decreased GDP.

e. Global atmospheric carbon dioxide emission rates also *cannot* be *unlinked* from economic production (wealth) through new or predicted gains in energy efficiency. Greater energy efficiency does not invalidate Garrett's research demonstrating that greater production (wealth) *always* equals greater atmospheric carbon dioxide emissions.

f. According to Garrett's research, even a 50% reduction in total fossil fuel use over the next 50 years will not be enough to keep us below carbon 425-450 ppmv.[114] Even with this 50% reduction, we will still hit 600 ppmv by the year 2100 (or sooner) and enter Phase 4 of the Climageddon Scenario, leading eventually to Phase 5 extinction.

g. Keeping carbon emissions at or below the already unsafe level of carbon 450 ppmv will not be achieved by any conservation, *increased energy efficiency*, or other *gradual* fossil fuel reduction tactics currently being implemented. To maintain our current standard of living with our growing population without further exacerbating global warming, a new, non-carbon polluting nuclear power plant would have to be built every day. Because this is not currently happening and, in fact, may be impossible (even if it was a desirable solution), the only remaining solution to radically reducing fossil fuel use is economic collapse.

h. For atmospheric CO2 concentrations to remain below 450 ppmv, Garrett's research suggests there will have to be some combination of an unrealistically rapid rate of energy decarbonization (reduction of fossil fuel use) and its consequent and near-immediate reductions in global wealth. Effectively, it appears that civilization may be in a double-bind. If civilization does not collapse quickly this century, then CO2 levels will likely end up

---

[114] Note: ppmv is different from carbon parts per million [ppm and CE carbon equivalent, CO2e]. The distinction is that ppmv is used to describe all trace gases found in the atmosphere such as sulphur dioxide, carbon dioxide, nitrogen, and other pollutants by volume.

exceeding 1000 ppmv.[115] At the same time, if CO2 levels exceed 1000 ppmv, then civilization will gradually tend toward total collapse. (For more about Garrett's research on the physics of long-run global economic growth issues, see this link.[116])

i. Garrett also does not envision that we will ever be able to reduce carbon emissions fast enough. In his paper "No Way Out," [117] he says that "reducing carbon emissions may be a bit like asking an adult to once again become a child. Over millennia, we have collectively built an enormous global infrastructure designed to consume massive amounts of energy. Without destroying this infrastructure, energy will continue to be consumed. Without energy, the circulations and transactions defining the global economy stop. And because so much of this infrastructure is tied to fossil fuel consumption, our economy is wedded to carbon emissions."

j. Although it is counter-intuitive, Garrett also states energy consumption rates can rise about twice as fast with rapid decarbonization as with no decarbonization. The reason is that decarbonization aids society health by limiting global warming. Better health means greater energy consumption, which then leads to a partial offset of any environmental gains that came from decarbonizing in the first place. (Going green is a form of global decarbonization.)

---

[115] Tim Garrett, interview by Alex Smith, *Radio Ecoshock*, October 19, 2011, transcript. http://www.ecoshock.org/downloads/climate2010/ES_Garrett_101119_LoFi.mp3

[116] Tim Garrett. "The physics of long-run global economic growth." *Utah.edu.* 2014. http://www.inscc.utah.edu/~tgarrett/Economics/Economics.html

[117] Tim Garrott. "No way out? The double-bind in seeking global prosperity alongside mitigated climate change." *arXiv.* January 9 2012. https://arxiv.org/pdf/1010.0428v3.pdf

k. Garrett also turned his new prediction model on the IPCC's global warming predictions and discovered two major errors. He demonstrated that the IPCC's current global warming prediction scenarios *substantially* underestimate how much carbon dioxide levels will rise for a given level of future economic prosperity and wealth. The two reasons for the IPCC errors are that global carbon dioxide emission rates cannot be *unlinked* from economic production and wealth creation through any efficiency gains, and our continuous future global warming can be expected to act as a *significant* inflationary drag on the real growth of wealth. Because neither of these two essential economic factors was properly accounted for within previous IPCC prediction scenarios, the IPCC has once again, *substantially* underestimated the relationship of projected future increased prosperity to increased carbon dioxide levels. By forwarding this falsely rosy belief that economic prosperity can be maintained while dramatically reducing fossil fuel use, it seems the IPCC was trying to "have its cake and eat it too." These serious miscalculations by the IPCC mean their predictions are even more unreliable than has already been discussed in Chapter 7. This also means most of the world has no idea how bad the current global warming emergency really is or that to solve it, we will *have to* go through a massive global economic downturn. (For more on how ongoing global warming disaster-related inflation will eventually reach 100 percent, see Chapter 3 in the financial consequences section.)

Garrett does give us some hope in his research for a possible solution when he mentions that if civilization's ability to adapt to rising global warming and its consequences is extremely low, "...then only a combination of rapid civilization collapse and high decarbonization comes close to achieving a 450 ppmv goal."[118] (Here rapid civilization collapse refers directly to the rapid reduction of all fossil fuel use.)

Garrett's unsettling research can also suggest that the only remaining possible way that we may be able to maintain or go below the carbon 450 ppmv[119] target to avoid irreversible global warming and keep our economy going fairly well is:

- sudden and drastic global fossil fuel use reductions, and simultaneously

- all nations immediately and fully switching to non-carbon-dioxide-emitting green power generation sources. (Neither of which is currently happening.)

It appears Garrett may not believe we currently have either the technical ability and/or the political will to enact the painful solution to replace our fossil fuel energy consumption in time to avoid irreversible global warming. He states that "as the current climate system is tied directly to its unchangeable past, any substantial near-term departure from recently observed acceleration in carbon dioxide emission rates Is highly unlikely."

This creates a real dilemma. If we can't scale up a full global green energy generation replacement in time, while we are also making all of the required global fossil fuel reductions, the steep crash of the global economy will financially destroy us. If we continue as we are now, and civilization does not collapse quickly (within this century), carbon dioxide levels will likely exceed carbon 1,000 ppmv and condemn us to the the last phases of the Climageddon Scenario.

---

[118] Tim Garrett. "No way out? The double-bind in seeking global prosperity alongside mitigated climate change." arXiv. January 9 2012. https://arxiv.org/pdf/1010.0428v3.pdf

[119] (Note: ppmv is different from carbon parts per million [ppm and CE carbon equivalent, CO2e]. The distinction is that ppmv is used to describe all trace gases found in the atmosphere such as sulphur dioxide, carbon dioxide, nitrogen, and other pollutants by volume.)

Assuming Tim Garrett's research is correct about how the gross world product (GWP) and civilization's accumulated wealth is intrinsically linked to the total carbon levels present in the atmosphere, without building a nuclear reactor every day, or fully scaling up global green energy generation to replace all global fossil fuel reductions, our only remaining solution is to let the economy crash in stages now, or completely collapse later, bringing most of civilization down with it.

Ethically, this is a simple choice, but in reality, it is a logistic nightmare. How do we educate the people of the world that to save the future and future generations, they must now expect less, have less, and be less economically comfortable?

In a world that has already conditioned us to demand and expect more, the message that we must all make painful sacrifices for the survival of future generations and civilization will be a very hard sell. This educational task might be nearly impossible because it requires a degree of personal maturity to delay immediate self-gratification for a collective reward in the future. It is completely unrealistic to think most people will voluntarily make the required sacrifices without enforcement by the governments of the world.

As outlined in part of the Job One solution in Part 2, while we are doing our best to help scale up global green energy generation to levels never seen before in human history, we will also need to ready ourselves for the coming drastic fossil fuel use reductions, as well as the equally drastic and hopefully temporary losses of both productivity and wealth.

Very few individuals, corporations, or nations are ready to hear this tough message, much less act upon the drastic fossil fuel reductions we now need to make. But this is exactly what we all need to hear, begin discussing, and start preparing for and doing to survive. It will be difficult to ride out a temporary economic downturn as we go through this fossil fuel to green energy generation transition. (This also does not even take into account dealing with the many other global warming-related financial losses from consequences discussed in Chapter 3.)

Although many new jobs and businesses will be created in transferring to green energy generation, these new sources of revenue will not protect the economy from the loss of old fossil fuel industry-related jobs and businesses. As we ride out the coming economic hardships, and as we transition from reliance on fossil fuel energy generation to green energy generation, we will have to learn to accept these harsh financial realities.

Unless we immediately scale up and shift to full global green energy generation and radically reduce fossil fuel use to carbon neutral before the end of 2026, there is no way to save ourselves from Climageddon and keep our economies prosperous. This should help motivate us to avoid crossing the critical carbon 425-450 ppm threshold.

There is both bad news and good news in Garrett's research. The bad news is that even if we radically reduce fossil fuel use that currently sustains a viable rising economy, unless we also switch to non-fossil fuel green energy generation sources at an exponentially rapid rate, our atmospheric carbon ppm concentrations will continue to rise past carbon 425-450 and we will continue moving toward the later phases of the Climageddon Scenario. The good news is that we can secure a prosperous economy and a safe future if we persuade our politicians to realize there will be no possible long-term economic prosperity without immediate and complete transition to global green energy generation for our energy needs.

In summary, Garrett's research points toward the unbearable idea that the short-term collapse of our economy may become a required action if we are going to save ourselves from global warming catastrophe. If you still don't believe this is valid and you are scientifically minded, take a look at Garrett's paper called *"No Way Out."*[120] (Be sure to go to the end of his study after the references and also look at his many prediction graphs.)

We are caught in a terrible transitional energy, economy and survival dilemma. Assuming there is no quick global green energy generation transitional fix, if we drastically cut fossil fuel use now, we will soon suffer financial hardship. If we don't drastically cut fossil fuel use now, we will still suffer even greater financial hardship in the near future.

If the economy is going toward a steep recession or depression no matter what, it is wiser to get the needed painful changes out of the way as quickly as possible and save the future. Even though Garrett doubts it can be done in time and will collapse one way or the other, *Climageddon* takes the position that this dilemma *is escapable* by taking the only viable option open to us—scaling up green energy generation in the greatest mobilization of human history while we are simultaneously scaling down fossil fuel energy generation. If we do this and do not cross the carbon 425-450 ppm levels, we still have a chance.

You are now ready for what may be the toughest news of *Climageddon*.

The super shocker

Migrating above the 45th parallel north and below the 45th parallel south is only a *temporary survival solution*. (The generally safer northern and southern zones come from computer models and future climate projections.)

---

[120] Tim Garrett. "No way out? The double-bind in seeking global prosperity alongside mitigated climate change." *arXiv.* January 9 2012. https://arxiv.org/pdf/1010.0428v3.pdf

Migrating North or South of the 45th Parallel

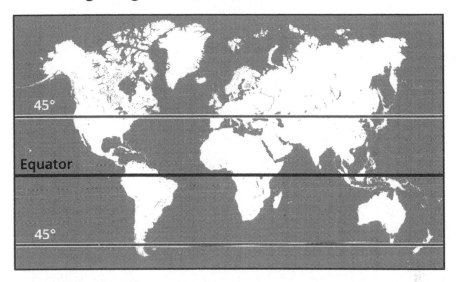

If the global warming emergency spirals further out of control into the later stages of the Climageddon Scenario, it will be the end of everything—no matter where you are or how wealthy you are. Without in any way diminishing the tremendous value of any person wanting to extend their quality of life for as long as is possible, it is also critical to realize that long-term survival will not be possible in the far north or far south indefinitely.

Saving civilization by temporarily moving people to the far north or far south is simply not a viable long-term solution to the escalating global warming emergency. Here's why.

It now appears that the only way to reverse the current global warming emergency may in part be to radically and suddenly reduce fossil fuel burning. Doing this will quickly lead us into a global economic recession or depression.

That may eventually be the lesser of our challenges because enforcing the required level of immediate global economic hardship in the 6-10 years we have left is nearly impossible. It is more likely all warnings will be ignored, and escalating global warming will continue until we have entered the endgame stages of the Climageddon Scenario.

In Phase 3 or 4 of the Climageddon Scenario, the greatest mass migration of climagees in human history will be well underway, and vast amounts of land between the 45th parallel north and the 45th parallel south will be all but abandoned. People will migrate because of unbearable heat, the global warming cluster of consequences, crashing economies, failing governments, scarce food and resources, as well as *Mad Max*-like chaos ruled by criminals and those forced by poverty or other circumstances to remain where the onset of suffering or death is only a matter of time.

As those vast dead zones are abandoned, the highly skilled technicians who oversaw the ongoing safety of the many nuclear power plants and hazardous chemical plants will no longer be there to prevent meltdowns or toxic chemical spills. Governments will also no longer function, providing the security necessary to prevent the remaining individuals from raiding military weapons storage facilities and biological, chemical, or nuclear weapons development centers.

While the damage from toxic chemical spills or conventional military weaponry will initially be limited, it will be only a matter of time before *hundreds* of water cooled nuclear power plants in the global warming dead zones melt down and, like Chernobyl, spew their unsurvivable levels of toxic radiation around the world. Worse yet, this accumulating radiation will remain in our atmosphere for hundreds to thousands of years, far past the survival capabilities of any underground shelter ever constructed.

This massive amount of toxic nuclear radiation means that eventually there will be no survivors. It will not matter how well the ultra wealthy individuals, corporations, or nations stock their underground shelters in the far north or far south.

We do not currently have any self-sustaining and continuously repairable energy generation, mechanical, or oxygen-creation technologies that could run continuously underground for hundreds to *thousands of years*. There are no current technologies that could meet all of the continuous needs for any underground survival group. (There is a book about an eventual global warming-caused extinction because of abandoned nuclear reactors melting down. It is called *Going Dark* by Guy McPherson, Professor Emeritus of Natural Resources and Ecology & Evolutionary Biology at the University of Arizona.)

Additionally, the actions of well-armed angry climagees will eventually overcome any border defense strategy. Any mined and reinforced border walls or other attempts to secure borders from the hundreds of millions of initial climagees will not hold, no matter how well-defended.

Conventional weapons caches as well as biological, chemical, and nuclear weapon caches from abandoned or broken nations located between the 45th parallels north and south will be used against any wall or fortified border area. Desperate climagees will do *anything* to get themselves and their families into temporarily safer zones.

Once these climagees get through the last border defenses, they will quickly locate any underground bunkers and force them open one way or the other for the critical survival resources inside. (In most cases, all they need to do is find and seal off the above-ground air intakes until those inside are forced to flee or suffocate.)

If massive unsurvivable toxic radiation circulating the Earth for hundreds to thousands of years and hordes of vengeance-seeking climagees are not enough to convince you that irreversible global warming is not survivable, here are additional facts about the situation we will face:

a. A drastically reduced population will not have enough genetic diversity to survive the onslaught of continuous new bacteria and viruses being released from the melting permafrost or from the northerly and southerly migrating diseases that will flourish in the global warming-created wastelands between the 45th parallel north and the 45th parallel south.

b. Gradual starvation. It is currently estimated that lands above the 45th parallel north and below the 45th parallel south, because of poorer soils, reduced hours of sun, and shorter growing seasons, will be capable of producing enough food for only 200 to 800 million people.

Things will be particularly bad for the ultra-wealthy individuals, corporations, or nations who did little or nothing to prevent the global warming crisis other than secure themselves a place in the temporarily safer far north or far south. (For more on this, see Part 2, Chapter 3 in the section called *The factors defining the practical responsibility of the world's wealthiest individuals and corporations for global warming.*)

This preceding means:

a. There really is no backup plan that is a *long-term* workable alternative to ending the global warming emergency.
b. The only remaining viable and rational plan to resolve the global warming emergency is to stay below carbon 425 to 450 and execute the critical action steps of the Job One Plan.

We're now left with the key fact in this book:

The one and only way *for any of us* or our children to survive long term is to solve the near impossible task in front of us.

Luckily, when there truly is only one way to solve an impossible task, we almost always choose that way. In part, this is because we are fully motivated and fully focused. We know the truth that there is only one way out!

There is a story from an ancient Chinese military manual called the *Art of War* by Sun Tzu that reinforces the idea that, even though the task is nearly impossible, when you are fully motivated, focused, and committed to a single remaining course of action, you will often surprisingly succeed.

In this story, a wise Chinese general was cornered at the banks of a large river by an opposing army many times larger than his own. His only means of escape was to get his army across the river before they were attacked. This general had also previously placed enough boats on the bank of the river for escape with his army should that need arise.

As the larger army approached, pushing the smaller army closer to the river, this general gave the order to his most trusted lieutenants to rush to the boats and burn them. When his army saw their only means of escape was being destroyed, they became wildly angry and charged toward the general. The army demanded to know why their trusted general had burned their escape boats and condemned all of them to certain death at the hands of a vastly superior army.

The general calmly said, "We will win this battle or we will die. There is no other alternative and no escape."

His army now knew their only option was victory or death. Filled with such clarity and single mindedness of purpose, they fought with such reckless intensity, they defeated the opposing army many times their size.

Now that you truly understand the rapidly approaching end game consequences of our global warming emergency, you too should no longer retain any illusion of escape. What you may not have realized yet is that our failure thus far to control the escalating global warming emergency and its many consequences means that we too have, in effect, *already burned* our escape boats.

This is the perilous point that we have come to. If we are lucky, we have 6 to 10 years left to exercise meaningful control over the accelerating emergency.

What do you have to lose and what rational alternative do you have? By doing nothing, even if we fail, your inaction will only shorten the critical time frame necessary to move people, technology, and infrastructure to the far north or far south so that you or those you love can be *temporarily* saved and live a little bit longer.

Most people would agree that living for a temporarily longer period is far better than dying now. Better yet, if we act wisely together and we are lucky, humanity and civilization will continue.

The last critical battle line of the global warming emergency

Everything you have read thus far has led you to our last battle line. Crossing carbon 425-450 ppm can act like a tipping point for the Climageddon Scenario process itself. Because of numerous contributing global warming factors, it was also disclosed earlier that if we cross the carbon 450 ppm range *we will eventually:*

1. raise temperatures 5°- 6° C (9°-10.8° Fahrenheit)

2. melt all remaining ice on earth (as has been done repeatedly in our distant climate past whenever we crossed that mark)

3. push ourselves into phase 4 and 5 of the Climageddon Scenario.[121]

---

[121] Hansen, James, et al. "Target atmospheric CO2: Where should humanity aim?" *The Open Atmospheric Science Journal* 2, no. 1 (2008): 217-231. DOI: 10.2174/1874282300802010217

If we cross this carbon 425-450 ppm battle line, we will go over the climate cliff where we will no longer be able to exert sufficient meaningful control, and our risk of irreversible global warming escalates *exponentially!*

We have 6 to 10 years remaining to slow and stop the processes that will eventually cross that carbon 425-450 ppm battle line. There will be many who say this task is impossible because of things such as pre-existing climate momentum and human systems inertia issues, as well as the 2.2-2.7°C of already committed temperature rise. It doesn't matter. We either do the nearly impossible or we will die.

If you take away nothing else from this book other than knowing that carbon 425-450 ppm marks the critical tipping point in the irreversible global warming process, your reading of *Climageddon* will have been a successful education and crucial warning.

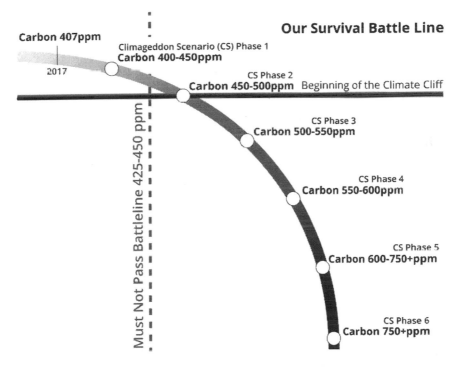

The best way of staying below the carbon 425 to

450 ppm battle line

At this unique moment in time, the following two targets are mission critical. With a bit of luck they *should* keep us from crossing either a keystone global warming tipping point or other tipping points that will lead us into and through Phase 2 of the Climageddon Scenario into the death spiral of Phase 3.

Based on where we are now, the following are our only valid *initial targets* that *must be* integrated into all new verifiable and enforceable laws or treaties that are needed:

1. Scale up and transition globally to nearly 100% renewable global green energy generation by 2026.

2. Scale down and reduce global fossil fuel use to ensure achieving carbon neutrality (net zero carbon) for all greenhouse gases by 2026.

Failure is no longer an option. We have to find the ways to scale up and scale down in time! Staying below carbon 425 to 450 ppm is our last fail-safe. (Do also keep in mind that carbon 425 to 450 ppm is nothing close to a safe level. It is the last "line in the sand" we cannot go beyond. A carbon 270-350 ppm level would be our ideal threshold, but at the current time, it is impossible to get back to those levels for possibly centuries.)

Because of the inherent counter momentum and inertia within our climate and human systems, our only remaining hope for survival is to make the immediate, radical, and painful changes described in steps 1 and 2 above (and in Part 2 of this book).

The good news about the two above 2026 targets is that they are also our best chance of minimizing the effects of global economic recession or depression due to radically reducing fossil fuel use over the next 10 years. Scaling up to 100% renewable green energy generation as fast as possible appears to be our best and most realistic cure for what will happen to the economy as we radically cut fossil fuel use. Scaling up while scaling down may not fully prevent a deep global economic crisis predicted by Garrett's research, but at the minimum, it should significantly reduce it.

There is no doubt that scaling up the needed amount of green energy generation for the whole world will be full of both anticipated and unanticipated problems. There will be those who swear scaling up enough new green energy generation in time to stay close to counterbalancing fossil fuel reductions and their economic consequences will be impossible.

In spite of those voices, we must still begin the largest coordinated global mobilization in human history and do the impossible. What other choice do we have?

The entrepreneur Elon Musk, founder of Tesla electric cars and SpaceX, has just built a new Giga factory for mass producing the newest technology in storage batteries. He has said that with just 100 more Giga factories being built, *all* of the world's green energy generation battery storage needs could be met. If every major government begins subsidizing or building such factories as an immediate national security and economic top priority, it should not take long to get them up and running. Here's a little bit of more good news.[122]

In addition to lessening the powerful economic downward push on the world's economy as we radically cut fossil fuel usage, do not forget that the sooner we reach 100% green energy generation, we will also:

    a. slow and lessen the escalating emergency,

    b. save many more lives,

    c. many more people will live longer,

---

[122] Adam Vaughan. "Renewables made up half of net electricity capacity added last year." *The Guardian*. October 25, 2016.
https://www.theguardian.com/environment/2016/oct/25/renewables-made-up-half-of-net-electricity-capacity-added-last-year?utm_source=esp&utm_medium=Email&utm_campaign=KIITG+series+2016&utm_term=198093&subid=15013304&CMP=ema-60

d. suffer fewer of the non-financial consequences of global warming, and

e. steeply reduce the risk of going over carbon 425-450 ppm climate cliff into a no man's land of escalating, unpredictable, and uncontrollable human and climate system variables.

Please keep in mind that the two above 2026 targets do not mean that if we fail, 2026 is the immediate end of the world. It is just a major process tipping point severely narrowing the window of meaningful control over preventing irreversible global warming.

Many people should still be alive over the first few decades after 2026. If we enter Phase 3 and Phase 4 of the Climageddon Scenario and cross that next Climageddon process tipping point, for decades after 2026 we will be dealing with the escalating consequences and processes described in detail throughout this book.

A motivational boost to counter the nearly impossible global warming challenge

If there were a large extinction-level asteroid rapidly approaching the Earth, we would immediately come together as one human family to mobilize and share resources and intelligence to overcome this common global extinction threat. It would not matter what nation we came from, what religion we held, or what race, ethnicity, or gender we were. We would immediately pull together in hopes of resolving this shared extinction threat because of our mutual desire for self-preservation.

At this moment, escalating global warming is racing toward crossing more tipping points and irreversible global warming. Although global warming moves at a slower pace, it is just as big and as real of a threat as an extinction-level asteroid steadily approaching Earth.

When deeply felt and understood, our common global warming threat also offers the motivation and clarity needed to compel our coming together as one human family and mobilizing to do what is necessary to resolve it. Once we realize that:

a. this threat is imminent and

b. no one will survive unless we utilize the remaining 6 to 10 years of meaningful control, it will be far easier to face the painful, costly, and radical changes together.

Your next vaccination—if you are a person of faith

Your faith provides a unique opportunity to help end global warming

The "benefits" for persons of faith are:

I. Your spiritual faith will help you to endure the hardships and sacrifice as the global warming process escalates until it is finally resolved.

II. There is a personal spiritual growth benefit in the evolutionary process itself whenever you overcome significant obstacles and challenges. You grow in both character and in spirit.

III. Restabilizing our climate will give you a powerful opportunity to live your deepest faith in relation to what many refer to as the Great Mystery of Ultimate Reality (God, Buddha, Allah, etc.).

IV. You can demonstrate that ending global warming and being a good steward for the Earth is fully compatible with your best understanding of the Great Mystery and its intentions to sustain life on the planet (as believed in many faiths). As this happens, you will be demonstrating the power and influence of your faith and the world's religions.

The best and biggest silver lining here is that when most individuals of faith and most of the great religious groups of this world collectively *demand* we do what is necessary to stop catastrophic global warming, an unimaginably *great moral leverage* will be in place to help ensure we are successful.

Your strong personal faith shared with others will also help demonstrate that humanity is completely capable of lessening, slowing, and eventually resolving the global warming challenge if:

I.   we are realistic about what is effective and what is not in the time we have left,
II.   we do the "first-things-first" on critical path actions,
III. we cooperate together as a *unified and coordinated* force.

Together, faith and spirit communities can help extend the existence, stability, and quality of life for the present generation, as well as for future generations.

> "A thing is right when it tends to preserve the integrity, stability and beauty of the biotic community. It is wrong when it tends otherwise."
> — Aldo Leopold, American author, ecologist and environmentalist

What's next

In the next chapter, you will find startling research on how people respond emotionally and philosophically to the idea of the end of civilization and extinction of humanity. The next chapter will also help you wisely evaluate and manage the urgency of the risk levels presented throughout previous chapters. In this chapter, you will also discover the 4 most commonly taken actions in response to this emergency.

Summary

- If we are lucky, there may still be time to act, but there is <u>no time left for delay!</u>

- By the time that the increasing damage of global warming becomes undeniable for many people, it will be far too late to do anything about it.

- If we want to save our economy, we need our politicians to realize there will be no continued or long-term economic prosperity without an immediate and complete transition out of fossil fuels and into global green energy generation.

- If we cannot rapidly scale up green energy generation to replace all required fossil fuel reductions, our only remaining choices are allowing the economy to collapse now and suffering severe and immediate economic pain, or collapse later and suffer complete economic collapse and the end of humanity and civilization.

- By this time it should be a no-brainer for any rational and mature individual to see that our best remaining chance to survive is to scale up green energy generation in time to replace *all* of the required fossil fuel reductions.

- If we reach the later phases of the Climageddon Scenario, no government, ultra-wealthy individual, or corporation will survive more than temporarily in the far north or far south. The unresolved global warming emergency leads directly to a no-win end game for everyone!

- Global warming as it exists now is not a one-time natural disaster. It is a continuous, continually escalating human-magnified disaster that, like getting too close to a black hole, will eventually suck in all of our resources and destroy our lives.

- Our global warming emergency exists because we have wasted 30 years failing to make the necessary changes to avert what is coming.

- The Phase 5 end game of the Climageddon Scenario may be as little as 54-89 years away, but it still may be averted and controlled if we act together and effectively within the next <u>6 to 10 years</u>.

- In addition to lessening the powerful economic downward push on the world's economy as we radically cut fossil fuel usage, do not forget that the faster we scale up to 100% green energy generation, the faster we will save many more lives, ensure many more people will live longer, suffer far less of the non-financial consequences of global warming, and steeply reduce our risks of going over the critical carbon 425-450 ppm battle line.

- We cannot allow ourselves to reach the carbon 425-450 ppm level before 2026. Crossing carbon 425-450 ppm acts like a tipping point. Like any crossed tipping point, it brings about an acceleration of the underlying processes.

- Most people do not yet know that the escalating global warming emergency and its many cascading consequences will soon or have already burned our escape boats. If we fail, soon there will be no real hope of any *long-term* escape from this emergency—no matter where we migrate to.

PART 1, CHAPTER 9

WHAT YOU CAN DO ABOUT THE GLOBAL WARMING EMERGENCY

Overview:

- Unknown to the general public, escalating global warming will eventually wreak the same level of death and chaos as thermonuclear war.

- Denying the realities of global warming is not a solution and it will not help us escape it. Escalating global warming will eventually impose its reality of escalating consequences *on everyone*.

- Accepting the realities of global warming and examining the facts will allow us to work toward the best possible outcome.

- There is a new, workable plan that deals with all the facts.

This chapter offers new ways to envision, evaluate, and personally manage the escalating risks, threat level, and urgency of the unfolding Climageddon Scenario phases. It will also help you decide what you can do about escalating global warming and our imperiled future. It describes the options other people have chosen to act upon.

Another perspective on the global warming risk and its ultimate consequences

A good way to think about the combined risks and consequences of continually escalating global warming is to go back to the asteroid metaphor presented previously. Imagine these combined risks to be much like a slow-moving but very large comet or asteroid headed directly for Earth. (The main difference between asteroids and comets is only their composition.)

To help you envision how risk evaluation is relevant in this scenario, it is useful to look to a 1998 Hollywood science fiction disaster film called *Deep Impact*. It depicted humanity's combined efforts to prepare for and destroy a 7-mile (11 km) wide comet set to collide with Earth and cause a mass extinction.

To prevent the comet from reaching Earth, Russia and the United States send a spacecraft with nuclear weapons to destroy it before it reaches the critical minimal distance from Earth. The spaceship reaches the proper critical distance in time, but the nuclear weapons' first attempt fails and instead splits the comet into two smaller masses, both still heading directly for Earth. After the U.S. President announces the failure, he declares martial law and reveals that in anticipation of this possible failure, governments worldwide have secretly been building underground shelters.

The U.S. government then conducts a lottery and selects 800,000 Americans under age 50 and 200,000 secretly pre-selected individuals (government officials, top military brass, key scientists, and powerful corporate elites). Around the world, the selected few go to the underground shelters, which contain seeds for every species of plant, important viable animals, as well as massive food supplies for the would-be shelter survivors.

The first comet mass impacts Cape Hatteras in the Atlantic Ocean, causing a tsunami up to 3,500 feet (1,100 meters) high. The second mass is due to impact western Canada, creating a cloud of dust that will block out the sun for two years, killing all unsheltered life on Earth in a remaining matter of weeks. At the last minute, the damaged spacecraft carrying the remaining nuclear weapons hits the larger second mass in a suicide mission, breaking it up so that most of it burns up in the atmosphere or misses the planet completely.

After the survivors come out of their shelters, the President speaks to a large crowd, telling them they've been blessed with a second chance to call Earth their home.

In the preceding story, the most obvious risk parallels to the global warming emergency are two: 1) if we keep going as we are now and somehow survive the emergency, most of humanity will die anyway and there will have to be a massive, difficult, and costly rebuilding of civilization by the few remaining survivors; and 2) as global warming consequences continue to worsen, governments will be forced to declare martial law, and there will be quotas for who will be able to move near or above the 45th parallel north or near or below the 45th parallel south to escape the chaos occurring within that middle zone a little longer.

This movie also depicted many of the consequences that occur within a society when it faces its end. Some of those are noble sacrifices, others widespread panic, chaos, looting, and crime.

As you continue to read this chapter designed to help you find the right decision for your circumstances, please keep in mind the *Deep Impact* end-of-the-world scenario because of its risk similarity to those of the Climageddon Scenario's most serious consequences.

Evaluating the Climageddon Scenario's threat and urgency levels

Here is an additional perspective different from the risk, threat, and urgency described in the previous planet-killer comet story...

Comparative threat and urgency levels are highly relevant to the unfolding Climageddon Scenario. Before we talk about urgency factors, let's explore threat levels by comparing escalating global warming to something else we absolutely know is catastrophically dangerous at a *global level*.

Escalating global warming and its unfolding Climageddon Scenario will eventually create a potential threat, hazard, and risk level similar in severity and potential destructiveness to *global thermonuclear war*. That may seem like a jarring comparison, but it is a highly appropriate one.

It has been over 70 years since the bombing of Hiroshima and Nagasaki. Because of the enactment of many nuclear treaties and nuclear weapons safeguarding systems, we have effectively managed and controlled an unconscionable nuclear threat level and the frightening outcomes of nuclear war for 70+ years.

Unlike the well-controlled and well-managed threat of nuclear war, the escalating global warming emergency is not being effectively managed, despite the fact that it is already wreaking escalating havoc upon greater and greater portions of humanity and it poses extinction-level probabilities. Here's where this disparity in comparable threat management becomes even more shocking.

Most people already know the nuclear powers of the world will go to unbelievable lengths to achieve 100% risk and threat management for all possible global thermonuclear war risks. This is because the consequences from a global thermonuclear war would likely cause the near extermination of the human race, and would make the planet a living hell for centuries to millennia for any unlucky survivors.

No nation or rational political leader would ever allow the slightest risk of global thermonuclear war to go unmanaged and uncontrolled. They would never allow their staff who manage or control nuclear weapons to be inadequately trained or unprepared for any nuclear weapons threat or freak security situations. Far too much is at stake to not take the nuclear threat, hazard, and risk *deadly serious.*

Additionally, because of the near certain extinction-level consequences of a global thermonuclear war, nations possessing nuclear weapons employ vast numbers of people to plan and prepare for every possible scenario where nuclear weapons could be used, damaged, mistakenly fired, lost, stolen, or activated in any possible scenario (including what are called rare tipping point, fat tail, outlier, or Black Swan scenarios.)

When it comes to protecting us against the threats of global thermonuclear war, no amount of national treasure, time or personnel is spared. *Excuses are never accepted* by our nation's leaders for less than continuous, 100% effective threat, hazard, and risk management.

Over time, global warming is also fully capable of producing a scale of global death and destruction similar to that of nuclear war. Unfortunately, outside of a small group of climate scientists and those aware of the Climageddon Scenario, the general public remains nearly completely unaware that the growing threats of escalating global warming now parallel the risk and consequence levels of global thermonuclear war.

These risk and urgency factors are even more compelling for escalating global warming because the consequences are not far off in the future—nor can they be successfully delayed for 70 years in the same way nuclear treaties and nuclear weapons security protocols keep nuclear war at bay. Global warming consequences are already occurring and will escalate as more tipping points are crossed.

After 30 years of warnings from our best scientific minds, we have thoroughly failed to develop the necessary 100% commitment to executing *effective* threat, hazard, and risk reduction actions for global warming. We have also not mobilized our global resources to manage and control the rapidly escalating global warming threats, hazards, and risks in any *adequate* manner, as we have done with *any and all* aspects of nuclear weapons and nuclear war.

Seeing the threat level of escalating global warming from the framework of your normal daily decisions

To help you put the growing probability of the end-of-the-world Climageddon Scenario into the perspective of your own daily decisions (if we do not act effectively now), ask yourself the following question:

Would you get on an airplane where there was a 10% risk of crashing? a 5% risk? a 1% risk? or even a 0.5% risk?,

If you wouldn't take such risks on an airplane and our most powerful nuclear armed governments wouldn't leave the smallest risk of nuclear war less than *100% managed*, why are we allowing a projected 10% or higher risk of going over more global warming tipping points leading to irreversible global warming and the later phases of the Climageddon Scenario to be so poorly managed?

The urgency level of the escalating global warming emergency

Now that you have several ways to view the threat and risk levels of the escalating global warming emergency, it's time to explore the urgency level of global warming using once again to the comet/asteroid analogy. Imagine that a single comet large enough to destroy almost all life on Earth has been just discovered to be on a collision course with Earth and it is 6-10 years away. Now imagine that our best scientists have worked out all of the calculations necessary to send rockets into space to deflect or break up the comet so that it does not hit us.

Next, imagine the scientists tell us we have a window of only 6 months in which we must launch and intercept the comet or all life on Earth will end. In this story, there is a time-limited, critical, life-and-death urgency. If we do not launch our rockets and arrive at the comet within the 6-month window of effective meaningful control, we lose *all* control over our future and reach the end game for humanity.

Although it is easy to understand the time-limited 6-month urgency for launching the rocket and arriving at the comet, it is very difficult for many people to understand a similar level of urgency to resolve global warming if they do not have access to the information in this book. As global warming continues to escalate and move toward the Climageddon Scenario end stages, without understanding the true critical urgency of this time-limited scenario, most people falsely believe we are making progress, that things are okay, or there is no particular rush.

This is one of the biggest problems we face. If we do not act immediately and make the radical, costly and difficult changes required (as described in Part 2 of this book), and we do not do so within this very limited window of remaining meaningful control, we will find ourselves needing to immediately begin moving infrastructure, technology, and as many people as possible to the far north above the 45th parallel and far south below the 45th parallel.

We will also need to prepare for deepening economic chaos, governments declaring martial law, and the suspension of many hard-won freedoms and civil rights. Governments will be forced to maintain law and order as desperate people realize they must migrate immediately or they will soon not be able to cross the national borders they must cross to survive.

The precautionary principle of risk management

It's time to discuss another piece of information about how to manage risk levels wisely and ethically. It should now be clear that there is an *extreme level* of risk related to consciously or unconsciously crossing more global warming tipping points and crossing the carbon 425-450 threshold. Accordingly, the *precautionary principle* of professional risk management must also be considered.

The precautionary principle of risk management states that if an action or policy has a suspected risk of causing harm to the public or to the environment, *in the absence of* scientific consensus that the action or policy is *not* harmful, the burden of proof to demonstrate that it is *not harmful* falls on those taking any proposed action. At the minimum—especially because there is no lack of scientific consensus about the harm burning fossil fuel is doing—this means that fossil fuel companies have a burden to prove *scientifically* that burning fossil fuels is *not* harmful to our shared environment and its various inhabitants.

Conversely, when and where scientific investigation has found a plausible to probable risk for some activity, the precautionary principle implies there is both a social responsibility and a legal responsibility for our government officials to effectively act to protect the public from exposure to harm. (In Europe, the precautionary principle is already being used in law.)

In the case of global warming, the obligations of the precautionary principle upon our national politicians can be relaxed *only if* further verifiable scientific findings provide *compelling consensus of evidence* that *no harm* will result. This is obviously not the case. As we continue on our escalating global warming path, we are *certain* to cross more global warming tipping points, and bear the harm that will result.

Now that you have reviewed multiple perspectives and comparisons on the threat, risk, and urgency levels of the escalating global warming emergency, it's time to begin exploring what *your* action (or inaction) options might be to prevent the later stages of the Climageddon Scenario from unfolding.

Startling research on how people respond to the possibility of the end of civilization and the extinction of humanity

Research done by Melanie Randle and Richard Eckersley[123] in the U.S., UK, Canada, and Australia investigated the perceived probability of threats to humanity and our different responses to them (nihilism,[124] fundamentalism,[125] and activism[126]).

Overall:

1. A majority (54%) rated the risk of our way of life ending within the next 100 years at 50% or greater.

2. A quarter (24%) rated the risk of humans being wiped out at 50% or greater.

3. The remaining study participants rated the risk of humans being wiped out within the next 100 years from 0 to less than 50%.

Across countries, age groups, gender, and education levels, the responses were relatively uniform.
Here's what they also discovered:

---

[123] Melanie J. Randle and Richard Eckersley, "Public perceptions of future threats to humanity and different societal responses: a cross-national study." *Futures*, 72 (2015): 4-16. doi: http://dx.doi.org/10.1016/j.futures.2015.06.004

[124] Wikipedia contributors, "Nihilism," *Wikipedia, The Free Encyclopedia*, https://en.wikipedia.org/w/index.php?title=Nihilism&oldid=757224924 (accessed December 29, 2016).

[125] Wikipedia contributors, "Fundamentalism," *Wikipedia, The Free Encyclopedia*, https://en.wikipedia.org/w/index.php?title=Fundamentalism&oldid=758581120(accessed January 6, 2017).

[126] Wikipedia contributors, "Activism," *Wikipedia, The Free Encyclopedia*, https://en.wikipedia.org/w/index.php?title=Activism&oldid=750786662 (accessed November 21, 2016).

1. Almost 80% agreed "we need to transform our worldview and way of life if we are to create a better future for the world" (activism).

2. About 50% agreed that "the world's future looks grim, so we have to focus on looking after ourselves and those we love" (nihilism).

3. Over 33% believed that "we are facing a final conflict between good and evil in the world" (fundamentalism).

Keeping these findings in mind about how people see the future when faced with the end of civilization and the extinction of humanity, it is paramount to examine your possible personal options below in responding to the global warming emergency that can lead to the same result.

Your options for what to do about the global warming emergency

The A-F options below are those most commonly chosen after someone understands the true gravity of the rapidly unfolding Climageddon Scenario. You may choose more than one of these responses in some combination.

The denial strategies and options:

a. <u>Deny it and do nothing because it's overwhelming.</u> Denial is an *understandable and legitimate* psychological defense mechanism when the reality is too much for that particular mind to bear. From experience at the Job One for Humanity organization, it was seen that many people struggle with the disheartening and difficult information of this book. For some individuals, complete denial is *initially* necessary to continue to survive with some semblance of psychological and emotional equilibrium. (At some later date, as their psychological and emotional equilibrium becomes stronger regarding this emergency, some of these individuals will choose to begin working on parts of the plan found in Part 2 of this book.)

b. Deny it and do nothing because you believe the inaccurate or incomplete media coverage and advertisements deceptively forwarded by the fossil fuel industry. These media generate *doubt and confusion* regarding the global warming science or the seriousness of the global warming emergency. At some point, when the real and personal costs of escalating global warming finally hit close to home, or individuals in this mindset are exposed to more global warming science, many of these individuals will leave the denier category and may also join efforts to resolve the emergency.

c. Deny it and intentionally do nothing because you are profiting from the fossil fuel-related industries. These organizations and individuals will flat out deny *almost everything* in this book. These organizations and individuals almost always have a direct or indirect vested interest in the continued profitability of the fossil fuel-related industries, or are being secretly or openly paid by the fossil fuel-related industries to create doubt and misinformation about areas of settled climate science. These "merchants of doubt" and misinformation are using many of the same tactics that were effectively used by the tobacco industry to delay laws regulating tobacco product use for almost 50 years.

To one degree or another, the denial strategies listed above are like the proverbial ostrich sticking its head in the sand, hoping that by not seeing a threat it will be spared. Denial strategies do not work for the ostrich and they will not work for us. The escalating global warming emergency *will* eventually impose its painful consequences upon any and all worlds of carefully constructed partial or complete denial.

Reality always seems to have the uncanny ability to impose itself and overcome any attempt to deny it. Denial *almost always* adds additional pain and suffering on top of the original delayed or denied consequences.

> "Resistance (denial) is what you add to pain to make it last longer and hurt more." —Errol Strider

The acceptance strategies and options:

a. Accept the facts of *Climageddon*, but do nothing about it. This option is taken when individuals feel they have no real influence or control that could significantly improve the situation, or they are so preoccupied with other more pressing personal problems they have no time or bandwidth left for *any* other life problems. These individuals simply go about living their lives trying to have as much peace and enjoyment as is possible by simply focusing on their daily problems and ignoring the situations they believe they cannot effectively influence or control.

b. Accept the facts of *Climageddon* and do nothing more than prepare one's loved ones, business, community, or nation for what is coming. These individuals strongly believe that the hope of resolving the escalating global warming emergency is so slim that it would be wiser for them to take whatever time and resources they have and dedicate all of them to preparing the appropriate emergency reserves and migration plans while also still trying to enjoy their lives every day as best they can for as long as they can. At some level, these individuals also believe they do not have the influence or control to make a real difference anyway.

c. <u>Accept the facts of the Climageddon Scenario and work for the best possible outcome for resolving the global warming emergency.</u> There are many mature adults who understand that difficult conversations, facts and situations are just another part of navigating the challenges of life. They understand that if they do not have all the accurate facts, they cannot properly do whatever is necessary to make the best out of *any* difficult situation. These individuals are strong enough emotionally and psychologically to bear the weight of disheartening truths like those found in this book. They are also the same individuals who will quickly seek out and use the best plans and strategies available. They will not deceive themselves as to the costs, pain, or suffering that resolving any difficult situation entails. While these individuals work for the best, they are also wise enough to prepare for the worst. However, they will not make personal emergency preparation their *main* priority. They will focus the majority of their attention and resources on resolving the escalating emergency using the best possible strategies.

Before you decide which strategy and option you will use, please do not forget that there may be still some time and hope left to avert climate catastrophe even though the process will be extremely costly, difficult, and painful. There is also much we do not know about the global warming systems and subsystems that could provide some positive wild cards in our favor.

If you have chosen the denial strategies and options

If you're one of those individuals who is:

a. a denier or is overwhelmed by all this bad news, or

b. who believes that things are truly hopeless, or

c. who believes that you don't have to worry about what you can't control and you can just enjoy the present, or

d. who is preparing for what is coming by protecting only yourself and loved ones without acting to help slow, lessen, and resolve the situation, then there are two more important ideas to carefully consider:

I. By doing nothing, you shorten the critical time frame needed for more people, technology, and infrastructure to be successfully moved to the far north or far south so that more of the population can live a bit longer.

II. Your inaction and/or your seeking personal comfort or escape from your moral, ethical, and spiritual obligation (if you are of a spiritual nature) to act is in fact, by omission, a form of contributing to the end of civilization and humanity as we know it.

Still not convinced the Climageddon Scenario is already happening? Watch "The Most Terrifying Video You'll Ever See, Version 2."[127] (10 minutes) This video examines what we should do with the risk in front of us from a completely different risk management perspective than has been presented anywhere else in the book. It examines the arguments of the global warming *deniers and critics,* as well as those who believe global warming-caused climate destabilization is occurring. It brilliantly summarizes what will happen to us if we do not effectively confront the escalating global warming emergency. This video has been viewed over 1 million times.

If you are *still* a denier of the global warming emergency, your denial will also slow or prevent your own necessary

---

[127] "The Most Terrifying Video You'll Ever See." YouTube video. 9:33, posted by "wonderingmind42," June 8, 2007. https://www.youtube.com/watch?v=zORv8wwiadQ

preparation and protection because you believe there is no problem. Once our governments are overwhelmed by global warming's continuous disasters, reality will rear its harsh and ugly head. Because of denial and your lack of preparation, you and those closest to you will receive the likely reward of suffering more and longer.

On the other hand, if you're one of those brave and mature individuals who wants to slow and lessen escalating global warming and then eventually work to end it (option F above), please continue to the section directly below. If you have not chosen option F, please read Part 2 and the book's conclusion.

If you choose option F, here is what you can effectively do to avert the worst of the Climageddon Scenario *before it's too late*

There is still a reasonable hope that we have enough time (about 6-10 years) to resolve this emergency and hit the critical global warming reduction targets discussed previously and in more detail in Part 2 of this book. It's also time to fully acknowledge and face a painful and bitter fact. What we are doing now and what we have been doing for the past 30 years is *not working* as proven by our continually rising carbon ppm measurements.

Luckily, there is a new, practical, effective, and comprehensive plan that may be our best hope to end escalating global warming and prevent us from crossing more global warming tipping points. This plan is based on current science. It provides prioritized and *emergency-appropriate* action steps you can start right now. It's called the Job One for Humanity Plan, and it is found in the next part of this book.

If we complete the radical, difficult and costly action steps of the new Job One for Humanity Plan *within 6-10 years*, it may not be too late for us to resolve the current global warming emergency or, at the least, slow and lessen it enough so that some of us may survive a bit longer.

Your next vaccination

Here is your next vaccination:

Scientific research is educating and mobilizing more individuals for resolving the global warming emergency

The spread of broad scientific consensus concerning the escalating global warming emergency means many of us will no longer be able to continue planning our futures based upon past inaccurate beliefs or fossil fuel industry misinformation. This is a subtle but important silver lining because once one can no longer deny the global warming facts, the urgency to find the best processes for ending it will more forcefully emerge and more likely be executed.

Intelligent, rational people want to know the facts no matter how bad they might be, and no matter how strongly they might want them to be something else. This is because mature, clear thinking persons have learned if they don't honestly face and deal with painful facts, eventually the facts will painfully deal with them.

> "Let us not pray to be sheltered from dangers, but to be fearless when facing them."
> — Rabindranath Tagore,
> 1913 Nobelist in literature

Once individuals have a deeper, more accurate understanding of the facts about the escalating global warming risks, they can then begin to manage and adapt to those new global warming realities to the benefit of themselves, their families, businesses, communities, and nations.

Summary

- Most people develop their global warming opinions from random news stories and studies from many different perspectives and conflicting sources. These scattered news stories and studies make it difficult to see the dangerous progression and patterns of our expanding emergency. One of *Climageddon's* greatest values is that it solves that problem by connecting the dots from these random news stories and research studies so that it is easier to see the dangers and the developing patterns to show where we are going through the 6 phases of the Climageddon Scenario.

- We had about 40 years to make the necessary global warming changes when we were warned 30 years ago by scientists. If we are lucky, we have about 6-10 years left to make radical, costly, and painful changes that would have been far easier, cheaper, and less painful had we begun them 30 years ago.

- Once we lose meaningful control over escalating global warming, there is no way to reverse the fatal consequences that humanity will endure for centuries or thousands of years, if we even survive.

- At a global level, the scale and severity of long-term global warming harm is so unthinkable that every emergency solution we enact must be on the critical path necessary to effectively get us out of this unconscionable risk level while we still have time.

- If we do not protect the gameboard of life by preserving the stability of our climate against the threats of escalating global warming, our personal, business or national "games" in life will first be disrupted, then eventually ended.

- It is now time for the painful and costly cure found within the radical action steps of Part 2.

Congratulations, you have just finished Part 1 of *Climageddon* and are ready for Part 2.

In Part 2, you will explore a comprehensive plan of prioritized new solutions to the global warming emergency. If we are going to be successful in saving our future, we will need to quickly manage the formidable challenges presented in Part 1.

CLIMAGEDDON
PART 2

The Key Action Steps of the
Job One Plan to End Global Warming

PART 2, CHAPTER 1

THE JOB ONE FOR HUMANITY PLAN TO END GLOBAL WARMING

Consider allowing what you have absorbed in Part 1 of *Climageddon* to steep and to settle, before you begin the Job One Plan in Part 2.

Part 1 is mostly science, and its many chains of reason-based conclusions can be disconcerting and take some time to digest. The Job One Plan in Part 2 presents a different type of content. Compared to Part 1, it is more theoretical.

It offers a series of suggestions and choices—strategies to respond to and resolve the multi-dimensional global warming crisis. It was developed because we believe that it is unconscionable to illuminate the massive challenge of escalating global warming and then fail to offer plausible responses and strategies that match the problem's scale. Job One does offers a menu of plausible responses and in doing so, it provides some measure of hope and reassurance.

The Job One Plan

Welcome to Part 2 of *Climageddon*. In many ways, this is the most important part of *Climageddon* because it describes critical action steps that may be our last best chances to respond to the scope, scale and urgency of the global warming emergency before we pass the final thresholds whereupon global warming becomes irreversible.

The new Job One Plan is designed *only to*:

   a. first slow and lessen global warming, then eventually

b. end the emergency before global warming becomes irreversible and we enter the later stages of the Climageddon Scenario.

It is a comprehensive "first things first" plan using innovative strategies and the most current science available. It is a fully prioritized plan deadline-driven designed to do *only what is absolutely necessary* in the most effective sequence of steps.

It is *significantly* different from other global warming resolution strategies and programs being presented today. It is not the intention of the Job One Plan to negate other current programs. The Job One plan hopes to augment and refine the existing programs of other organizations with a fresh infusion of information, ideas, strategies, and perspectives so that we are best equipped to succeed on the monumental collective task in front of us.

The Job One Plan will disrupt our normal lives, businesses, nations, and economies, exactly as the escalating global warming emergency will be the "Great Disruptor" over the balance of the 21st century.

While working on the Job One, never forget that there is always still hope left until we have crossed:

a. more points of no return, or
b. a keystone tipping point, or
c. more tipping points that trigger the later stages of the Climageddon Scenario (late Phase 2 or entering Phase 3).

To take advantage of our remaining window of meaningful control, we must act together immediately.

Getting real about the Job One for Humanity Plan

As we have been candid about how bad the global warming emergency, we will also be candid about strengths and weaknesses of the components of the Job One Plan you are about to explore:

a. It is not a complete, nor is it a "finished" plan. It is a series of last chance responses and solutions that will require continuous adjustments.

b. It is designed to be able to evolve and to adapt quickly to discovered weaknesses or strengths as relevant research or verified information is realized.

c. It candidly examines our personal action options. In essence, we have two main choices: 1) giving up because the global warming emergency looks impossible to resolve in the time we have left, or 2) doing our best to tackle it, all the while knowing that we still may fail and at best be able only to buy ourselves a little more time.

d. It is also meant to be a catalyst and igniter of virally expanding, effective action around the world.

e. It offers no 100% guarantee it will of itself resolve the current global warming emergency.

f. It is not the only global warming elimination plan being promoted by sincere and intelligent individuals and organizations around the world, but in many ways it may be the most unique. What is unique about the Job One Plan is that:

    1. It is straightforward about our 30+ years of failure to end the escalating global warming emergency.

2. It offers innovative new strategies to confront severe challenges that appear nearly impossible to resolve within the deadlines we have left.

3. It invites you or your organization into what *must be* a collaborative process for resolving this seemingly unsolvable emergency.

4. Anyone can contribute to or expand this collaborative effort. Anyone can experiment and adapt, exchange feedback with us and, wherever possible, assume a self-organizing, leadership role wherever they or their organization might reside.

The Job One Plan is not perfect, but it is an innovative, flexible, and evolving starting point for quickly changing course away from our 30-year history of failure.

The biggest potential weaknesses of the Job One Plan

The Job One Plan can be criticized from many different perspectives. What follows is a partial listing of the important criticisms we have received:

1. "You'll never get it done because huge vested interests with vastly superior resources will crush you before you ever get going. These vested interests will tie up every major effort you make for at least 2-3 more decades."

2. "You'll never get the nations of the world to cooperate at the levels that are needed to execute key elements of your plan."

3. "You're making demands for actions to be done in which you have little to no influence on those your demands are directed toward."

4. "The agents whom you are relying on to help solve the emergency will not act in the public interest at the expense of their own interests."

5. "Those agents your demands are directed to have little incentive, much inertia and many countering incentives that facilitate them not acting in your favor."

6. "The agents you are relying on to act are already overloaded with current local crisis demands they must deal with *today*, making them unlikely to tackle a catastrophic global transition point that is 6 to 10 years in the future."

7. "What you're saying needs to be done is simply not feasible within the critical deadlines presented."

8. "Your plan introduces questions of fairness, equity, and justice without resolving these issues in any meaningful way."

9. "Your plan is so radical that not even the existing environmental, sustainability, and global warming educational organizations will adopt and promote its strategies."

10. "You have labeled so many of today's popular green-oriented efforts as essentially futile in the fight against escalating global warming deadlines that it will result in alienating large numbers of your greatest potential allies when you need those same allies to achieve your plan."

11. "On one hand, you say climate systems are complex, dynamic, and interdependent and therefore not easy to predict yet, on the other hand, you discount the cumulative positive effects of many small individual going-green activities related to meeting the critical deadlines of the emergency. You may be dead wrong and these cumulative small positive effects may have a

much bigger effect in complex adaptive climate systems than you are allowing for."

12. "You state that politicians, corporations, and nations have extensive, well financed, well honed resources and skills for resisting global warming lobbying. Yet, some of your action steps amount to little more than innovative new approaches to 'lobbying' the very individuals that you say are highly resistant to such lobbying."

13. "Your 'when all else fails' migration strategies insufficiently describe the practical difficulties of such migration or the resistance that will be mounted by those fortunate nations temporarily advantaged by increased global warming."

14. "The plan is unrealistically idealistic. It assumes too many positive results to be achieved too easily, compared to what is actually more likely to happen."

15. "*Climageddon* is too apocalyptic. Nobody wants to hear this much bad news. While society is grateful to the person who yells fire in a real burning building, few if any can deal with the warning that the whole world is burning up."

As you can see, we have heard many well articulated, reasonable concerns about the following Job One Plan. By the time you finish reading it, you may see some of the Job One solutions as, at best, a stretch or, an iffy plan landed upon because nothing else seemed even remotely possible. You may also believe you see gaps, contradictions, overly-optimistic assumptions, and wobbly logic in Part 2.

Beyond that it's also normal and natural to doubt that neither the Job One Plan nor anything else can for that matter can resolve the current conditions causing this emergency. Nevertheless, that does not change the reality that if we fail to meet this challenge in the next 6 to 10 years, the future will not only become more and more unpleasant, it will become more and more unbearable as we move closer to extinction and the end of civilization.

Sometimes life imitates art. Recall the movie, *Apollo 13*, when the astronauts' capsule suffered a critical mission breakdown in its oxygen scrubbing and electrical systems. Whether we know it or not, we are all now also mission co-engineers—but with a planet as our endangered capsule and billions of lives as our "space crew" hanging in the balance.

We too have been walked into a room by the head of Apollo 13 mission control, who tells us he will not let anyone out of that room until we come up with a solution using *only* the supplies currently present inside the capsule. The mission control director looks at us and says the famous line of the *Apollo 13* film: "failure is not an option." He departs and locks the door.

Like in the movie, failure to resolve our escalating global warming emergency is also not an option! We are all locked in the same and now must somehow resolve this crisis before it's too late. True, the odds are not good, but the consequences of not resolving it are immeasurably worse.

After reading the Job One Plan, if you do have criticisms, please forward them including your deadline-sensitive better solutions for the strategy you are criticizing. Additionally, after *Climageddon* is published, a discussion forum and FAQ will be created on the Job One website where you can join an ongoing dialogue and help resolve the gargantuan challenge before us.

How to get the best results with the Job One Plan

Now that the Job One disclaimers are out of the way, it's also good to know:

a. It is best to focus on the critical *primary* action steps in Part 2 of this book. They are the most effective action steps on the critical path for resolving the escalating global warming emergency in time to save us.

b. Don't be afraid to experiment with the Job One action steps. Wisely use any feedback from your own experiments (and those of others) to quickly adapt and tweak all action step tactics into better, faster solutions. Experimenting with alternate solutions not foreseen in the Job One Plan is good *provided* such solutions will also achieve the critical goals and 2026 targets outlined in the Job One Plan, keep us from crossing the climate cliff and do not repeat steps that are already known to be ineffective. We actively invite you to improve the Job One Plan with your own critical path action steps we have not considered.

c. If you have tested a more effective way to complete any step, or you have tested a new solution to some step, please collaborate and let the Job One team know about your success by emailing them at manage@JobOneforHumanity.org. Job One staff will do their best to help spread your successes around the world in our newsletters.

Three easy and fast Job One Plan warm-up steps

Athletes go through a brief but important warm-up procedure before engaging in a challenging practice session or competition. Like an athlete, you also are about to begin a challenge. To help you prepare for this challenge, try the following three easy warm-up actions.

1. Start talking about global warming as it really is.

We need to change how we talk about global warming to reflect the real challenge. One important thing you can do is to stop saying "climate change" and use more accurate and informative terms.

There are several reasons why "climate change" is misleading. It has been a term employed primarily by the fossil fuel industry and its lobbyists, advocates, and climate denial apologists to lull both the media and the public into a false sense of safety concerning the global warming emergency. This near-invisible global warming counter-propaganda is designed to make something very dangerous to your future well-being appear as common and non-threatening as normal everyday changes of our usual climate.

The fossil fuel industry lobbyists and PR firms are strategically exploiting the public's accurate experience that climate is always changing. Promoting the term "climate change" cleverly reframes the danger and creates the false impression that escalating global warming is nothing more than another benign and expected normal change in the weather and certainly nothing to worry about. What is occurring is not benign climate change, however, but climate *destabilization* and climate *disruption* caused by escalating global warming and our use of fossil fuels.

In order to overcome any challenge, we must be able to see it without false illusions. Unfortunately, climate change is a term that feeds false illusions and fosters *intentional* confusion about what is really happening to our climate.

The climate is not only changing as it always does, *it is destabilizing and violently disrupting the lives of more people every month!*

If we are ever going to create the necessary awareness within the public to help slow down and eventually reverse global warming, it is imperative we stop using the term "climate change." Going forward, please use the terms "climate destabilization," "escalating global warming," or "global warming emergency" in place of that deceptively benign term forwarded by the fossil fuel industry.

Words do have power! How you frame things with your word choices does make a difference. How you frame an issue also directs and guides the conversation. Watch what happens as you start using more accurate terminology and *re-framing* your global warming conversations in this manner. To help you solidify this action, we encourage you to sign the stop saying *climate change* online pledge, which you can also forward to your friends.[128]

2. Stay informed on the rapidly changing news and progress.

The battle to save the future from the expanding consequences of global warming and the unfolding Climageddon Scenario is constantly changing. Some areas are getting better and some areas getting worse. Consequently, if we are going to overcome the immense challenge before us, it is wise for you to stay up-to-date, motivated, and supported.

To stay informed, motivated, and supported, we *strongly recommend* you do the following three things:

a. Sign up to receive regular email blog posting summary updates from the free *Global Warming Blog*.[129] These interesting and entertaining blog article summaries are a great way to increase your knowledge of the constantly evolving progress, problems and research.

b. Sign up for the Job One For Humanity email list.[130] You will receive free monthly newsletters and other information tracking who's doing what and the progress we are making together to end global warming.

---

[128] Job One for Humanity. "Stop saying climate change pledge." *JobOneforHumanity.org*. Accessed March 9, 2017.
http://www.joboneforhumanity.org/stop_saying_climate_change_pledge

[129] Job One for Humanity. "Blog Signup Page." *JobOneforHumanity.org*. Accessed March 10, 2016. http://www.joboneforhumanity.org/blog_signup_page

[130] Job One for Humanity. "Sign up." *JobOneforHumanity.org*. Accessed April 19, 2017. http://www.joboneforhumanity.org/sign_up

c. Check out our growing list of partners and allies also aligned with the core Job One For Humanity Plan and message.[131]

3. Call it what it is. We are currently in a global warming State of Emergency.

(If you have signed the emergency petition in an earlier chapter, you can skip this step.) We are currently in an undeclared global warming state of emergency. It is now vital to have the world *publicly declare* that fact. There are two important reasons for this public declaration of a global warming State of Emergency:

a. Having this become a formal national and international declaration puts those in power on notice that they are responsible to begin allocating resources for resolving the escalating global warming emergency.

b. It puts those in power on notice that they are fully responsible for making and enforcing all necessary new global warming reduction laws *on an emergency priority basis.*

Please read and sign the global warming State of Emergency Petition.[132] We also ask you to forward this emergency petition to everyone you know, particularly other nonprofit organizations concerned about the global warming emergency. (If you are uncertain in any way about why it is critical to declare this emergency, review Chapter 5 in Part 1.)

---

[131]Job One for Humanity. "Mobilization Partners and Allies." *JobOneforHumanity.org.* Accessed March 20, 2016. http://www.joboneforhumanity.org/mobilization_partners_allies

[132] Job One for Humanity. "Declare a Global Warming State of Emergency." *JobOneforHumanity.org.* Accessed March 20, 2016. http://www.joboneforhumanity.org/declare_a_global_warming_state_of_emergency

What's next

The next chapters of Part 2 contain the *most critical* action steps we must accomplish. For your convenience, in Appendix 1 you will also find a master plan and checklist for all Job One Plan action steps.

Summary

- The Job One Plan was designed to focus exclusively upon correctly answering the most important global warming question: What will actually work in the limited window of effective control we have left to save ourselves from crossing more global warming tipping points, which will eventually bring about irreversible global warming and the later phases of the Climageddon Scenario? With your help, the Job One Plan may be our best hope to resolve the escalating global warming emergency.

- Escalating global warming is the single most urgent threat humanity must act upon and resolve to continue to survive and thrive.

- Even with using Job One's new strategies, there are no guarantees we will be able to end global warming in time to avoid global catastrophe. But if we successfully collaborate and innovate together on the key primary action steps of the Job One Plan and, if we are very lucky, we might just be able to slow and lessen the worst of the coming catastrophes so that some may survive.

- Stop using the term "climate change!" "Climate change" is a term that feeds false illusions and confusion about what is really happening with escalating global warming. If we are ever going to create the necessary awareness within the public to slow down and eventually reverse this emergency, it is imperative that we all stop using the term "climate change" and refer instead to "climate destabilization" or "escalating global warming."

PART 2, CHAPTER 2

THE CRITICAL PRIMARY AND SUPPORTING ACTION STEPS OF JOB ONE

Before you start the Job One Plan, it is important to grasp the core reasoning behind the new Job One Plan action steps:

1. We don't have much time left. Therefore,

2. We have to *ruthlessly prioritize* our *every* action using the strict criteria of taking *only* the most *effective and correctly sequenced*, first-things-first actions essential to succeed within the necessary deadlines.

At first, the Job One Plan action steps and substeps below may seem difficult to achieve, but in Chapter 3 of Part 2, you will discover innovative ways to accomplish them, and *you* won't be doing most of the heavy lifting.

By completing the key action steps found in the Job One Plan, we preserve an honest and rational hope of saving humanity from irreversible global warming and the later phases of the Climageddon Scenario. We also should be able to keep from crossing more global warming tipping points within the next 6-10 years—our last window of remaining meaningful control.

Job One Primary Action:

Demand an *immediate* emergency meeting of the world's political leaders to declare an international *State of Emergency* and enact new global warming reduction laws or treaties.

There is no longer any excuse or time for delay. We cannot afford to waste another year, much less another 5-7 years, waiting for the next *ineffective* global climate conference like the UN Paris Climate Conference of 2015[133] (COP21). Because we are already in an unacknowledged and dangerous global warming State of Emergency, we need to demand an immediate emergency meeting of the world's leaders to *finally* face and resolve this crisis. These world leaders will need to stay in session in this emergency meeting until the key actions listed below are accomplished.

The key goals to accomplish at this emergency global warming meeting will be to:

A. Have the world's political leaders declare a worldwide "Global Warming State of Emergency."

> With a public declaration of a worldwide global warming State of Emergency in place, the world and all its nations will be on notice, fully authorized, and legally and morally obligated to create necessary new laws or treaties and allocate sufficient resources to resolve this escalating emergency before it is too late. Supported by this worldwide declaration of a State of Emergency, we, as corporations, organizations, and individuals, will be better able to mass-mobilize the necessary top-down-driven global actions before it's too late. In case you're wondering, the next chapter will explain how we will get reluctant politicians into an emergency meeting to make this declaration.

B. Have the world's political leaders declare new national and international goals that, when reached, will resolve the global warming emergency.

---

[133] Job One for Humanity. "The dirty secrets behind the new Paris Climate Conference (COP21) agreement they don't want you to know." *JobOneforHumanity.org*. Accessed December 9, 2016. http://www.joboneforhumanity.org/climate_change_conference

Those new goals are:

1. To do only what is critical and effective in the properly prioritized sequence to slow and lessen global warming enough to keep us from crossing carbon 425-450 parts per million (ppm) and more global warming tipping points. (Crossing carbon 425-450 ppm and more global warming tipping points or any keystone tipping point could quickly move us into *irreversible* global warming and the later phases of the Climageddon Scenario.)

2. Once the currently escalating global warming emergency has been resolved, to then begin the necessary secondary actions to reduce atmospheric carbon to the long-term temperature and climate-safe maintenance level of carbon ppm between 325 and 350 ppm.

The two essential subgoals that should keep us from crossing carbon 425-450 ppm, keystone global warming tipping points, or more non-keystone tipping points taking us into Phase 2 of the Climageddon Scenario are:

1. **Scale up** and transition globally to *ensure* nearly 100% renewable global green energy generation by 2026. We need to bring new and existing green energy generation technology online and to *full capacity* at a speed of infrastructure transformation, deployment, and mobilization never before achieved in human history. Achieving this subgoal may now be possible because of the many improvements in green energy generation technology. For example, solar panels and storage batteries are becoming more efficient, and they are significantly dropping in price each year. Wind and other green energy generation and storage technologies are also making significant technological

and pricing reduction advances. (Please note that this subgoal is focused only on global green energy generation, not merely building more efficient, less polluting electric appliances or electric cars that will still be getting their electricity mostly from fossil fuel energy generation. The 2026 date relates directly back to the remaining 6-10 years of meaningful control described in Part 1.)

2. **Scale down** and reduce global fossil fuel use *to ensure* achieving carbon neutrality (net zero carbon) for all greenhouse gases by 2026. Job One's use of the term carbon neutrality, or having a net zero carbon footprint, means achieving net zero carbon emissions by balancing any measured amounts of carbon dioxide released into the atmosphere with an equivalent measured amount of carbon dioxide taken from the atmosphere and being captured for long-term storage (see carbon sequestration). In the Job One Plan, this critical carbon capture and sequestration should happen almost exclusively through our already-existing *natural* biological, chemical, and physical processes (described in Chapters 2 and 3 of Part 1). Net zero carbon emissions by 2026 is a difficult subgoal to achieve. It will require that huge financial disincentives be placed on fossil fuel use and keeping 90% or more of *all existing* fossil fuels (coal, oil, natural gas, tar sands, etc.) *in the ground* and never burned. Please note that the Job One Plan for achieving carbon-neutral does not endorse Cap and Trade methods of arriving at carbon-neutral. Current Cap and Trade methods are too often a disguise for "business as usual" and will not get us to the radical fossil fuel reduction levels we need in the extremely limited time left to keep us safe. In Job One's own targeted version of carbon neutral called Fee and

Dividend, you will not be able to buy Cap and Trade carbon credits to make up the difference and achieve net zero carbon emissions because that inevitably promotes more fossil fuel burning.

Collectively attaining the above two subgoals is the necessary *minimal* global warming reduction work that *must be* accomplished by at least the end of 2026 to maintain any realistic hope for meaningful control over our future.

C. Have the world's political leaders create essential new, verifiable, and enforceable laws and treaties to achieve adequate global warming reduction in time to save us.

Once our politicians have declared a worldwide global warming State of Emergency and have agreed upon national and international global warming reduction goals and subgoals, several categories of new national and international laws or treaties will be needed to ensure effective action rapidly resolves the global warming emergency in time.The categories of laws or treaties described below must be enacted simultaneously because they function as an *integrated system*, which will have the highest probability of success in the little time we have left.

The many categories of new laws or treaties below are required in part because both the climate and human society are complex adaptable systems, so resolving the global warming emergency will require an *integrated systems level approach involving many categories of laws or treaties* covering these areas. These new laws or treaties are also needed to successfully reach the critical subgoals of net zero carbon and 100% green energy generation by 2026. Please note some temporary but *strictly limited* critical exceptions in immediate or complete reductions of fossil fuel use may also need to be *temporarily* allowed within these new laws or treaties for military use, space exploration, air travel, as well as other critical, medical, and chemical uses of these fuels.

If any area of the following categories of verifiable and enforceable laws or treaties is not enacted, the probability of achieving the necessary level of success in time to save us from going over the carbon 425-450 ppm battle line or one or more of the critical global warming tipping points is perilously lessened. If you think of enforceable and verifiable international and national laws or treaties as the most essential and critical fulcrum point that helps to maximize successful top-down-driven leverage to resolve the emergency *before* we go over the climate cliff, you will have fully grasped their true importance. This single step is by far the most important action step we must succeed in if we are to survive.

How we can quickly get these new national and international laws or treaties passed without an effective global governing body in existence will be covered in the next chapter. For now, here are the key areas of new, verifiable, and enforceable global warming reduction laws or treaties we must demand:

1. Demand new national and international laws or treaties to create a revenue- neutral, Fee and Dividend-based global warming reduction program.

The Fee and Dividend plan will work because it puts a price on carbon fossil fuels use equal to their environmental damage and accomplishes this through market economy mechanisms. The Fee and Dividend plan's rising fee on carbon pollution incentivizes a rapid shift from toxic fossil fuels to clean green energy. Its *direct dividend payments* to all those individuals, companies, and nations that reduce their fossil fuel use is the profit motive and self-interest key that will strongly incentivize the rapid transition to green energy generation essential to our survival.

This Fee and Dividend plan is also revenue neutral and not the investment banker-friendly, grossly flawed Cap and Trade program continually promoted by the fossil fuel industry, its lobbyists, investment bankers and the fossil fuel-related, owned, or influenced media.

Fee and Dividend laws or treaties would quickly reduce greenhouse gas emissions by placing a fee on carbon dioxide (CO_2) or equivalent gases. This fee would be levied against *all* fossil fuels at their *point of entry* into the economy.

Almost 100% of the collected revenue would be returned as a monthly, quarterly, or annual direct payment to *every* citizen, business, or nation that uses less fossil fuel energy or moves to green energy. Hence the concept that this fee is *revenue-neutral*. This revenue-neutral feature would protect low and middle class citizens from the rising consumer costs associated with the carbon fee and the critical rapid transition to green energy generation. It will quickly spread the financial benefits of green energy transition to every area of the world.

In the U.S. current proposals would start the fee at $15 per ton of CO_2 equivalent (3/4 of a penny per pound) and rise $10-$20 per ton each year (1/2-1 penny per pound). The fee would continue to rise until total U.S. CO_2 equivalent emissions had been reduced to 10% or less of U.S. CO_2 equivalent emissions in 1990. (The projected carbon fee is estimated to quickly reach $40-$100 per ton.)

To protect national businesses from actions of other countries that do not have or enforce equivalent carbon Fee and Dividend pricing mechanisms, a compensating border adjustment would be enacted. All goods coming from countries without a Fee and Dividend carbon price equivalent would be subjected to an equivalent compensating fee at the border of the fee compliant nation. Goods leaving a compliant nation for sale in a fee noncompliant country would be reimbursed that fee at the compliant nation's border at the time of export.

No other program will be more effective and faster to adopt globally than the Fee and Dividend plan because it:

a. Financially stimulates low-carbon innovation and the creation of jobs in green energy generation.

b. Is the fairest current revenue-neutral method of motivating and mobilizing the critical and necessary high-speed transition to green energy generation and away from fossil fuels.

c. Offsets citizens' higher energy costs with direct dividend payments for conservation and going green.

d. Immediately and radically reduces emissions in all sectors and areas globally, thereby moving toward carbon neutrality (net zero carbon) by strongly incentivizing carbon pollution reductions and efficiencies.

e. Creates a stable, predictable carbon price benchmark for business planning and puts the carbon fee *at the source* (well, mine, or port). This way businesses don't directly absorb costs. Carbon fee border adjustments will also encourage other nations to price carbon similarly to avoid paying the difference at other national borders. This will help create a competitive and level fossil fuel *reduction* playing field amongst the nations.

f. Is not easily exploitable by investment bankers and other wealthy special interests who could easily use current Cap and Trade plans to delay or defer expanding green energy generation while continuing carbon pollution and while making vast fortunes buying and selling Cap and Trade credits for owners and Wall

Street brokers. Think of Cap and Trade as the "business as usual" scheme of the wealthy few to maintain the status quo for as long as possible. Think of the Fee and Dividend plan as the fairest plan for the well-being of the many as well as the fastest possible transition facilitator to green energy generation *for almost all of our energy needs.*

g. Is quickly implementable and is a rational, transparent, and simple policy.

h. Will quickly generate widespread public support because of its direct and near immediate financial dividend payments.

i. Is a great policy tool that actually has an excellent chance of being implemented politically. This is because both liberals and conservatives can support it. What makes it an attractive policy for conservatives is that the program creates minimal bureaucracy and does not expand the size of government. Citizens are free to use their dividend as they choose, presumably in part to reduce their use of carbon, to offset the increased cost of carbon due to the carbon fee. Its appeal to liberals is that it will help keep the environment safe.

At every level where rapid and effective change away from fossil fuel dependence will be necessary, the Fee and Dividend program has the greatest hope of motivating and immediately mobilizing the necessary green energy generation, use, and effective energy conservation changes that will keep the greatest possible amount of fossil fuels in the ground forever. More importantly, no other known fee measure will as quickly or effectively lessen the escalating global warming emergency and avert crossing more global warming tipping points. (If you are still uncertain about the details of how the Fee and Dividend plan will work to finance the various actions listed above, please read this Wikipedia article here.[134])

What some of the carbon fees from the new Fee and Dividend program will be used for

In addition to paying dividends for reducing fossil fuel use, part of the Fee and Dividend plan proceeds will also help finance the following critical activities:

a. Create employee job retraining as well as a business and national recovery fund that would assist all individuals, businesses, and nations that will suffer significant financial losses because of the rapidly falling use of fossil fuels. For example, Fee and Dividend revenues will assist developing nations to leapfrog over building or expanding any current carbon energy generation systems directly into building or expanding green energy generation. We cannot forget to actively assist those who will be harmed financially in this rapid transition.

b. Fund global education and public relations campaigns on why we all have to comply with many new, difficult, and costly global warming reduction laws or treaties and other changes that will be enforced by our governments. The general public is not ready for the rapid transition required, and resulting radical changes in energy generation and energy distribution. It will take a massive global public relations and education program to help the general public understand why these rapid changes are needed, why these changes are beneficial to their futures, why individual self-directed

---

[134] Wikipedia contributors. "Fee and dividend." *Wikipedia, The Free Encyclopedia,* https://en.wikipedia.org/wiki/Fee_and_dividend (accessed December 6, 2016).

actions alone are not enough, and why escalating global warming is everyone's worst common enemy.

- o We can never forget that change usually evokes fear. The financial dividends of the Fee and Dividend program will help lessen that fear and help stimulate adoption, but any sudden, radical, and costly large-scale change will still evoke initial fear, resistance, and counteraction. The successful use of large-scale public education and public relations is not unprecedented. A large-scale education and public relations program is exactly what was used to mobilize the United States in World War II and was foundational to its later victory.

- o Over time, the citizens of the world will be brought to understand, through these education and public relations programs, the severity, and immediacy of the challenge that the global warming emergency presents. These education and public relations programs must take place concurrently with top-down enforcement of the new global warming reduction laws or treaties. Although many individuals will quickly comply with their national laws or treaties, many others will not commit themselves to any collective effort to remedy this emergency unless they better understand why it is necessary. Over time, this global education and public relations campaign will help the current culture's transition from the *dying* fossil fuel age into the *life-promoting* green energy age. If this global education and public relations campaign is done correctly, the population of the world will begin to feel a powerful sense of common and collective destiny and high moral purpose, knowing their rational actions are saving themselves, their children, and future generations.

c. Fund *appropriate* technologies to help us rapidly achieve complete global green energy generation by 2026. Appropriate new technologies will have a major role in the long-term retooling and reorientation of our economy to facilitate the final transition to green renewable energy. It can improve smart grid systems, energy storage capabilities, electricity-based mass transportation, retrofitting buildings, sustainable agriculture, zero waste, and more. Appropriate green technology can even help provide access to cleaner and greener cooking for the poorest 3 billion people who spend hours each day collecting solid biomass fuels and burning them for cooking.

d. Fund other new technologies as an emergency backup if we fail to meet the two critical 2026 targets (mentioned above); but only after we have funded the actions detailed above. This is our last-chance-plan for when all other remedial actions of the Job One Plan have failed to slow or lessen escalating global warming and we are about to go over the climate cliff into irreversible global warming and Phase 2 of the Climageddon Scenario.

In spite of the grand promises new technologies may offer in helping us reach 100% global green energy generation faster, there are critical warnings about any rushed or desperate implementation of new and unproven technologies. A myriad of unsolved problems attend the proposed "geoengineering" technologies, not the least of which is they are still in the "theoretical drawing board stage," have no economically proven working models, they cannot be scaled to draw down carbon as modeled, and much more. Negative Emissions Technologies (NETs) are particularly troublesome, and they are built into many international IPCC models. One overwhelming reason they are not feasible any time soon is that they require growing carbon crops on land the size of India, each and every year for decades. The world does not have anything close to this amount of land to lend to a carbon capture scheme, because the land is already being used for food crops for human use and consumption. When the choice is starving hundreds of millions of people to grow carbon-capture crops to remediate what humans did in the past, then we must say that this plan is non-sense and look for other technologies. And as Professor Kevin Anderson explains in his lucid video in March, 2017, [135] that nonsense is just what many of the international IPCC models now suggest.

The key warnings about planning new, undemonstrated and economically unproven technologies to resolve the global warming emergency are:

- We cannot allow new, undemonstrated and economically unproven technologies to lull us into a false sense of comfort that we can continue to pour more carbon and methane pollution into our atmosphere—or preserve the dying fossil fuel energy generation business model. The emphasis on the development of these new technologies must always be to move past the fossil fuel energy generation age. There can be no turning back! We have entered the age of green energy generation, and we need to go forward

---

[135] "Kevin Anderson: Paris, climate & surrealism: how numbers reveal another reality." YouTube video. 52:38, posted by "Cambridge Climate Lecture Series," March 14, 2017. https://www.youtube.com/watch?v=jIODRrnHQxg

full speed to get us out of the existing escalating global warming emergency.

- Before demonstrations at scale with proven economic viability, we cannot expect that "theoretically drawing board" of geoengineering technologies will save us from what is coming. Relying heavily on miraculous new technologies to save us is a dangerous strategy and should never replace the primary focus of doing the most *in-harmony-with-nature* actions and the other systemic actions recommended in the Job One Plan. These actions do not carry the potential disastrous side effects of many new technologies employed as *last chance solutions* suggested in the most desperate of times and situations.

- We must never forget that almost all new technology is based on mechanical, three-dimensional engineering principles that are far simpler than the principles of complex adaptable systems like the biological and climate systems of our precious planet. Engineering is generally a simple and linear three-dimensional set of cause-and-effect actions. Biology and the climate are complex adaptable systems with nonlinear, self-organizing, and unpredictable spontaneously *emergent* qualities. They should be seen as having many more non-cause-and-effect "dimensions." They also have far more *unknown* and complex tipping points, interconnectivities, and interdependencies than are found within the limited mechanical rules and solutions characteristic of the nonliving, mechanical world. Frequently,applying mechanical solutions to complex adaptive systems such as our biological and climate systems, results in unpleasant surprises in the form of unintended negative consequences.

- We cannot allow our individual or collective *hubris* about our many great mechanical engineering accomplishments to blind us to the risk of overlooking the possibility that new mechanical technology solutions applied to global warming's complex adaptable systems may in fact produce *equal or even greater* damage than the problem they're meant to solve. For example, placing massive amounts of sun-reflecting particles into the complex adaptive system of the atmosphere and global climate is being widely discussed as a mechanical *new technology* solution to the global warming emergency. What if, as an unintended side effect, those particles blocked the normal rainfall in a nuclear-armed country like China and caused immediate mass starvation and death? With its own population dying before its eyes, where do you think the Chinese government would point its nuclear weapons, or from whom would they demand immediate restitution? The unintended risks could easily and quickly get out of hand, leading to unpredictable and potentially worse consequences if any of the nations harmed have nuclear weapons. Additionally, once our ecological and climate systems have been stressed beyond their respective tipping points and points of no return, it will be far too late to develop or deploy any technologically useful geoengineering repair or *cooling* mechanism. For additional information on the many problems and dangers of geoengineering solutions to the global warming emergency, see these articles by Andrew Revkin,[136] Chelsea Harvey,[137] and John Vidal.[138]

---

[136] Andrew C. Revkin. "Can humans go from unintended global warming to climate by design?" *New York Times*. October 18, 2016.
http://dotearth.blogs.nytimes.com/2016/10/18/can-humans-go-from-unintended-global-warming-to-climate-by-design/

- We cannot expect to extend the use or lifespan of fossil fuels by increasing fossil fuel consumption efficiency. Collective experience and research has repeatedly shown that using technology to increase fossil fuel consumption efficiency or conservation frequently increases overall fossil fuel use rather than reducing it. This is because of the economic savings that increased fossil fuel energy efficiency or conservation provides, acting to create more cash resources to buy or use more things dependent upon using more fossil fuels. This is known as Jevons's paradox.[139]

2. Demand world political leaders require their respective national intelligence agencies and national security agencies take immediate and full responsibility for re-analyzing current global warming research and rapidly reporting the updated security threats, predicted consequences, and new timetables.

It's time to stop engaging in the false hope that the underfunded Intergovernmental Panel On Climate Change of the United Nations (IPCC) can or should be taking on the lead research and analysis responsibility for the future of humanity or producing accurate reports which include tipping points!

---

[137] Chelsea Harvey. "We're placing far too much hope in pulling carbon dioxide out of the air, scientists warn." *The Washington Post*. October 13, 2016.
https://www.washingtonpost.com/news/energy-environment/wp/2016/10/13/were-placing-far-too-much-hope-in-pulling-carbon-dioxide-out-of-the-air-scientists-warn/?utm_term=.7443bd74ae95

[138] John Vidal. "Time to listen to the ice scientists about the Arctic death spiral." *The Guardian*. August 18, 2016.
https://www.theguardian.com/commentisfree/2016/aug/18/ice-scientists-arctic-ice-disappearing-reduce-emissions-peter-wadhams

[139] when technological progress increases the efficiency with which a resource is used (reducing the amount necessary for any one use), but the rate of consumption of that resource rises because of increasing demand. From Wikipedia contributors, "Jevons's paradox," *Wikipedia, The Free Encyclopedia*,
https://en.wikipedia.org/w/index.php?title=Jevons%27s_paradox&oldid=759401245
(accessed January 10, 2017).

It's time to recognize and publicly "reassign" the full final responsibility for creating a complete and accurate risk analysis for the current and future security threat levels of the global warming emergency to our respective national intelligence agencies and national security agencies.

There are many good reasons for "transferring" those senior global warming research and analysis responsibilities:

1. The IPCC has failed to carry out its mandate effectively. (See Part 1, Chapter 7.)

2. Escalating global warming is the one common security threat to *all* nations, which if not managed correctly, will eventually destabilize our global civilization. The best and brightest of the intelligence agencies analysts already know much of what's in *Climageddon*. They also know that if they continue to fail to properly inform their politicians to protect the world, they also fail to protect their nation and their own families. In general, there is sufficient intellectual capability and access to accurate information available, along with qualified, self-interested people within intelligence agencies. They know escalating global warming is the ultimate no-win game where we will all come to a painful end if their politicians do not have all of the non-politicized facts and then act effectively to protect and preserve our common well-being. The intelligence agencies already know that if the global warming emergency reaches late Phase 3 or Phase 4 of the Climageddon Scenario, it is the beginning of the end of civilization itself! Because of the sheer power of self-preservation, it is realistic to believe many courageous individuals within our intelligence agencies will fight through whatever

bureaucratic or political resistance exists to ensure their respective politicians fully understand that global warming is the largest single *and* escalating security threat the world faces in the 21st-century.

3. Intelligence agencies have the mandated first and final legal responsibility *to speak truth to power.* Excluding global thermonuclear war, escalating global warming is the single most serious risk to both national security and humanity. Therefore, the responsibility for global warming risk analysis and reporting to our political leaders must be "re-assigned" to respective national intelligence agencies and national security agencies.. These intelligence agencies are also ethically obligated to present this security information clearly and simply enough to their respective politicians so that they fully understand the scope and scale of *all* risks, time frames, and consequences involved.

4. Intelligence agencies of the world have the budgets, resources, research capabilities, and expert analytic capabilities to do these annual risk analysis updates *far better* than an easily politically influenced and grossly underfunded agency like the IPCC. Our well-funded intelligence agencies are far more capable of accessing and hiring the best climate scientists and related researchers to quantify the escalating security threat of global warming than any other existing entity or organization.

5. The politicians of any nation whose intelligence agency has produced such reports and briefings will tend to give those reports and briefings *more credibility* and legitimacy than any presented by an underfunded, under-resourced, and expertise-challenged UN agency.

Consequently, it would be immeasurably more difficult for our politicians to ignore these credible dire warnings.

6. Having global warming reports produced by national intelligence agencies would also help to educate and motivate the public. The key issue is "believing" the truth that we are in the middle of a global warming emergency of the scope, scale, and urgency presented here. In the 1941, the Japanese attacked Pearl Harbor. President Roosevelt used this as the catalyst to engender a US mass mobilization for warfare. Most people don't recall that Roosevelt had begun planning and preparation for this mass mobilization and the military was ready to swing into full-scale action. Business was ready to support the effort. Currently, with our fractured political system, and with mobilization to leave the fossil fuel era remote and still only a suggestion, the first issue is to provide the optimal credibility mechanism so that the US and the nations of the world, along with their citizenry can "believe" that immediate mass mobilization is truly necessary. The Job One Plan suggests that national intelligence and national security agencies can best substantiate the reality of the dire crisis we find ourselves in as described here, and that they are the most likely organizations and entities that can be "believed." Having these highly credible sources educate the public on why radical fossil fuel reductions must take place immediately is critical. This public education factor could also have the beneficial side effect of creating a more accurately informed citizenry, which will better hold their politicians to account for any delays in taking immediate action to resolve the global warming emergency.

7. Regular reports and briefings from respective intelligence agencies may well be crucial for political systems and their respective publics. For some time to come, it will likely be necessary to both combat and neutralize the anti-science, climate denial propaganda machine abundantly financed by a dying fossil fuel industry. These intelligence agency reports would also serve to validate and confirm good climate science, as well as accurate consequence prediction models and time frames. This validation and credibility factor will be indispensable to politicians as they ask their citizens to make the many costly, difficult, and radical sacrifices now needed in order to save humanity and civilization.

8. Despite the military entanglements and extreme nationalism that pervades the histories of national security and intelligence agencies, the Job One Plan asserts that humanity has no better current mechanism for persuading the world's political systems and public that the common enemy the escalating global warming emergency is real. There are no more credible organizations available to illuminate the overwhelming common plight we all face. While climate scientists and related disciplines have provided the complex information basis that asserts that the global warming emergency is actually at the scope, scale, and urgency explained herein, the unfortunate reality is that the "relatively" uncomplex information related to the global warming emergency is both disputed and obscured by vested financial interests. Trillions of dollars are at stake for the dying fossil fuel industry, and it will be defended. Therefore, the world's intelligence agencies are the best remaining option for both correcting the IPCC's underestimations and other flaws described previously in Part 1, Chapter 7 as well as for establishing high credibility for the correct global warming information.

3. Have the world's political leaders demand *annual* global warming updates from their respective intelligence agencies, which going forward will always include projection scenarios related to crossing more tipping points.

In spite of the escalating emergency, global warming update reports are far too infrequent (about once every 5 to 7 years from the IPCC). Carbon ppm levels are rising when they should be dropping dramatically. Each increase in carbon ppm in our atmosphere again tolls the warning bell of IPCC failure.

Unfortunately, by continuing to rely on the IPCC for accurate global warming information, we are doing the same thing over and over and expecting a different result—the classic Einsteinian definition of insanity. Our escalating emergency is far too dangerous and moving too fast to not have annual updates by the most qualified parties with the greatest resources and vested security interests.

We must also create a comprehensive global warming annual risk report that will include the consequences of crossing global warming tipping points. By having every intelligence agency in the world produce an annual national update on the current state of the escalating global warming emergency for both politicians and the public, we would also be creating inherent checks and balances against underestimation, errors, or intentional deceit by rogue intelligence agencies, outlier governments, or conflicting nongovernmental organizations.

These multiple annual reports coming from many different intelligence agencies would quickly expose any nation hiding critical global warming information for their own temporary benefit. In time, these national intelligence agencies and the individuals within them would also see the many benefits of cooperating on research and sharing confirmable and comprehensive risk analyses.

Similarly, it would be against the interest of rogue national intelligence agencies to be caught hiding critical information or falsifying information for a perceived temporary national benefit when the other nations' intelligence agencies publish their contradicting annual global warming reports. As an extra safeguard against deceptive practices, once the multiple intelligence agency annual global warming reports have been made publicly available, leading climate scientists from around the world can review them, looking for common patterns, omissions, or errors within and between these multiple intelligence agency reports.

Similar to the way the scientific method works in advanced scientific systems, peer review and consolidation by non-intelligence community scientists would reveal additional valuable information that single intelligence agencies might miss or misrepresent, as well as reveal omissions that could serve to inequitably benefit any single nation. The intelligence agencies that produce the most accurate annual global warming reports will gain prestige around the world and become the standard for credibility and reliability. For the best agencies, this will likely result in increased funding and budget discretion.

4. Demand new international and national laws or treaties that will provide government subsidies and incentives for expanding green energy generation.

We have to radically scale up green energy production and use—at *least as fast as or faster* than we are reducing fossil fuel energy use and generation—to meet the 2026 fossil fuel reduction goal mentioned above. If we do not complete this massive transition to green energy quickly enough, we risk the danger of economic collapse (see Chapter 8, Part 1).

Specifically, we will need to mass-mobilize the production and use of green technologies such as wind turbines, solar panels, high capacity non-toxic battery storage, hydrogen fuel cell or electric light-duty vehicles, and more efficient end-use devices, especially in appliances, lighting, air conditioning, and industrial processes.

5. Demand new international and national laws or treaties to increase natural carbon sequestration.

In order to save ourselves from the worst consequences of escalating global warming, we must also rapidly engage and expand carbon sequestration actions that directly and effectively reduce the existing carbon ppm levels in the atmosphere while we are also radically reducing the global use of fossil fuels. Surprisingly, we *can* do this while avoiding new technologies with risky outcomes.

By harmonizing with nature's existing mechanisms to reduce and "eat" carbon in the atmosphere and investing globally in reducing deforestation, promoting reforestation, land/soil restoration, restoration or enhancement of carbon sinks and agroecology, we can avoid the use of risky new technologies. We can also wisely use these existing natural technologies to increase the use of biochar, and the successful implementation of other non-natural means of carbon sequestration such as improved and expanded carbon farming. For more information on carbon sequestration, see this article by Umair Irfan.[140]

The global deployment of the above atmospheric carbon reduction and sequestering measures has the

---

[140] Umair Irfan. "Engineers work to cut costs and emissions in geothermal power." *E&E News.* July 29, 2016. http://www.eenews.net/stories/1060040959

potential to reduce and offset 20% of the current emissions of CO and other greenhouse gases. As a side benefit, the more natural methods mentioned above will also create wealth for the poorest 3 billion. (Many of the above carbon sequestration actions will occur in our poorest nations and help provide work for many in those nations. Also see "the global climate's heat-controlling systems and subsystems" in Part 1, Chapter 2 for more information on the Earth's natural systems, many of which can be used to remove massive amounts of carbon from the atmosphere.)

6. Demand new international and national laws or treaties that will rapidly remove government subsidies from fossil fuel energy generation.

The fantastically wealthy $28 trillion a year global fossil fuel industry is much more dependent on global government handouts than is widely realized. In 2015, governments worldwide subsidized the fossil fuel industry with an estimated $5.3 trillion,[141] giving this dying industry 50 times more than the $120 billion[142] that went to renewable energy subsidies. Governments are thereby unconsciously paying for their nation's global warming caused self-destruction!

Amazingly, some fossil fuel subsidies went to <u>boost</u> oil consumption. In effect, taxpayer dollars from around the world are being used to subsidize more toxic fossil fuel pollution, escalating global warming and its catastrophic and unhealthy consequences.

7. Demand new laws or treaties that will incentivize divestment from the dying fossil fuel energy

---

[141] David Coady, Ian Parry, Louis Sears, and Baoping Shang. "How Large Are Global Energy Subsidies?" *International Monetary Fund.* May 2015. http://www.imf.org/~/media/Websites/IMF/Imported/external/pubs/ft/wp/2015/_wp1 5105pdf.ashx

[142] Sara Matasci. "What are Some Renewable Resources? Examples of Alternative Energy." *EnergySage.com.* August 12, 2016. http://news.energysage.com/examples-of-renewable-resources-and-alternative-energy/

generation industry.

The fossil fuel industry is dying as the green energy revolution continues to grow. While it may be difficult to accept these radical changes, this is as it should be. One important realization related to this change is to understand that the fossil fuel world will, by necessity die, if for no other reason than we cannot continue to run our world economies on lower quality, harder to get, dirtier, and more expensive fossil fuels. The reliance on tar sands, super-polluting processes like fracking, and dangerous super-deep drilling systems will only get worse in the near future. So, it is not a matter of "if" the fossil fuel era will end, but "when." As the public begins to understand the urgent necessity of leaving fossil fuels behind, and as global warming emergency is increasingly illuminated and substantiated, fossil fuel-related industries will go the way of dinosaurs. Consequently, many people heavily invested in this dying industry will sooner or later suffer huge financial losses.

To prevent the unscrupulous from trying to unfairly profit on this dying industry, new laws or treaties need to be enacted to:

a. incentivize fossil fuel divestment and
b. punish those "gaming the system" to stop windfall profiteering on the sudden and rapid changes in production, pricing, distribution, carbon fees, or inventories that this dying industry will experience as fossil fuel use radically shrinks and the green energy revolution rapidly expands.

How might the system be gamed? As an example, the fossil fuel industry might hear ahead of its competitors that Fee and Dividend per ton carbon fees are going to go up again on a certain date on any fossil fuels that will be subsequently removed from the ground. Before the new carbon fees take place, a fossil fuel producer could accelerate its extraction process many times beyond normal by creating an out-of-the-ground large non-taxable inventory. This would allow that business to "game the system" and obtain windfall profits on the fossil fuels it just quickly stockpiled. The new laws or treaties must prevent all such activities.

8. Demand new laws or treaties to tax all fossil fuel profits at significantly higher rates.

Governments will need to provide a massive retraining of fossil fuel industry-related employees, as well as funding many retooling projects while subsidizing new green energy infrastructure. Considerably higher taxes on remnant fossil fuel profits may also need to be authorized and legislated.

9. Demand new international and national laws or treaties that mandate the creation of emergency recovery reserve funds equal to 5% of national GDPs.

This is necessary in order for each nation to cope with the rapidly rising costs of escalating global warming catastrophes. The modern world has never experienced the rising scope, scale, and frequency of loss and destruction that will continue to accumulate as global warming moves toward crossing more tipping points and deeper into the Climageddon Scenario phases.

Some estimates have suggested that _if_ we survive, it will eventually take $200-$600 trillion dollars to repair the damage. To put that amount in perspective, that is roughly 4-6 times the total annual GDP of the entire world's economic systems.! Unless we create a minimum 5% emergency reserve fund for each nation, it is difficult to conceptualize how will be able to constructively ameliorate continuing and escalating global warming catastrophe costs.

10. Demand new laws or treaties mandating that

fossil fuel corporations pay for past and current environmental and health damages caused by their products.

It has been recently discovered that some fossil fuel companies like Exxon appear to have known their products were causing global warming damage and degradation for over 30 years. This suggests that a reasonable interpretation of their actions could be seen as *knowingly harming or intentionally harming* the health air, water and land belonging to all of us.

If these allegations are "proven" by legal action, Exxon will be guilty of offloading the pollution damage and health costs of their products onto the citizens and taxpayers of their respective nations while they kept *all the profits* from their knowingly destructive acts. If this is demonstrated, the intentional harm projected upon the public should be seriously penalized, and appropriate restitution should result.

New laws or treaties requiring fossil fuel-related companies to pay for past and present health and environmental damage should be enacted at the same time as the other global warming reduction-related laws or treaties mentioned in this chapter. The governments of the world will need restitution payments as part of the funding to repair past fossil fuel damage and to facilitate the fast migration to clean green energy generation.

11. Demand the International Monetary Fund, the World Trade Organization, and other power centers call for the immediate emergency meeting of world's leaders, as well as facilitate verification and enforcement of global warming reduction laws or treaties.

Without a global government that has verification and enforcement powers, individual nations or corporations will have incentives to "cheat," thus gaining competitive advantages. This is because they believe they are immune to outside verification, enforcement, or punishment.

Unless some kind of effective international mechanisms are put in place for global verification and enforcement of these new global warming laws or treaties, they will be as ineffective and toothless as the reduction pledges, promises and intentions of the various IPCC conferences. Without strong verification procedures and globally enforceable penalties evenly applied across all structures and negotiated agreements, there is little hope we will change our ways in time and we will still go over the climate cliff (carbon 425-450 ppm).

Luckily, there are several strategic and innovative ways to ensure all global warming cheaters, treaty violators, or treaty non-signers gain no competitive or other advantage. Some individuals may initially be uncomfortable with bypassing the failed IPCC structures in the manner described below, but please keep an open mind.

We are in a desperate corner and forced to utilize the most effective methods with the right resources—even if the agents of this new solution are not perfect or have checkered histories.

If the solution proposed below makes you uncomfortable, after reviewing it ask yourself: What other current options have any proven track record or realistic hope of being *more* effective? We are potentially going to be trapped in the perfect storm of perfect storms. To adapt an old saying, we need to consider *any port in a superstorm.*

In the title of this section, we mention the World Trade Organization (WTO) and the International Monetary Fund (IMF). These organizations already have a track record of facilitating the negotiation of international agreements and treaties. They also have a history of managing and In some cases, assisting with enforcing those international agreements or treaties. Additionally, many of the world's largest corporations and nations have already developed some level of trust and confidence in their existing relationships with these organizations. If requested to do so, the World Trade Organization (WTO) could be tasked to:

a. help negotiate the necessary international global warming reduction laws and treaties with adequate verification and enforcement penalties,

b. arbitrate disputes over execution or implementation of resulting law or treaty enactment issue areas, or specific parts of these.,

c. set up mechanisms to verify that nations or corporations are complying with the negotiated global warming laws and treaties, and

d. impose fees and penalties on trade deals or trade items from any nation or corporation shown to be violating the global warming reduction laws or treaties; increasing trade penalties could accompany repeated violations to always insure the prompt removal of any profit incentive for ongoing violations.

Also, if requested to do so, the International Monetary Fund (IMF) could:

a. collect and hold in trust all global warming law or treaty violation penalty fees,

b. Disperse global warming fees and penalties collected,

c. impose additional interest penalty fees on every existing bank loan for any nation or corporation caught violating the new global warming reduction laws or treaties; these increased interest penalty fees could also independently escalate with repeated violations to a level that replaces any cheating profits with equal cheating penalties, and

d. on the basis of repeated gross violations of global warming laws or treaties, nations or corporations could even be denied loans.

Additional tools and power centers for enforcing and collecting penalties on cheaters:

There are other well-established international power centers capable of penalizing any corporation or nation—across international borders—that might seek to cheat and violate the negotiated international global warming reduction laws or treaties. Among these power centers are the international and national banking transaction clearinghouses that handle clearing and processing of the world's banking transactions.

Once these and similar international organizations act to collect violation penalties, here's how it would work. These ibanking transactional clearinghouses would impose a small additional penalty fee on every banking or checking transaction of any nation or corporation caught violating the new global warming reduction laws or treaties.

All collected transactional interest penalty fees, Fee and Dividend fees, and other fees or penalties could eventually be directed into the IMF or some other similar international banking organization that would act as trustee for holding all collected funds. These collected funds could then be dispersed to various areas (as mentioned above in the Fee and Dividend section). Proper dispersal of these funds could be overseen by qualified legal and accounting administrators, as well as a panel of global warming experts chosen from all nations.

As mentioned before, how we will make this happen will be covered in the next chapter. For your convenience in getting started on the plan, all Job One Plan action steps have been put into a simple checklist, found in Appendix 1.

Why top-down mobilization is critical for ending global warming

By this time it should be clear that to be successful with the Job One Plan, we need to effect massive high-speed change through top-down action. We cannot resolve this global warming emergency *and* save ourselves in time without a mass mobilization of the world through:

a. government and/or internationally verified and enforceable laws and treaties and

b. massive education and public relations programs on governmental, corporate, and social levels to convincingly explain why the painful new changes are required as well as the amazing survival, health and economic benefits this transition to green energy will produce.

This does not mean that *only* top-down action is required to achieve the Job One goals. Because *some* bottom-up public actions to get things happening on the Job One steps will also be required, but it will be primarily top-down action that will give us the necessary laws or treaties, enforcement, and verification in time to save us.

Important bottom-up actions will also involve the public learning why such radical and costly changes are needed immediately and demanding changes be made by those with real influence. Bottom-up actions will also involve all of us doing what is necessary to maintain a stable climate once we are successful in ending the global warming emergency.

Because our window of opportunity for effecting meaningful control over the emergency is short (6-10 years), we are in essence *forced to* start with a top-down approach using the legitimate power of governments to verify and enforce compliance with laws or treaties necessary to save us in time. Educating and then changing individual behavior one person at a time or even in groups is doomed to failure because there is not enough time left to break through the massive inertia and resistance by almost almost all of the population to the radical changes we will be required to make. Only change derived from the legal, structural and cultural power of *universally* enforced and verified laws or treaties has any hope of being successful.

The simple beauty of enacting the previously mentioned types of national and international laws or treaties before it is too late is that these laws or treaties, with their financial and non-financial incentives, dividends, disincentives, and penalties, will provide the fastest stimulus for the greatest mass mobilization of national and international, governmental and nongovern-mental, corporate and other resources in human history. Enacting these new global warming remedial laws or treaties responds effectively to the uncomfortable reality that only top-down regulatory action coordinated with a top-down global public relations and education program will be able to save us in time.

The good news here is that at national, regional, and local levels, governments, corporations, and individuals will rapidly reorganize themselves to take advantage of the dividends and incentives and avoid the disincentives and penalties related to the new global warming remedial laws or treaties. This will serve to reduce both national and international fossil fuel pollution of our atmosphere at the fastest possible rate because *cooperation* is rewarded at every level, and failure to cooperate is *penalized at every level*.

Some challenges regarding the needed new laws or treaties

These are some additional challenges:

1. All of these various types of international and national laws or treaties in the different categories must be *enacted together* to create an effective, comprehensive, and integrated systemic solution to escalating global warming. If laws or treaties in only one or two of the above categories are passed, it will greatly slow the pace of solving our global warming emergency, as well as seriously imperil the probability of achieving success.

2. There will likely also have to be some emergency deficit spending by many governments in order to make the transition from fossil fuels to green energy to prevent unthinkable disaster. Deficit spending is not a dirty word or an unusual or unproven thing.

    Deficit spending was used in World War II and specifically in the United States to help save a great portion of the world in a previously declared State of Emergency called war. Deficit spending is currently happening in almost every nation of the world.

    If deficit spending were such a morally or financially bad thing, the greatest portion of the population would not be given credit cards and most of the world governments wouldn't be be able to function. When one accepts the reality that this emergency is far worse in total eventual damage than World War II and parallels the global extinction threat level of nuclear war, deficit spending by our governments is not only appropriate, it is demanded. If our governments do not deficit spend in this even greater emergency, as they did in World War II, it would be a gross dereliction of their legal and moral responsibilities to protect the lives, livelihoods, and futures of the members of their nations.

The challenge of our fossil-fuel-free future

Within a decade or less, we must eliminate the use of fossil fuels and begin the process of drawing atmospheric carbon levels back down to safe levels (carbon 325-350 ppm). Within a decade, we must be functioning worldwide on green energy generation, almost exclusively, except for a few special exemption areas. This will require nothing less than a heroic effort and a massive global warming emergency mobilization. It will also create a great sense of moral purpose, because we know that to save humanity and our civilization this is what *must be done*. Because of the scale and immediacy of this emergency, it is to be expected that *both* fact and fear are utilized to help motivate us to be successful.

One small act you can do right now

If you have not do so already, there is one quick, small act you can do immediately. Sign the petition [143] calling for an immediate gathering of world leaders to resolve the escalating global warming emergency and enact steps like those called for in the Job One Plan above. We need to do what we can to get this emergency meeting going fast!

Your next vaccination

The global warming emergency will inevitably force us into new levels of local, national, and international cooperation

---

[143] Job One For Humanity. "Petition to demand an immediate emergency meeting of world leaders for action on the escalating global warming emergeny." *JobOneforHumanity.org.* Accessed January 6, 2017.
http://www.joboneforhumanity.org/petition_to_demand_an_immediate_emergency_meeti ng_of_world_leaders_for_action_on_escalating_global_warming_emergency

In the past, humanity has cooperated successfully on critical climate issues. We have successfully created international laws, treaties and agreements regarding the pollution of the atmosphere caused by the gas/liquid refrigerant Freon®. Freon was formerly used in refrigeration and air conditioners. When it leaked out, it rapidly degraded the ozone layer of the atmosphere and created holes in it. Those rapidly-widening holes in the atmosphere's protective layer of ozone would have greatly increased incidence of skin cancer in the areas directly beneath them.

We acted quickly because of the escalating danger of a "hole in the ozone" that would have eventually harmed almost everyone on earth. If we did this successfully before with Freon's pollution, *we should be able to do it again* with the fossil fuel industries toxic carbon and methane pollution!

The solution to reversing escalating global warming depends upon radical and immediate global changes in how we produce energy, how we pollute the atmosphere, and how we cooperate collectively as humans. These needed changes are far larger and needed far faster than any change of this scale has ever been previously achieved in human history. Consequently, resolving global warming will require more of Earth's inhabitants to mobilize and cooperatively work together than has ever occurred in the past.

The silver lining bonus for trying to survive escalating global warming is that human global cooperation itself will have to rise to a new and higher evolutionary level that has never been seen before!

To survive the threat of escalating global warming, which transcends national interests and national borders, we will be forced to create a new and greater international cooperative union of nations and peoples that will form an enforcement and verification-empowered global governance well beyond any existing international cooperative structures like the United Nations. This itself would also be a huge evolutionary advantage and advance for humanity!

"The most powerful force ever known on this planet is human cooperation—a force for construction and destruction."
— Jonathan Haidt, social psychologist, professor of Ethical Leadership, New York University

What's next

For some of you, the preceding action steps may seem too difficult for you to achieve by yourself. In the next chapter you will discover there is a new and achievable way to get the necessary action steps done by working through those with the real influence and power.

Summary

- Which would you rather learn about: what is easy and makes you feel comfortable, or what will save your and your family's lives?

- The new and ongoing risk analysis and reports for escalating global warming must be assigned solely to those most responsible, those most qualified, and those whose advice has the highest levels of rational influence on our national politicians. Ongoing risk analysis for escalating global warming must be wholly placed in the intelligence agencies of every nation—the correct place of highest responsibility for all national threat and risk analysis.

- We cannot resolve escalating global warming in time to save ourselves unless we can mass mobilize the world from the top down through new verifiable and enforceable national and international global warming reduction laws or treaties.

- We need to come to the collective realization there is no such thing as an allowable amount of carbon and methane emissions anymore or *any* remaining carbon budget that we can safely burn. Today, there are only damaging carbon and methane emissions to our health and future. Climate catastrophes are already occurring with increasing frequency, scale, and severity at as little as 1°-1.5° degree Celsius (1.8°-2.7° Fahrenheit) of temperature increase. We need to hit the critical Job One Plan 2026 targets for scaling up green energy generation and scaling down fossil fuel use.

- The new national and international Fee and Dividend laws or treaties will help the world to change its fossil fuel behavior at the greatest possible speed.

- We cannot resolve escalating global warming in time unless we mobilize the world through the proven power of financial incentives and penalties. Financial incentives and penalties are time-proven facilitators for rapid and radical behavioral change.

- Without the new global warming remedial laws or treaties having strong, enforceable penalties, some nations or corporations will always cheat. Without strong penalties, cheating will spread into the nations and corporations that would be unfairly penalized by the economic advantages accruing to noncompliant nations and corporations. If this is allowed to happen without sanction, we will not solve the global warming emergency in time.

- Among the proposed global warming laws or treaties that need to be passed, the verification and penalty enforcement mechanism laws or treaties are *the most critical* to making all of the other global warming reduction laws or treaties work.

- New, enforceable, and verifiable international and national laws or treaties to end global warming are the most critical maximum fulcrum and leverage point within the Job One Plan to ensure ending global warming in time. Getting these new laws or treaties passed is *by far* the most important action we must achieve to survive.

- We have a choice: immediately decommission the world's largest conglomerate, the fossil fuel industry, with all of its related painful costs and problems—or lose humanity and civilization. We either go *all-in* on green energy generation, or we watch everything we love suffer and be destroyed.

- By completing the Job One Plan action steps within the remaining 6-10 year window of opportunity for effecting meaningful control, we preserve an honest and rational hope of saving ourselves. If we act effectively, together, and *immediately*, we should be able to keep from crossing more global warming tipping points, going into irreversible global warming and entering the later stages of the Climageddon Scenario.

- Make the commitment to help end global warming. It will change your life for the better. It will also release powers, potentials, and opportunities that simply would not have appeared had you not made that decision and committed to put it into action.

PART 2, CHAPTER 3

HOW TO GET VERIFIABLE AND ENFORCEABLE GLOBAL WARMING LAWS OR TREATIES PASSED

You're probably still wondering how we will ever get the needed international and national global warming reduction laws or treaties passed without effective global governance or global courts that have cross-national border enforcement and verification powers. You're also likely to be questioning how a person like yourself can ever ensure that an emergency conference of national leaders convenes immediately to start the process of passing all the needed verifiable and enforceable new laws or treaties.

To properly answer these questions and deal with this emergency, we need a creative work-around. We need a last-chance solution that *bypasses* our current deficiencies and failed structures to innovatively use whatever we do have. To help you see the value of Job One's creative work-around, it is necessary to briefly discuss who is *really responsible* for the escalating global warming emergency.

Who is responsible for global warming

Moral and ethical responsibility is a relatively simple concept:

> *The more you created or contributed to the problem, the greater your moral responsibility for fixing it.*

When we talk about who is responsible for global warming, we need to think about it in two distinct ways—*moral or ethical* responsibility (climate justice as it is often called) and *practical* responsibility (someone who *has responsibility* and *can do something about it*).

The moral or ethical responsibility for resolving global warming lies *proportionately* with those individuals, corporations, and nations that have created the fossil fuel burning global warming problem since the First Industrial Revolution in the 1880s. While this is morally true, in practical terms it presents a considerable challenge.

We could spend many more decades we do not have trying to determine or litigate the proper proportion of moral and ethical global warming responsibility for every nation, corporation, and individual on earth. Next, we would have to try to enforce that moral and ethical responsibility on the nations, corporations, and individuals all over the planet. This alone could take many decades, if it could even be done.

This presents another imposing dilemma. Because many of these individuals, corporations, and nations have varying and frequently conflicting cultural, religious, or other value criteria and definitions for responsibility, morality, ethics, and justice, finding some kind of agreed upon determination of the common and universal meaning of moral and ethical responsibility is all but impossible within the dwindling time window for meaningful control we need.

In other words, as wonderful, fair, and reasonable as it sounds to simply enforce moral and ethical responsibility proportionately on all of the creators of global warming to achieve true climate justice, the practicality nightmare is that we could *still be* arguing about implementing such enforcement issues many decades from now after we have tumbled into irreversible global warming and extinction.

If we can't successfully take a moral and ethical responsibility approach to solve the global warming emergency in the time that is left, we need to find another approach. Job One proposes the *practical responsibility* approach.

Practical responsibility in the context of global warming is defined by several factors:

1. Who has enough influence and power to create the verifiable and enforceable global warming remedial laws or treaties *in time* to avoid irreversible global warming or extinction-level climate destabilization.

2. Who has the *most* to gain or lose.

3. Who has good reasons for also bearing at least some additional moral and ethical responsibility.

4. What will take into practical account the unbearable reality that we do not have enough time left to bottom-up educate the masses about the incredibly complex and difficult issues of global warming as a complex adaptive climate system. We also do not have enough time left to slowly build political will *person-by-person* from the bottom up until the growing *public will* finally demands that its self-interested politicians create these critical new laws or treaties.

So this then leads us to the 600-trillion-dollar question: Who has the greatest *practical responsibility* for resolving global warming? You and I as average individuals do have moral and ethical responsibility for global warming to the degree that we have contributed to it in our lifetimes, but we do not hold much effective practical responsibility for resolving it, as we have so little real influence in the necessary areas.

Because the United Nations, the IPCC, and our national governments have failed so horribly over the last 30+ years, the 5 key entities that now bear the greatest practical responsibility for resolving the global warming emergency in order of priority are:

a. the world's wealthiest nations
b. the world's wealthiest corporations
c. the world's wealthiest individuals

    d. the world's wealthiest celebrities

    e. the world's intelligence agencies (as discussed in preceding Chapter 2)

To explain the reasons for this, we must first explain what this does *not* mean. We are not talking about the world's wealthiest nations, corporations, individuals, and celebrities *individually* setting up new companies and/or research projects to find new technological and non-technological solutions to global warming. That will never work in time without globally enforceable and verifiable warming reduction laws or new treaties and a global Fee and Dividend program already in place.

This also does not mean that the world's wealthiest nations, corporations, individuals, and celebrities cannot privately invest in global warming remedial solutions; it just means we can't exclusively or primarily rely on their individual or private wealth to solve the global warming problem. That being said, there is successful experience the world's wealthiest nations and corporations can bring to the table to help other national governments plan and execute the largest energy generation transition project in human history.

As far as the world's wealthiest celebrities are concerned, their importance in educating the masses about the seriousness of the emergency and the necessity of the changes we must all endure cannot be overestimated. The celebrities of the world command the attention needed to be successful.

We also have to be diligent

From many experiences over the last 30 years, we have learned that some of the world's wealthiest nations, corporations, and individuals greenwash their political and profit-making activities to make themselves look like good citizens while not actually doing anything. Their real motivation for the greenwashing remains to increase profits, often in some other area of their existing carbon-polluting activities. For more information on greenwashing, see this article by Tim McDonnell.[144]

Greenwashing allows wealthy nations, individuals, and corporations to look like good global citizens in public while continuing to do business and pollute as usual. In the Job One collective action steps we steer away from this fatal flaw that, unfortunately, too many previous big environmental groups have embarrassingly fallen prey to.

Wealthy nations, individuals, and corporations should not be allowed to greenwash. Rather they need to be educated and inspired to use their influence and control to get the politicians of their respective nations to enact the necessary global warming remedial laws or treaties previously mentioned. If they try to greenwash with insincere and hypocritical actions, they need to be exposed.

While not ignoring the greenwashing risk—in fact, being vigilant about it instead—it's still true that the world's wealthiest corporations, individuals, and celebrities *without a doubt* have the necessary influence and control to get the attention and/or compliance of the world's political leaders to create and enforce the new laws or treaties that must be enacted if we are going to survive.

The reason they should or will want to use that influence is because they are the ones who have the most to gain or lose. These wealth-endowed entities control 90 percent or more of the world's wealth and assets. They do in fact have the *very most to gain or lose* as escalating global warming continues toward irreversible global warming or extinction-level climate destabilization.

As we move closer to irreversible global warming and worse, millions and then hundreds of millions of their citizens or customers or fans (not to mention themselves) will begin to

---

[144] Tim McDonnell. "The fossil fuel industry is bankrolling the Paris Climate talks." *Mother Jones*. December 2, 2015. http://www.motherjones.com/environment/2015/12/climate-change-summit-paris-cop21-fossil-fuels-sponsors

suffer and die. First weak and then stronger national economies will begin to crash. As national economies crash, so will governments.

Normal business as we have known it will become impossible to conduct because the safe, stable, and consistent environment needed for any kind of reliable and continuous manufacturing, supply distribution, retail, or other business operations will be so unpredictable and so disrupted that maintaining a continually profitable business of any kind will be all but impossible.

Irreversible global warming is a no-win game for everyone, no matter how much wealth you have. The wealthy corporations, individuals, and celebrities who are already buying land and facilities in northern countries will eventually not be safe there. Mass migrations of desperate, aggressive, and armed climagees and national armies will eventually overrun any and all border security measures, angrily take their fair share of what's left, and punish anyone who by either commission or omission had any significant part in letting this horrific global warming meltdown and catastrophe occur.

Eventually the private security companies of the ultra-wealthy corporations, individuals, and celebrities will turn against their affluent bosses, realizing that they now live in a late-phase Climageddon Scenario world where only firepower and military-style personal training determine survival, final ownership, and safety. Worse yet, and worth repeating, the climagee survivors of the most painful and devastating catastrophe in human history will be so angry and traumatized they will seek a horrible vengeance on everyone and anyone they hold responsible for causing or contributing to the catastrophe, or for failing to act when they reasonably could have prevented the worst of it.

In their unimaginable anger and pain, some of the remaining climagee survivors who desperately fight their way into the remaining temporarily safe zones, like some survivors of the Holocaust, will relentlessly hunt down anyone who they believe knew about the escalating global warming emergency and had the influence or resources to address it, but did not. Things will be even worse for wealthy corporations, individuals or celebrities who acted to protect *only themselves*, did nothing, or intentionally sought to profit from the escalating global warming catastrophes and chaos as they developed.

When those individuals are identified by the enraged climagee survivors for their unconscionable commissions and omissions, it is highly likely that all their wealth will be removed from them as well as from their trusts, heirs, and businesses. They will be imprisoned for what will be defined later in the history of the global warming emergency as *crimes against humanity and the future.*

The above-mentioned entities also have good reasons for bearing more moral and ethical responsibility. This is because they have caused measurably more fossil fuel pollution in the creation and maintenance of their vast wealth than any of the rest of us have, and because they continue to use far more fossil fuels than any of us do in the maintenance of their current jet-setting lifestyles and business activities.

Another component of their moral and ethical obligation resides within the concept of "wealth obliges," similar to the old French concept of noblesse oblige. The updated concept of noblesse oblige also implies the moral and ethical obligation that possessing great wealth extends beyond mere economic influence, comforts, and privileges. It also requires the person or entity who holds such status to take on reasonable and rational social and leadership responsibilities to promote and protect the *common well-being.* Under this updated concept that wealth obliges, the world's wealthiest nations, corporations, individuals and celebrities are in fact *more* morally and ethically *bound to act* and lead.

And, finally, there isn't enough time for anyone else with sufficient influence over the world's politicians to remedy the situation. Yes, we really are out of time.

We should have started making the necessary changes 30 years ago. Now there is no one else available with the necessary levels of immediate controlling influence over today's self-interested politicians other than the world's wealthiest corporations, individuals, and celebrities.

To solve escalating global warming before we cross *more global warming tipping points* (see tipping point Chapter 4 in Part 1), we need to act at levels of effective coordinated global action and mobilize like we've never seen before in human history. We simply do not have *adequate time* left to build a movement of individual citizens from the bottom up as was done in the past to influence our politicians to pass the new laws or treaties to resolve this emergency.

If you are not one of the world's wealthiest individuals, corporations, or celebrities and you are not a high-ranking member of an intelligence agency cognizant of the damage being created, you now know you are *not* the one who is *primarily* responsible to fix this mess. With that in mind, let's explore what you are responsible for getting done by seeing the challenge in a new way.

To bypass the failed solutions of the past, new solutions are needed

If we are going to solve this global warming emergency, we have to let go of old solutions that no longer work in the unique circumstances and time limitations we now face. We must surrender all such illusions or die.

Only a top-down solution that begins with immediately enacting verifiable and enforceable national and international laws or treaties will work. There's really no other way to say it. Laws or treaties driven into existence by the far superior direct access, influence, and control of the world's wealthiest individuals and corporations have the best chance of resolving global warming in time. (See chapter 8 in Part 1 for more about why top down driven solutions will not work in the time frame remaining.)

The power of self-interest

Politicians and governments are *highly susceptible* to the influence of the world's wealthiest individuals, corporations, and celebrities as evidenced by the lavish ongoing favors, subsidies, and special interest laws they have passed—actions which *greatly* favor wealthy individuals and corporations over the interests of common citizens and our collective well-being.

We can count on the deep evolutionary truth of driving self-interest. The world's richest nations, corporations, individuals, and celebrities *will want to save themselves and their futures* first when they finally realize that escalating global warming is a no-win game for their nations businesses, themselves, and their heirs. All we have to do is thoroughly convince the politicians of the world that this really is a no-win game and *they will save us* as they save themselves *first*.

Because of this, it is now our individual and collective job to repeatedly and compellingly work to convince the world's wealthiest individuals, corporations, and celebrities that it is also in their highest self-interest to embrace our cause as their own. This means motivating them in turn to convince the politicians to immediately enact the necessary laws or treaties to resolve the global warming emergency and to sustain this lobbying until they are successful.

If we fail to educate and motivate those who have the power to immediately remedy this situation, there is no long-term or viable backup "Plan B" here. If the world's wealthiest nations, individuals, corporations, and celebrities don't turn this Titanic of a disaster immediately away from the iceberg of crossing more tipping points, all will be lost in the ensuing climate meltdown and chaos.

More about how the world's wealthiest individuals and corporations will lead the rapid global transition out of fossil fuels and into green energy generation

It's important to qualify the preceding statement. It will not be all of the world's wealthiest individuals and corporations. It will only be about two thirds to three quarters of them.

The reason is simple. Approximately a third to a quarter of of all of the world's wealthiest corporations and individuals derive their wealth from fossil fuel related operations and industries. They are not going to give out that wealth or watch it dissipate without a long drawn-out fight.

The good news is 2/3 to 3/4 of the rest of the world's wealthiest individuals and corporations do not derive the greatest portion of their wealth from fossil fuels or fossil fuel related industries. This means that they will not want to see their wealth destroyed as global warming escalates beyond any controllable level. This also means they will have considerably more resources and far greater numbers to defeat the counter efforts of those unwise wealthy individuals and corporations who obstinately link their futures to a rapidly dying industry.

All we have to do is communicate to those two thirds of the world's wealthiest individuals and corporations that their financial survival depends upon overriding any and all well funded counter efforts to stop the rapid transition to 100% green energy generation.

This tactic is an ironic turnabout. Since time immemorial, the world's wealthiest individuals have been playing other classes or groups against each other to forward their own interests. This time, we as the general public are doing it to them, not for private gain, but to protect and preserve everyone's ultimate self-interests.

The supporting action steps found below will help us begin educating the world's wealthiest individuals, corporations, and celebrities about why they will want to lead the call for an emergency meeting of world leaders and push for new enforceable and verifiable laws or treaties to remedy escalating global warming. The following supporting action steps will make the primary actions described in the previous chapter both possible and successful.

The supporting action steps that *will* get Job One done

You're now ready to see how we will resolve the great evolutionary challenge of the global warming emergency. In the rest of this chapter, you will find our current best options for maximizing and optimizing the influence leverage needed to achieve the Job One Plan. The sequence in which these steps are done can be altered by local circumstances as well as individual preference.

Supporting Action Step A:

Help Job One contact 1,000 of the world's wealthiest celebrities through email and personal letters.

There are already many celebrities like James Cameron and Leonardo DiCaprio speaking out publicly, telling the world that we have to solve the global warming emergency now. See this video clip by James Cameron[145] and this article by Katie Kilkenny.[146] In addition to being able to quickly educate massive audiences on the basics of the global warming emergency and get more individuals involved, celebrities in areas like entertainment, sports, the media, etc., can also have immediate and effective influence in getting the necessary new global warming reduction laws or treaties passed.

Getting more celebrities to publicly come out, speak, and act against global warming as the largest single security threat and disruptor of the 21st century has important benefits in several areas:

---

[145] "Not Reality TV by James Cameron." YouTube video. 5:27, posted by "Democratic National Convention," July 28, 2016. https://www.youtube.com/watch?v=zORv8wwiadQ

[146] Katie Kilkenny. "What can celebrities do for climate change?" *Pacific Standard*. October 8, 2016. https://psmag.com/what-can-celebrities-do-for-climate-change-d7800b032447#.ij2p2goh7

- They are often friends with or attend functions given by the world's wealthiest individuals, politicians, or senior executives of the world's wealthiest corporations. Because of their celebrity, they have unique access to promote the benefits of resolving the global warming emergency and advocate that the world's wealthiest individuals, corporations, and celebrities use their access and influence on the world's politicians to get the necessary laws or treaties passed.

- They also have the attention of and are a voice to billions of people around the world. If they come out and actively endorse resolving the global warming emergency and promote effective steps similar to those in the Job One for Humanity Plan, people all over the world will be discussing the global warming remedial steps and strategies and will soon get involved to help resolve this survival-critical issue. For more information, see this article[147] documenting how celebrities can and do capture public interest.

Here's how to begin this celebrity contact step. You do not need to have friends, family, or direct or indirect connections with any celebrity to help in this action:

a. Before you begin writing the celebrity you have chosen, go to the Climageddon Book Support Navigation Center page[148] and click the link that supports celebrity

---

[147] Chris Mooney. "People really do pay attention to climate change — when Leonardo DiCaprio talks about it." *The Washington Post*. August 5, 2016. https://www.washingtonpost.com/news/energy-environment/wp/2016/08/05/the-leo-effect-when-dicaprio-talked-climate-change-at-the-oscars-people-suddenly-cared/?utm_term=.6129fadf4b36

[148] Job One for Humanity. "Climageddon Book Support Navigation Center." *JobOneforHumanity.org*. Accessed March 20, 2016. http://www.joboneforhumanity.org/climageddon_book_support_navigation_center

campaigns, addresses, and updates. You will find sample celebrity letters there as well.

a. Use the best letter writing advice given a bit farther down this page, then send personal letters and emails. Directly ask them to:

1. assist and facilitate an emergency meeting of all world leaders, and

2. contact and pressure the politicians in their circles of influence to act now on the steps like those described in the Job One Plan.

b. Send them a copy of *Climageddon* if you think it will help educate them.

If you do have friends, family, or direct or indirect connections to celebrities, use the information above with your connections.

It is always good to personalize and modify any sample "template" letters we have provided to have a better chance of effecting an impact. It's vital they not be seen as obvious "form letters." They should be personalized with appropriate recipient-related details, much like a cover letter to a potential employer, where the applicant demonstrates they took time to learn about the employer and his/her business.

Here are our suggestions for essential personalization that can be used in many of the supportive action steps below:

1. Spend the first part of the letter "connecting" with the celebrity recipient before talking about what you want as far as desired actions. In your unique introductory section, answer the reader's question: Why should you care about this? If the reader then feels that sense of risk and responsibility that you connect him or her to, there is a much better chance they will read the

requested actions with more interest. If you put these the other way around, you would lose the reader in most cases because they may think they have heard it all before.

2. Offer some positive strokes to the recipient where possible. Who doesn't like hearing a compliment?

3. You can still use our basic templates for about 80% of your letter content, but for the rest of your letter text, take some time to do the research based on the celebrity recipient.

4. Always request that the celebrity publicly express what they are doing or will do to help get the emergency meeting of world leaders called to enact the global warming reduction laws or treaties and indicate that you will interpret no public statement on the issue to be inaction on their part.

5. At the end of the letter, be sure to include a unique personal closing, your name, and your contact information. You may be surprised by who responds to your personal appeal.

6. If the celebrity you have contacted responds, don't forget to send a thank you and let the Job One for Humanity team know about your letter as well. We will put the most successful letters on our website or in our monthly newsletter to help motivate and inspire others.

Keep in mind that if you're going to go to the trouble of writing to celebrities, give it the best possible shot you can. Personal letters are far more effective than emails. If you are emailing, always use unique, non-trite subject titles so that "gatekeeper" support staff do not use automatic email filters to delete your expression of deep concern.

Once the celebrity you've contacted takes a *public stand* against escalating global warming and uses their influence on the world's politicians to help begin that emergency meeting to enact new global warming reduction laws or treaties, move on to contacting other celebrities.

Do not worry if they try to act like they're doing something and are really doing nothing. Once it becomes known that they are publicly saying they are doing something for global warming, it is highly probable the media and other watchdog individuals will verify that this is not just another greenwashing public relations tactic. If the individuals or corporations you are contacting do not act to use their power and effective influence to help resolve this extreme threat to our common well-being, move to Action Step G below.

Supporting Action Step B:

Help Job One contact 1,000 of the world's wealthiest corporations through email and personal letters.

Some of the world's wealthiest corporations are already onboard and active in fighting global warming. In addition to the addresses and campaigns being put together at the Climageddon Book Support Navigation Center page, there are long lists such as the Fortune 500 and Fortune 100 of the world's wealthiest corporations available online and at most public libraries.

The world's wealthiest corporations are a good place to send your email and personal letters because they are:

- more agile than governments in their ability to respond quickly to changing conditions;

- highly motivated to preserve and grow their businesses, as well as to secure both customer bases and markets;

- less constrained by national borders;

- better able to raise and control the expenditure of large sums of money;

- subject to stakeholder pressure if they do not respond to our initial letters and emails;

- always looking for projects that will enhance their brand's reputation and goodwill in the eyes of the public. (As the global warming catastrophes continue escalating, any corporation helping to resolve this emergency will be viewed favorably by the public and negatively if not aiding the cause.)

Those corporations whose senior executives understand that losing this battle will quickly eradicate their customer base will help lead the way. They already know day-to-day normal business and financial markets will be all but impossible to conduct in the later phases of the Climageddon Scenario.

Here's how to begin this wealthy corporation contact step. You do not need to have friends, family, or direct or indirect connections within any wealthy corporation to help in this action.

a. Go to the Climageddon Book Support Navigation Center page [149] and go to the link that supports this action for additional information, updates, or actions. (Job One may already be helping to facilitate getting and prioritizing addresses for which wealthy corporations to contact. You will find sample corporation letters there as well.)

b. Use the best letter writing advice given previously and send personal letters and emails. Directly ask them to:

---

[149] Job One for Humanity. "Climageddon Book Support Navigation Center." *JobOneforHumanity.org.* Accessed March 20, 2016. http://www.joboneforhumanity.org/climageddon_book_support_navigation_center

1. assist and facilitate calling the emergency meeting of world leaders,

2. contact and pressure the politicians in their circles of influence to act now, and

3. assist our often dysfunctional governments in the mass mobilization planning and implementation of the life-critical and lightning-fast transition from fossil fuels to green energy generation.

c. Get them copies of *Climageddon* if you think it will help educate them.

If you do have friends, family, or direct or indirect personal connections with any wealthy corporations, use the same instructions as above using your contact information.

To help you with this, see our sample letters. This sample letter or email is the starting point for selling the most positive reasons for the world's wealthiest corporations to follow their own highest and most enlightened self-interests in ending escalating global warming. These letters also contain specifics on what we want to have happen to resolve global warming.
As with letters to celebrities, it is good to personalize and modify any sample "template" letters we have provided to have a better chance of effecting an impact. It's vital they not be seen as obvious "form letters." They should be personalized with appropriate recipient-related details, much like a cover letter to a potential employer, where the applicant demonstrates they took time to learn about the employer and his/her business. Use the suggestions for essential personalization given in the celebrity letter writing section above.

Once we finish the first 5,000 contacts, we will begin the second 5,000.

Supporting Action Step C:

Help Job One contact 1,000 of the world's wealthiest individuals through email and personal letters.

It is really not that hard. Some of the world's wealthiest individuals like Tom Steyer, the technology billionaire, are already onboard and active. There are long lists such as the Fortune 500 and Fortune 100 of the world's wealthiest individuals available online and at most public libraries.

Here's how to begin contacting the world's wealthiest individuals. You do not need to have friends, family, or direct or indirect personal connections with any wealthy individual to help in this action.

a. Before you begin, go to the Climageddon Book Support Navigation Center page and go to the link that is most concerned with supporting this action for additional information, updates or actions. (Job One will also facilitate getting and prioritizing addresses for which wealthy individuals to contact first. You will find sample letters to wealthy individuals here as well.)

b. Use the best letter personal writing advice given earlier in the celebrity section and send personal letters and emails. Directly ask them to:

1. assist and facilitate the calling of an emergency meeting of world leaders, and

2. contact and pressure the politicians in their circles of influence to act now.

c. Send them a copy of *Climageddon* if you think it will help educate them.

If you do have friends, family, or direct or indirect personal connections with any wealthy individuals, use the information above with those personal contacts.

Supporting Action Step D:

Help Job One maximize leverage by contacting the heads and staff of your nation's intelligence agencies

If we want the politicians of the world to meet soon to declare a world global warming State of Emergency, pass the essential verifiable, and enforceable laws or treaties to save us in time as well as the other needed actions described previously, we have to maximize our influence leverage efforts by using a multi-pronged influence strategy. This includes:

a. convincing the world's wealthiest individuals, corporations, and celebrities to lobby their politicians,

b. getting the WTO and the IMF and other power centers to use their influence to facilitate and quickly convene the emergency meeting of the world's political leaders, and

c. ensure our national intelligence agencies take over global warming research, analysis, and reporting responsibilities and are *actively educating* our politicians (and the public) on all of the imminent security and economic threats the escalating global warming emergency poses to our world. (See Part 2, Chapter 2 for the reasons why the powerful and credible influence of our intelligence agencies with politicians is a key part of our strategy to get the new laws or treaties needed passed in time.)

Do not doubt that there are many brilliant and courageous high-level analysts and executives within the world's intelligence communities who already know much of what is in this book and its predictions for our future. Because of current political realities, they are restrained from speaking out. We need to give them the support and encouragement necessary for them to continue to champion the truth that will save all of our futures.

These brave individuals will have to fight through the opposing influence or resistance exerted by the fossil fuel industry, lobbyists, other vested interests, existing political partisanship or any fixed ideas and any antiquated systems or traditions within their agencies that would prevent them from credibly educating the politicians they serve before it is too late.

These brilliant and courageous individuals can never forget that not only is the future of their nation at stake, but the world's future is also at stake. If they fail to convince their respective politicians about the truth and full consequences of the escalating global warming emergency, no one will survive the Climageddon Scenario's later phases.

If the combined total influence of the world's wealthiest individuals, corporations, celebrities and the world's intelligence agencies is not able to convince our politicians to enact the needed enforceable and verifiable new laws or treaties, we will be facing *the beginning of the end.*
If you still need more convincing on why our national intelligence agencies must take the full risk analysis and progress tracking job from the United Nations, see Chapter 7, Part 1 and Chapter 2, Part 2 of this book.

After you have done that, go to the Climageddon Book Support Navigation Center page and go to the link that is most concerned with supporting this action for additional information, updates, or actions. You will find intelligence agency sample letters there as well as a petition you can sign immediately.

Supporting Action Step E:

Help Job One contact and demand the International Monetary Fund and the World Trade Organization and other power centers initiate an emergency meeting of world's leaders and facilitate the creation of verifiable and enforceable new global warming reduction laws or treaties

You do not need to have friends, family, or direct or indirect personal connections with anyone working at the WTO or IMF or other power centers to help in this action. Here are the steps:

If you don't have any direct or indirect connections within the WTO or IMF or other power centers:

    a. Before you begin, go to the Climageddon Book Support Navigation Center page and go to the link most concerned with supporting this action for additional information, updates or actions. You will find IMF and WTO or other sample letters here as well.

    b. Use the best letter writing advice given earlier in the celebrity section and send personal letters and emails asking they use their influence to get the emergency meeting called immediately and execute the meeting actions described in Chapter 2 in Part 2.

    c. Send them a copy of *Climageddon* if you think it will help educate them.

If you do have friends, family, or direct or indirect personal connections within the WTO or IMF or other power centers, use the information above with your connections.

Supportive Action Step F:

Quickly scale up education, collaboration, and mobilization

There is one last critical action step to make the Job One Plan successful. We have to massively *scale up* global education about the emergency and the unfolding Climageddon Scenario.

We also need to scale up collaboration and effective action within the urgent deadlines the global warming emergency demands.

But how does this scaling up or solution scalability step actually work? Scalability is defined as:

1. the capability of a system, network, or process to handle a growing amount of work, or

2. that system's potential to be enlarged in order to accommodate that growing amount of *anticipated* work.

At the minimum, this Job One Plan scale-up step means that the global warming challenge is so large that no single organization or group of organizations could handle the ever-increasing volume of communication and coordinated actions that will be needed to resolve this emergency. This also means that the Job One Plan and the Job One for Humanity organization will not be successful with its mission to end human-caused global warming *unless* it can ignite and catalyze independent *self-organizing*[150] global education, action and collaboration partnerships and alliances not just with other nonprofit organizations and NGOs, but also with anyone or any organization *anywhere* that wants to help in this nearly impossible challenge.

In the critical next 6 to 10 years, it will take a massive effort and the greatest emergency mass mobilization in human history by everyone—individuals, groups, NGOs, nonprofits, corporations, and religions, as well as governments around the world. All such organizations will be needed to quickly spread the word on Job One's best or similar ideas and to get the world's celebrities, wealthiest individuals, corporations, other power centers, as well as our national intelligence agencies leveraging our politicians to create and enforce verifiable new laws or treaties and get the needed critical actions executed

---

[150]Wikipedia contributors, "Self-organization," *Wikipedia, The Free Encyclopedia*, https://en.wikipedia.org/w/index.php?title=Self-organization&oldid=757928655 (accessed January 2, 2017).

before it's too late. It will also require involving the best and brightest minds to amend, adapt, and improve the Job One Plan, solutions and tactics as needed, using new research on the particulars and feedback on the ground at any given location.

Let's get started. The biggest first scale-up substep is to educate as many people as fast as possible about Climageddon and how bad the global warming emergency actually is. There are numerous ways for you to help save your own future and help Job One for Humanity do this:

1. Tell your friends about the new *Climageddon* book and the Job One for Humanity Plan within it.

2. Use our Spread The Word [151] tool where you can automatically share the Climageddon book link on Facebook, Twitter, LinkedIn, Gmail +, Reddit, Tumblr, and Digg. (Wherever you can, please add a personal note to your sharing of our link.)

3. Go to Amazon, Itunes, *and* Google Play (after April 14, 2017) and write a book review. Start with Amazon as they are the biggest bookseller. This small action can make a big difference particularly because the well-financed fossil fuel climate denial propaganda machine will do everything it can to author many, false, horrible and insulting reviews at these websites designed exclusively to discourage anyone from evaluating the book's information for themselves.

4. Sign up for our Global Warming Blog RSS feed to get new global warming articles, and the latest news and progress. There are several thousand news articles

---

[151] Job One for Humanity. "Spread the Word." *JobOneforHumanity.org*. Accessed March 20, 2016. http://www.joboneforhumanity.org/spread_the_word

already in this blog. (When you sign-up for the RSS feed on the Job One website, a Feedburner pop-up window may appear showing your email address asking you to enter the "no robots" code shown to prove you are not a robot. Once you enter the code, you will be sent an email to verify your email address with the email verification link in it. Once you click the link in the email sent by Feedburner you will automatically receive regular Global Warming Blog updates.)

5. If you know someone in any nonprofit or NGO that may be sympathetic to the information and action steps in *Climageddon*, talk personally with them about what you have learned and have them get a copy of the book. You might be the one who helps them refine and update their mission to the new global warming reality and then encourages them to join the emergency mobilization taking place.

6. If you are already involved in any organization sympathetic to the ideas and action plan steps of *Climageddon*, your organization can help by becoming an independent collaborating partner or ally in the *Global Warming Emergency Mobilization* (GWEM) currently facilitated at the Job One for Humanity website. There is much your organization can do to collaborate and mobilize with Job One for Humanity on critical path actions to help end global warming. It will take nothing less than a massive emergency mobilization and collaboration between hundreds of thousands of organizations to end this crisis in time to keep us safe. Visit our page [152] for more *Global Warming Emergency Mobilization* support, collaboration, and partnering information.

---

[152] http://www.joboneforhumanity.org/mobilization_partners_allies

7. If you know someone in any media-related organization that may be sympathetic to the information in *Climageddon*, talk personally with them about what you have learned and ask them to start covering information about how little time we have left in their media broadcasts. They are in the same boat as the rest of us. They and their families will suffer just as much as everyone else.

8. If you are already involved in an organization sympathetic to the ideas and Job One actions of *Climageddon*, you or your organization can also buy the book in bulk at a substantial discount and distribute it wherever you think it will do the most good. (For current bulk purchase discounts, email us at manage@JobOneforHumanity.org.)

9. If you are not already a member of an organization doing similar mission work to Job One for Humanity, please consider becoming a Job One volunteer and help us educate others. The Job One Plan needs all the volunteers it can get to be successful in the time we have left. To get started as a volunteer, fill in the online volunteer form by.[153] In the comments field, be sure to let us know about any special skills or experience you have or any specific projects that you would like to work on. One of our team members will get back to you with additional information. On the Job One Navigation Center page you will also find a listing of positions that are currently open for volunteers.

10. If you are not already a member of an organization doing similar mission work to Job One for Humanity, you

---

[153] Job One for Humanity. "Volunteer." *JobOneforHumanity.org*. Accessed March 20, 2016. http://www.joboneforhumanity.org/volunteer

can also set up and self-organize an independent Job One Plan meetup, study, and action group in your local area. We have website tools to help you do this, but you will be the main person creating and self-managing your own local area events and actions. Our newsletter and local area group coordinator will share planned larger scale actions and successful strategies as they become available.

11. Donate to support the nonprofit tax-deductible mission of Job One for Humanity. Your financial support will be wisely and frugally used to end global warming and to spread the word and educate others. Your donations also help subsidize discounted or free Climageddon books for students around the world. Never forget that well-financed vested interests in the fossil fuel industries and nations have nearly unlimited funds to impede our efforts. You can be certain they will use those resources against us as our new message gains traction. Help level the playing field, visit our page [154] to make a online or mail-in donation to support our mission to *effectively* end global warming. All of your donations are tax-deductible if you are a US citizen.

12. If someone has giving you your copy of Climageddon and, you can afford it, please make a donation to help us get more books into the hands of more people.

13. Here are a few additional quick supportive actions. Like the Job One website, [155] our Climageddon Facebook page [156] and follow our Climageddon Twitter feed. [157]

---

[154] Job One for Humanity. "Donate and Help End Global Warming." *JobOneforHumanity.org*. Accessed March 23, 2016. http://factnet.nationbuilder.com/donate_job_one_for_humanity

[155] Job One for Humanity. "Job One for Humanity." http://joboneforhumanity.org/

There truly is no other way we will be successful unless we can scale up education and action globally!

Please share whatever primary or supporting action step successes or adaptations you have with the Job One team by emailing them to us at manage@JoboneforHumanity.org. We will do our best to share them with everyone in regular newsletter updates.

For additional scaling-up information and strategy, go to the Climageddon Book Support Navigation Center page and go to the Scaling Up link that is most concerned with supporting this action. For your convenience, a simplified version of all Job One Plan steps is found as an action step checklist in Appendix 1.

Supporting Action Step G:

For the individuals, corporations, or celebrities or other power centers that *do not* act, begin contacting them directly at their public events.

Go to these events and set up a peaceful, nonviolent demonstration that would make Gandhi proud. Demand that they immediately use their direct access and effective influence with any and all politicians to whom they have access to enact all of the necessary global warming remedial laws or treaty types listed in the Job One Plan.

If it is a wealthy corporation not responding, you can also get a list of the largest stockholders of that corporation and begin writing them to use their voting leverage to change the policies of the corporation toward this emergency.

---

[156] Job One for Humanity. "Climageddon." *Facebook.com*. Accessed March 17, 2017. https://www.facebook.com/Climageddon/

[157] Job One for Humanity. "Climageddon." *Twitter.com*. Accessed April 19, 2017. https://twitter.com/climageddon

Please keep in mind that the Job One For Humanity Plan recommends *only* peaceful, nonviolent protest and demonstrations. We actively discourage any illegal or violent tactic. We also strongly recommend against going to any individual's private home for these protests. These demonstrations should be only at locations where the public can obtain some level of access.

Before you begin this step, go to the Climageddon Book Support Navigation Center page and go to the link that is most concerned with supporting this action for individuals or organizations who fail to act.

The above letters and actions involving those who have real influence and control *can save our future*. If large numbers of people from around the world engage in these critical action steps, the world's wealthiest individuals, corporations, and celebrities and other power centers will be educated on their practical responsibilities to end global warming and, to protect their own self interests, will do the right thing. They will use their direct or indirect access and effective influence on the world's politicians. When this happens, we will be able to resolve the global warming emergency with far less damage and hopefully secure a survivable future for humanity.

There will, of course, be those corporations, individuals, celebrities, and power centers so invested in the carbon and methane polluting fossil fuel industries that they will resist *all efforts* at evolving through peaceful education. As Upton Sinclair famously observed, "it is difficult to get a man to understand something when his salary depends on his not understanding it."

Do not be discouraged by or waste endless amounts of time on those who blindly and foolishly continue to choose their salary over the future of everyone and everything they love, the great works of our civilization, and the whole of humanity. Just keep the faith and continue executing the Job One Plan action steps.

Once the emergency meeting of world leaders enacts the needed verifiable and enforceable global warming reduction laws or treaties, we will have a real hope for the future and for preventing the later stages of the Climageddon Scenario from unfolding.

A wise and motivating personal launch action

Now that you understand both the urgency of resolving the global warming emergency and most of the logic of the Job One Plan goals and subgoals, it would be wise to make or confirm an important decision and pledge.

The Job One for Humanity 3-point pledge to help resolve global warming:

1. I will become an active part of the global warming solution by working effectively to help slow, lessen, and end the global warming emergency.

2. I will do my part to educate my friends and others about the global warming emergency and its effective solutions.

3. I will stay the course until we end the global warming emergency and set laws, treaties and policies in place so it never occurs again!

Gallup Poll reports show up to 87% of workers feel disconnected from meaningful and purposeful work. [158] Resolving global warming is this century's greatest and most meaningful challenge and *job one for humanity*.

"Until one is committed, there is hesitancy, the chance to draw back, always ineffectiveness. Concerning all acts of initiative (and creation), there is one elementary

---

[158] Steve Crabtree. "Worldwide, 13% of employees are engaged at work." *Gallup.com*. October 8, 2013. http://www.gallup.com/poll/165269/worldwide-employees-engaged-work.aspx

truth, the ignorance of which kills countless ideas and splendid plans: that the moment one definitely commits oneself, then providence moves too. A whole stream of events issues from the decision, raising in one's favor all manner of unforeseen incidents, meetings and material assistance, which no man could have dreamt would have come his way. Whatever you can do or dream you can, begin it. Boldness has genius, power and magic in it!" —Johann Wolfgang von Goethe

Making the above pledge will change your life for the better. It will also release potentials and opportunities that simply would not have appeared had you not done so. Click here to sign this pledge online and join the Job One for Humanity honor roll.[159]

If you understand how to use visualization techniques on the goals and subgoals mentioned previously, please visualize them as already being achieved. If you do not understand the process or importance of the goal visualization process for ending global warming, visit this page.[160]

Your next vaccination

We can work together and not make it a polarized battle of us versus them because we truly *are all in the same sinking boat*

If we hold a big-picture perspective and we are creative and smart, we really can work together and we really *have* to work together! We do not have to *"polarize to mobilize."*

Here's how addressing the global warming emergency can be inherently and ultimately non-polarizing:

a. Eventually everyone will be adversely affected in one way or another. Some will be affected less in the

---

[159] Job One for Humanity. "Honor Roll." *JobOneforHumanity.org.* Accessed March 23, 2016. http://www.joboneforhumanity.org/honor_roll1

[160] Association for the Tree of Life. "Visioning for a better world: why and how." Accessed December 11, 2016. http://www.tree-of-life.works/visioning

beginning. Some will even experience a few benefits in early stages, but as global warming escalates toward irreversibility or it moves toward the Climageddon Scenario extinction levels, we will all suffer nearly equally, no matter how rich we are or how insulated we thought we could make ourselves. Whether we know it or not, at this moment all of our long-term global warming remedial self-interests are aligned. We all win together, or we all lose together.

b. With the motive of survival ultimately aligning our self-interests, it is now just a matter of

   a. passing enforceable and verifiable laws or treaties to end global warming,

   b. conducting widespread education, and

   c. then executing those new laws or treaties.

   We do not have to play the "us vs. them" game or other win/lose games. We do not have to characterize those who do not understand the incredibly complex global warming information as bad, greedy, or evil people. We should also never forget that general ignorance of the climate system complexities is just where many people are now in their personal, corporate, or national evolution.

c. If we are tempted to polarize into us vs. them strategies, we need to remind ourselves that every person, every organization, and every nation is at a different level of evolutionary development and maturity. Evolutionary development or maturity depends upon physical, psychological, cultural, educational, and, if you are a spiritual person, even spiritual development and maturity.

No matter what position a seeming adversary may hold in resisting actions to end the escalating global warming emergency, they are just reflecting their current level of evolutionary development and maturity. Never forget that their current education, evolutionary development and maturity level is also part of an ongoing process that is in constant change. Given the right information and circumstances, their positions can change just as your past positions on other issues may have changed.

The big silver lining here is that addressing global warming ignorance among our lawmakers and power brokers *is* a challenge that can actually be met if we are skillful and determined!

What's next

The next chapter contains vital information on how you and your business, community, and nation can adapt to and prepare for increasingly frequent and severe global warming disasters. It contains essential emergency preparedness information, as well as advice on backup migration plans.

For your convenience, in Appendix 1 you will find a simplified master checklist of all the action steps of the Job One Plan.

Summary

- Because of the lack of truly empowered *global* governance and the little time remaining to save us, there is no perfect solution to the global warming emergency. But there are reasonable, creative options with an honest hope of success.

- We should have started making the necessary changes to end global warming 30 years ago. Now, no one else has the necessary influence over today's self-interested politicians than the world's wealthiest individuals, corporations, celebrities, and power centers.

- The global warming emergency must be put squarely on the shoulders and backs of the world's wealthiest corporations, individuals, celebrities, and power centers. It is not the little guy's responsibility! You and I simply do not have the necessary influence and control over our politicians, no matter how many of us unite together.

- We do not have enough time left to adequately educate the public, mobilize politically, and then use the public's bottom-up momentum and consensus to sway politicians. Our collective job is to get the world's wealthiest individuals, corporations, celebrities, and power centers to realize that immediately shouldering that responsibility is in their own highest self-interest!

- Irreversible global warming eventually is a no-win game for *everyone*, no matter how much wealth you have. The ultra-wealthy individuals, corporations, celebrities, and power centers who are already buying land and facilities in the global-warming-safer areas will not be safe there. Mass migrations of desperate, aggressive, and armed climagees and national armies from unlivable latitudes will eventually overrun any and all border security measures. They will angrily take their fair share of what's left and punish everyone who by commission or omission had any significant part in letting the horrific global warming meltdown and chaos occur.

- There is no ultimately viable backup "Plan B" if we fail to educate those who have the power to immediately remedy this situation. If the world's wealthiest individuals, corporations, celebrities and power centers don't turn this Titanic of a disaster immediately away from the iceberg of crossing more tipping points, almost everyone and everything will be disrupted or lost in the destabilizing climate chaos.

- If we provide *enough* creative influence and pressure at the correct points of maximum leverage as described in the Job One Plan, we can convince the world's politicians to do all of the needed actions to save humanity in time.

- All we have to do is convince the world's wealthiest individuals and corporations that escalating global warming is a no-win game for them too! They too _will_ lose their assets, their lives, _and_ their legacies. We just have to convince them of the truth that there is no escape for anyone, no matter how much money they have. Once the world's wealthiest individuals and corporations understand this, they will follow their highest self-interests to save themselves and, in doing so, they will save us all! Let's start convincing them they have to act <u>now</u> and let us not give up until they compel the politicians _they control_ to pass the enforceable and verifiable laws needed. We can do this. If we act wisely, there is hope. At its essence, the Job One Plan to end global warming _is_ this simple truth and action!

PART 2 CHAPTER 4

HOW TO PREPARE FOR ESCALATING GLOBAL WARMING CATASTROPHES AND THE CLIMAGEDDON SCENARIO PHASES

In previous chapters you discovered why we are in an undeclared State of Emergency, which phase of the Climageddon Scenario we are currently in, and what key primary and supporting action steps we *must take* to have any reasonable hope of saving ourselves before it is too late. Because of the still unresolved dangers and risks, however uncomfortable that might be, it is now appropriate to discuss *your* personal, business, community, and national emergency preparedness in this last Job One supporting action step.

> "No matter what we do, there will be very severe and unavoidable consequences, especially for the world's regions, peoples, and ecosystems most vulnerable to a hotter climate. That requires a keen focus on *preparing for* and adapting to the changes that are now inevitable..." —David Spratt, *Climate Reality Check.*[161]

Supporting Action Step H: Get prepared for what is coming!

Just as there are no guarantees in life, there are also no guarantees humanity will be able to resolve the escalating global warming emergency before it becomes irreversible and moves into the later phases of the Climageddon Scenario. Therefore, prudence dictates having an emergency survival

---

[161] David Spratt, "Climate Reality Check." *Breakthrough - National Centre for Climate Restoration.* March 2016.
http://media.wix.com/ugd/148cb0_87bbbc8197824d4ab66c85d059020ae8.pdf

plan for ourselves and loved ones as well as our businesses, communities, and nations at the ready.

If we enter the later phases of the Climageddon Scenario, we are in a no-win situation. No areas of the planet will be safe or secure *other than on a temporary basis.*

Despite knowing this outcome, it is still wise to plan for yourself and your loved ones in order to *extend* the quantity and quality of your lives for as long as possible. With good preparation and early migration, you should be able to live a while longer and more comfortably than those who are unprepared.

Even if we do not enter the later phases of the Climageddon Scenario and we manage to avert the end of humanity and civilization, it is wise and essential to read and use this chapter's information on preparedness. There will be many terrible and ongoing global warming-related natural disasters that will collide into our human economic, political, and social systems. These disasters will cause severe disruption of normal supply distribution (food, medical, etc.) and regular system collapses before we get this emergency under control.

In this chapter you will learn how to create a temporary global warming emergency survival plan for you, your family, and your business. Advice will also be offered for community and national emergency preparedness issues.

Other key reasons why it's smart to have an emergency backup plan

The ultra-wealthy and multinational corporations are far ahead of the global warming emergency preparation curve compared to the rest of us. Their top risk and investment advisers, who can access privately created and confidential global warming and climate research reports, have already told them to prepare for the escalating consequences of global warming. In fact, they are being advised not only to get prepared, but also on how to profit from the global warming emergency.[162]

Many ultra-wealthy individuals and corporations have begun to quietly sell off high-risk real estate in areas most affected by global warming consequences. Many ultra-wealthy individuals, corporations, and nations (such as Saudi Arabia) have already quietly purchased large amounts of arable and defendable land in the safest areas of Canada, Scandinavia, Russia, Ukraine, Alaska, the tip of South America, and parts of island areas of Greenland, Iceland, England, and New Zealand.[163] This land is for their high-security, well-stocked personal, global, and other emergency evacuation and survival compounds.[164]

The wealthiest and best informed individuals and corporations are already taking escalating global warming very seriously. They are already preparing for the worst of it while most average citizens haven't even thought about the escalating global warming emergency in terms of their personal emergency preparation.

This raises an important question. If the wealthiest individuals, corporations, and nations are aggressively and secretly protecting themselves against the many current and coming global warming consequences and emergencies, why aren't you doing the same? Why should only the ultra-wealthy have the necessary information to save themselves and their assets long before the rest of us?

Being unprepared for evolution's natural periods of emergency, catastrophic mistakes, or disasters is dangerously unrealistic.

---

[162] Kevin J. Delaney. "Bill Gates and investors worth $170 billion are launching a fund to fight climate change through energy innovation." *Quartz*. December 11, 2016. https://qz.com/859860/bill-gates-is-leading-a-new-1-billion-fund-focused-on-combatting-climate-change-through-innovation/?utm_source=nextdraft&utm_medium=emai

[163] Hayden Donnell. "Silicon Valley super-rich head south to escape from a global apocalypse." *The Guardian*. January 28, 2017. https://www.theguardian.com/technology/2017/jan/29/silicon-valley-new-zealand-apocalypse-escape

[164] Evan Osnos. "Doomsday prep for the super-rich." *The New Yorker*. January 30, 2017. http://www.newyorker.com/magazine/2017/01/30/doomsday-prep-for-the-super-rich

Human history is littered with the corpses of economic, social, and political catastrophes and collapses that our smartest ancestors were prepared for and our not-so-smart ancestors were not. Your gene pool is here today in significant part because your *smart ancestors* were, to some degree, prepared enough to make it through our emergency-filled human history of natural catastrophes and economic, political, and social collapses.

Prudent individuals could argue convincingly that based on humanity's extensive history of past large-scale challenges, humanity will not respond to this global warming emergency until it is too late, or the suffering and pain is so horribly severe that many of us will not survive to enjoy its eventual solution. History overflows with examples of individuals, businesses, and nations that did not adapt and change their behavior until the pain of going forward with the required changes was less than the pain of staying where they were. Unfortunately, that was often too late to prevent widespread suffering and death and the collapse of the economic, political, or social systems of the time.

Looking back into history you will discover that 99.9% of every species that has ever lived on earth has gone extinct.[165] To think that it could not happen to humanity in the 21st century is betting against very long odds.

It is easy to despair thinking about this if one does not know that in all of the past five major extinction events in Earth's history, there were always survivors. Even though 99.9% of every species that has ever lived is no longer here, the fact we are here *now* proves something always goes on.

The following emergency climate preparedness recommended in the Job One Plan is never wasted. The Job One Plan not only assists individuals with strategies to survive the current global warming emergencies and catastrophes, but also many of its

---

[165] W. E. Kunin, K. J. Gaston, eds. *The Biology of Rarity: Causes and consequences of rare—common differences.* December 31, 1996. ISBN 978-0412633805. Accessed January 19, 2017.

emergency preparation steps will help ensure you survive the many other major global challenges and emergencies we face in other areas.

In summary, the wisdom behind having your emergency backup plan ready for the consequences of escalating global warming is simple:

a. It is always wise to prepare for any real or probable emergencies.

b. Once you have completed prudent emergency backup plan preparations, you can be far more comfortable working on preventing those emergencies from ever happening.

You do not have to get your full emergency plan and supplies in place immediately. You can keep working on the preparation steps below while completing the primary and supporting action steps of the preceding Job One chapters.

Step 1: Build your necessary emergency supplies and resilience for global warming catastrophe survival and recovery.

While we still have time, practical wisdom dictates one should first prepare one's family, business, and nation for increasing disruptions in resource supply and distribution, as well as the economic, social, and political turmoil that will inevitably result as global warming steadily worsens.

This means building backup emergency supplies and resilience into your existing personal, community, and national systems. To establish your personal recovery backup emergency supplies and *resilience*, create at least a 30-day reserve (60-90 days would be much better as things get worse) of all necessary survival commodities (food, water, heat, energy, lights, communication devices, medicines, toiletries, self-defense, etc.). It is essential to include self-defense supplies because as we proceed through the phases of the Climageddon Scenario, local, regional, and national governments will begin to break down and you will need to become fully self-reliant for your own protection.[166] Having at least one firearm per adult with adequate ammunition for extensive periods of conflict and chaos will quickly become survivor or climagee *minimum essentials* in the highly unsafe later phases of the Climageddon Scenario.

Also build backup redundancies into your water, power, heating, sewage, and other critical systems. You can do this by having secondary and separate water purification systems, solar, or wind power backup systems,multiple fuel types and acquiring the tools and materials necessary to care for everyday needs, such as keeping warm, cooking, and managing waste with an old-fashioned latrine and safe garbage disposal. Water, sewage, and garbage-born diseases are major secondary death factors in an extended crisis. Prepare now so you and your loved ones will not suffer unnecessarily or die.

At the community, business, and national levels, building more resilience also means gathering emergency and essential non-emergency supplies and reserves as mentioned above for the many different consequences of escalating global warming. Adequate emergency preparation on the community and national levels also gives people more information and time to prepare for local consequences. Without carefully planned resilience and emergency backups built into every level of our interconnected and interdependent economic, social, and political systems and infrastructure, there will again be far too much *unnecessary* and avoidable suffering and death.

When you're ready to begin your emergency preparedness plan, go to http://www.ready.gov and click the navigation

---

[166] Although the author of Climageddon discusses possible scenarios involving global warming-related violence or retribution as potential consequences which must be considered, both the author and the Job One for Humanity organization do not directly or indirectly endorse, condone, or support in any way violence against any person or property. Both the author and the Job One for Humanity organization promote nonviolent peaceful protest that would make Gandhi proud.

link. It will provide you detailed guidance for each area of emergency preparedness.

Step 2: Create a global warming emergency cash or other valuable commodity reserve fund equal to 5%-10% of your monthly income.

A tradable cash, gold, silver, or other valuable emergency trading exchange reserve helps you build financial resilience. Building up and storing an easily exchangeable commodity that you can use or trade in the *beginning phases of the emergency* is also essential.

As escalating global warming continues, hundreds of millions, then eventually billions of climagees (climate refugees) will need to migrate closer toward the poles to survive a bit longer. No current government, charity, or corporation is remotely prepared for these massive human migrations and the unbearable economic, political, and social stresses that these climagees—as well as the consequences of escalating global warming—will cause to every climate, human, and biological system of our global existence.

As global warming escalates, the accelerating inadequacy of governmental or charity-based emergency assistance to protect *you and your family* dictates a need for radical individual responsibility and individual preparedness completed well in advance. This minimal 5%-10% personal and family tradable commodity reserve will help you cope with the many unpredictable consequences as our local systems go into severe stress, crisis, or an eventual collapse.

All *communities and governments* will also immediately need to work toward putting at least 5% of their total GDP into reserves each year. This level of tradable commodity reserve is essential if they hope to stay politically and financially stable while coping with the rapidly escalating global warming costs. (See Chapter 3 in Part 1, which explains the unbearable financial consequences of escalating global warming.)

Because no community or government will be able to keep up with the continually rising costs of escalating global warming and its consequences, *all businesses* must also create similar 5%-10% reserves to help them cope with global warming-related supply, manufacturing, distribution, and labor disruptions. Furthermore, if you are an individual, business, community, or nation with considerable debt, reduce that debt as soon as possible. Having lots of debt in a growing unresolved crisis is likely to make you, your organization, or nation far less adaptable and resilient. High resource liquidity, mobility, and flexibility are a few of the most needed and most useful resiliency qualities in an ongoing or long-term crisis.

Additionally, post-emergency rebuilding and repair will dramatically increase food and insurance costs, emergency housing costs, emergency transportation costs, and other migration costs to temporarily or permanently get out of crisis zones. If you are in a river or lake floodplain, near a coast, in wildfire, drought, or severe storm areas, or near a southern national border, your individual costs will most likely be higher than the 5%-10% suggested reserve. In addition, losses in real estate and farmland values, etc., will rapidly consume your 5%-10% reserves as we cross more global warming tipping points.

Creating these emergency reserves will be difficult in today's debt-encouraging climate. In the United States, an estimated 62% of all families are one paycheck away from bankruptcy, and one-half of *all U.S. households* are just one personal or family emergency away from bankruptcy. Even though it may be difficult creating your emergency reserves, it is *critical to surviving* this emergency. (If you have trouble saving money for these reserves, we recommend that you get and apply the information in the book *Your Money or Your Life* by Joe Dominguez and Vicki Robin.[167])

And finally, a tradable commodity or cash emergency reserve can easily be used while cash is still being accepted. In the

---

[167] Vicki Robin, Joe Dominguez, Monique Tilford. *Your Money or Your Life.* (Penguin Books; 2008.)

later emergency phases, when cash is no longer accepted or is greatly devalued, you will always need to have your five key survival items:

    a. weapons,

    b. water,

    c. food,

    d. medicine, and

    e. small tradable silver coins or other tradable commodities to survive in a new barter system, which will come into being out of necessity.

In the later Climageddon Scenario phases, as the world starts to unravel, your government will be stretched so thin that you will not be able to depend upon it for protection, water, food, medicine, or even a stable currency to acquire what you need. If you have not prepared for these contingencies long before they are needed, you and your loved ones will suffer far more than the growing number of individuals who are preparing for what's coming.

Step 3: Plan now for how you will adapt and/or move critical resources, technology, and infrastructure to handle the escalating consequences of global warming.

Because we have already begun crossing global warming tipping points, business planners, city planners, long-term corporate and governmental planners of all kinds need to begin restructuring their 5, 10 and 25-year plans, using the *least* optimistic climate prediction scenarios (found in previous chapters) on how the consequences of escalating global warming will unfold. Several good reasons for using the least optimistic predictions are:

    a. The many serious errors and underestimation problems in global warming prediction scenarios (see Chapter 7, Part 1 on IPCC underestimation).

b. The sudden, large-scale unpredictability which each additional crossed tipping point creates.

c. We will be very lucky if the *worst* we get are the IPCC's current least optimistic projections!

The amount of emergency adaptation work needed and the short amount of time available makes this adaptation and preparation step an immediate planning imperative. For example, in the San Francisco Bay Area, the headquarters of big tech corporations like Facebook, LinkedIn, Apple, etc., now have to readjust their long-term operational or relocation plans to deal with their low-lying international headquarters facing as much as 13 feet (3.9 meters) of sea level rise by 2100.[168] (A worst case scenario of a possible 10-foot [3-meter] rise was predicted by James Hansen's newest research, with the additional 3-feet [0.9 meters] accounting for coincident king tides and storm surges.)

Adapting and moving critical resources, technology, and infrastructure also means moving them into the safer areas near or above the 45th parallel north or near or below the 45th parallel south. During this massive move of critical people, supplies, and infrastructure, never forget that unless we fix this mess now, survival in those areas will only be temporary.

Step 4: Create your long-term migration plan.

Mobility will be a key life-saving capability during the worst aspects of the global warming emergency and the second and third Climageddon Scenario phases. Our crisis-surviving ancestors have repeatedly proven the validity and importance of the mobility principle.

The worst escalating global warming projections point to an average global temperature increase of 4°-6° Celsius (7.2°-10.8°

---

[168] Oliver Milman. "Silicon Valley Underwater." *The Guardian*. April 22, 2016. https://www.theguardian.com/technology/2016/apr/22/silicon-valley-sea-level-rise-google-facebook-flood-risk

Fahrenheit). This makes having a backup long-term migration plan a must for numerous reasons.

If it looks like we're going to hit the middle-to-late Climageddon Scenario phases, planning to migrate to extend your life and its quality a little longer is a major life decision that should be carefully considered by evaluating one's current location, all of one's personal circumstances, and the best projections for how the global warming emergency will affect your particular location over the coming years. You can also stagger the steps and levels of this emergency migration plan to meet the speed of global temperature increases, sea level rises, the closing of national borders, and the increases in severity, scale, and frequency of all of the other global warming consequences as they occur in your particular area.

Create a 30-day emergency migration plan and then extend it out to 60, 90, and 120 days or longer. Keep in mind that it is very difficult to migrate during the actual crisis when everyone else is trying to migrate as well. One can see examples of this in many of today's war zone migrations.

If you are under 30 and you and your family want to survive longer in relative peace, you will want to move north well before the worst of this emergency hits. If you are over 30 without a family or, if you are older than 50, you may feel that because of your shorter life expectancy or lack of dependents, migration to extend either the quality or length of your life may not be practical or necessary, no matter how bad it gets.

Where and when to migrate

Migration is a personal decision no matter what age you are. If you are going to migrate, here are some helpful things to consider:

- In general, moving north of the 45th parallel or south of the 45th parallel should be the safest, but always check the most current computer models and predictions because some areas above the 45 parallel north, particularly in Europe, will still be unsafe. "Safety" considerations always should include availability of water and defensibility.

Migrating North or South of the 45th Parallel

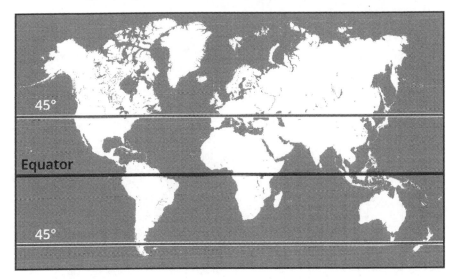

- Some existing areas between the 45th parallel north and south will remain safe and viable longer because of changes in weather patterns, ocean currents, temperatures, and the jet stream. Predicting where these areas will be difficult because of the continuous changes and corresponding consequences as global warming continues. Many climate researchers are already trying to predict these safer zones for various investment banking houses, commodity traders, and the ultra-wealthy.

- Countries like Canada, Scandinavia, Russia, Iceland, Greenland, England, New Zealand and the tip of South America and Alaska will most likely experience a warmer and longer growing season and improved weather conditions in the early stages of the global warming emergency. As global warming escalates, these countries and locations will most likely become the world's new richest and most powerful nations because of their more climate-safe locations and new "friendly" warming. These countries will likely form new military alliances that will initially attempt to ensure that other global-warming-challenged nations will not be able to take their land and sovereignty. These global warming-challenged nations will be motivated to extreme aggressive behavior because of starvation and chaos within their borders. Eventually, all borders previously thought to be safe will be breached, once again leaving migration just a temporary solution.

- If you choose to migrate and things don't turn around quickly, the good news is that most of us will still have at least 6-10 years before:

- We cross the carbon 425-450 ppm battle line as well as more tipping points where entering the mid phases of the Climageddon Scenario is *highly probable*. (Once we cross that point, tens if not hundreds of millions of informed and prudent individuals across the world will migrate to stay ahead of the ever-escalating catastrophe curve.)

- The temporarily safer areas and countries (or other luckily positioned areas) charge millions of dollars *per person* to migrate *legally, and/or otherwise restrict or completely close their borders to the ever-escalating masses of new climagees.*

- Land prices skyrocket in those areas and countries while real estate prices crash or drop steeply in the areas most negatively impacted by global warming.

- Trying to migrate to one of these temporarily safer areas after breaching carbon 425-450 ppm is a plan doomed to either fail or be plagued with hardship and suffering. If you think that is an overstatement, consider the hundreds of thousands of drought and political migrants from Africa and the Middle East who have been struggling in recent years to get into Europe, Scandinavia, Germany, or England.

- *Always* study the latest supercomputer global warming weather and other current prediction models at global, national, and local levels before you consider where to migrate! As new data on the emergency is released, the supercomputer weather models will continue to evolve to higher predictive accuracy. Be certain you are always looking at the latest data! A lasting change in the jetstream or an ocean current can consistently and radically affect weather all over the world.

- You will need to be highly certain that the rain, water sources, soils, and growing seasons will be adequate in the new area or nation that you want to migrate to. Carefully consider issues like wildfires, sea level rise, flood plains of rivers and lakes, as well as how defensible and safe your new location or nation will be as desperate climagees seek safety in the later phases of the Climageddon Scenario. Additionally, if you are considering migrating out of your home country, you will need to evaluate how your new country will receive, treat, and protect you as a new immigrant. Unfortunately, in many countries, immigrants are often treated as second-class citizens.

- Essential to any decision regarding whether to migrate or not is a need to evaluate if the new location you select will work for your long-term future—*even if there were not a global warming emergency* or we manage to resolve it later. In other words, if you have changed your life profoundly by migrating to this new location, will you still like living there if we were to resolve the global warming emergency before we go over the cliff into irreversible global warming?

- And finally, ask yourself if your new chosen location includes enjoyable and/or suitable work opportunities available for your knowledge, experience, or skill set.

For more information on short- and long-term migration to cities in North America, click here.[169]

The above global warming emergency preparedness information can seem a little scary unless you view it from a bigger perspective. Here are a few key points to remember about preparedness in general:

1. Being prepared for emergencies, catastrophic miscalculations, and future uncertainties by creating emergency plans, physical reserves, and backup system resilience is as old as humanity itself.

2. Being physically and psychologically prepared for emergencies is the most basic form of insurance. It existed long before we ever began paying premiums to today's insurance companies.

3. The history of emergency relief efforts during Hurricane Katrina and other climate catastrophes around the world *has demonstrated* most people will not have

---

[169] Jonah Engel Bromwich. "Where should you live to escape the harshest effects of climate change?" *The New York Times.* October 20, 2016.
http://www.nytimes.com/2016/10/20/science/9-cities-to-live-in-if-youre-worried-about-climate-change.html?_r=o

either the resources or time to create an emergency recovery program *during an actual emergency.* Just before or during the emergency, everything you will need to be safe will be long gone off the shelves, not working, or unavailable as others desperately struggle to quickly find what they need to survive. As a rule, if you're not well prepared *long before* the emergency, you're out of luck.

4. Emergency relief history has also shown people will initially be kind and share their resources up to the point they realize the essential life-sustaining resources have become scarce. Then they usually switch over to the Darwinian "do whatever you have to do to survive" mode.

5. No government or charity will have the ongoing capacity to respond to the ever-increasing global demands for more emergency resources and services as the costs and other consequences of escalating global warming increase in frequency, scale, and severity with each degree of temperature increase.

If you are seriously considering migration as a temporary solution to extend the length and quality of your life, consider all possible positive and negative factors before choosing any particular migration location. At this point, whether humanity is marching into a *silent future* unthinkably worse in threat, scale, and severity than the *Silent Spring* described by Rachel Carson[170] depends upon what we do now to execute the primary action steps of the Job One Plan.

---

[170] Rachel Carson. *Silent Spring.* (Houghton Mifflin, 1962.)

Step 5: Find ways to enjoy your life each day in spite of the escalating global warming emergency.

To stay motivated while you help resolve our global warming challenge and to survive the transitional catastrophes, you will need to preserve your psychological resilience and your emotional reserves. You can build and preserve this resilience and maintain these emotional reserves by:

1. taking time every day to do the normal things you enjoy and that renew you,

2. taking time for cultivating and enjoying your relationships,

3. taking time each day to do and experience things you may have delayed, and

4. taking time to draw strength and renewal from your faith and faith community, if you are of a spiritual nature.

As we move into greater global warming consequences and increasing climate destabilization, it is critical to take one day at a time and always make time to have fun, renewing experiences. The importance of taking one day at a time and doing whatever you can each day to fully enjoy the life that you have *right now* is that it will allow you to emotionally and physically survive, as well as effectively contribute toward the hopeful eventual resolution of the global warming emergency.

> "The art of life is to know how to enjoy a little and to endure much."
>
> — William Hazlitt,
> English writer, philosopher, and critic

Never forget that the scope of the task before us is daunting and unprecedented. If one fully understands how much has to change in the world *in so little time*, in such *major ways* within our lifestyles, livelihoods, and within our energy, political, economic, and social systems, one can get overwhelmed quickly. This is why it is important to embrace these perspectives of "one day at a time" and enjoy your normal life right now.

Because of the consequences looming over us and the fact that there are no guarantees we will resolve this emergency in time, another reason to enjoy each day now is because our current lives and conditions may in fact be *the best they will ever be*.

Your next vaccination

We can still work together to *significantly* slow and lessen the pain, suffering, and death of escalating global warming

The silver lining here is that no matter what, every *effective action* to rein in global warming that we do now will slow or lessen the suffering to come! The key is to focus on the most effective primary action steps in their prioritized order to first slow and lessen, then resolve this emergency. There is always something everyone can do within their "zone of influence" to reduce suffering for as long as possible.

What's next

The following chapter contains three more vaccinations that can be emotionally helpful and supportive as you finish Part 2 of this book.

Summary

- Build resilience into your existing personal, community, and national systems. To establish your basic personal recovery *resilience*, create at least a 30-day reserve (60-90 days would be much better as things get worse) of all necessary survival commodities (food, water, heat, energy, lights, toiletries, communication devices, maps, medicines, and self-defense, etc.).

- Build backup redundancies into your water, power, heating, sewage, and other critical systems. Do this now so you and your loved ones will not be unprepared, suffer unnecessarily or die.

- A cash and a tradeable commodity emergency reserve helps you build early phase financial resilience by building up and storing an easily exchangeable commodity now that you can easily use later when needed. In the later Climageddon Scenario phases, when cash may be no longer accepted or is devalued, you will need to have food, water, medicine, weapons and maybe small silver coins or other in-demand tradeable commodities to survive in a barter system that will surely evolve.

- Because we have already begun crossing global warming tipping points, business planners, city planners, long-term corporate and governmental planners of all kinds need to begin restructuring their 5, 10 and 25-year plans, always using the *least* optimistic climate prediction scenarios (found in previous chapters) for how the consequences of escalating global warming will unfold. We will be very lucky if the *worst* we get are the IPCC's current least optimistic projections!

- Mobility will be a key life-saving capability during the worst phases of the global warming emergency and mid-to-late Climageddon Scenario phases. Our crisis-surviving ancestors have repeatedly proven the validity and importance of this mobility (migration) principle.

- No government or charity will be able to respond to the ever-increasing global demands for more emergency resources and services as the costs and other consequences of escalating global warming increase in frequency, scale, and severity with each degree of temperature increase.

- Being physically and psychologically prepared for emergencies is the most basic form of insurance and is as old as humanity itself. It existed long before we ever began paying premiums to today's insurance companies.

- The more people who know when and where to migrate, the more people who will have better quality of life for a longer period of time.

- In addition to the necessary physical emergency preparations, to survive and thrive while dealing with what's coming, you will need to build and *preserve* your psychological and emotional *resilience*.

- The emergency climate preparedness recommended in the Job One Plan is never wasted. The Job One Plan not only assists individuals with strategies to temporarily survive the current global warming emergencies and catastrophes, but also many of its emergency preparation steps will also help ensure that you can survive after many other major global challenges and emergencies.

- Just as there are no guarantees in life, there are also no guarantees humanity will be able to resolve the escalating global warming emergency before it becomes irreversible or moves into the later phases of the Climageddon Scenario. Therefore, in this emergency if you would like to survive a little longer and a bit more comfortably, prudence dictates having an emergency survival plan for yourselves and loved ones, as well as having our businesses, community, and nation at the ready long before it will be needed.

- If we do enter the later phases of the Climageddon Scenario, we are in a no-win situation. No areas of the planet will be safe or secure other than on *a temporary basis.*
- Individuals who prepare to survive ecological catastrophes like the escalating global warming emergency are known as *eco-preppers.* There is an extensive network of Prepper websites dedicated to different survival and preparedness strategies and philosophies.

PART 2, CHAPTER 5

VACCINATIONS FROM OUR EVOLUTIONARY HISTORY TO HELP OFFSET ALL THE BAD NEWS

By this time, the gargantuan challenges of the escalating global warming emergency have probably invaded your thoughts and life. You may discover as others have that it is considerably easier to live with and through this emergency once you see the bigger picture from an evolutionary perspective.

To understand our global warming emergency from this bigger-picture perspective, consider a short overview of evolutionary history and a few relevant evolutionary principles. This may at first seem a little complex, but by the end of this chapter, you should glean enough to find significant relief and balance regarding the challenges of this emergency.

13.7 billion years of evolutionary success suggests we should be able to get through the global warming emergency

Life on Earth has *successfully* survived over 3.5 billion years of biological evolution. Through Earth's five previous Great Extinctions and First Evolutionary Bottleneck (described in Part 1, Chapter 1) life has survived, *and it will most likely go on now as well!*

When one sees our current trend toward irreversible or extinction level global warming from the perspective of 13.7 billion years of successful universe evolution, 4.5 billion years of successful planetary evolution, 3.5 billion years of successful biological evolution, as well as 10,000 years of successful human civilization, it once again puts things into perspective. From this very long-term evolutionary perspective, encouraging facts, trends and patterns emerge for dealing with the steep adaptive challenges of the global warming emergency.

In the previous Five Great Extinction Events, occurring long before the developing Climageddon Scenario extinction event depicted on the left in the illustration below, 50-90% of all the species that existed at the time became extinct. Yet, life and evolution still carried on by moving into new species, and some new species became the next dominant species.

Migrating North or South of the 45th Parallel

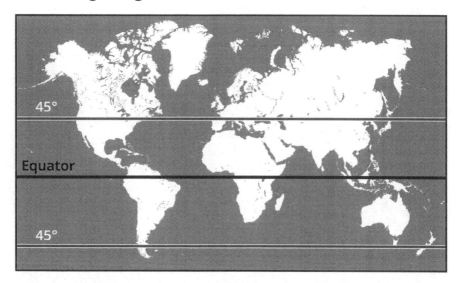

Some of these five previous Great Extinction Events occurred slowly, taking many thousands of years. The recovery of species density and population after each of the Five Great Extinction Events took an average of 10 million years.

Extinction, collapse, retrogression, and renewal are all built into the evolutionary processes. They are a natural and healthy part of normal evolution.

Looking at the *wide sweep* of our whole evolutionary history, we do have a few other valid big-picture reasons to offer hope that we can rise to overcome this great global warming adaptive challenge and evolutionary adventure:

a. What is unique today that did not exist in any of the previously mentioned Five Great Extinction Events is that our species can intelligently and rationally reflect upon its own behavior, as well as upon the evolutionary processes of the planet and universe it lives within. This species effectively gathers new knowledge and useful feedback from its environment, and is highly adaptable in modifying its behavior once it perceives a real threat.

b. Over history, this species has also organized cooperation on larger and larger scales. It has evolved from small hunter-gatherer groups, to agrarian villages, to warrior city-states, to great nations, and now to international cooperative alliances of multiple nations, such as the European Union. This unique species, namely us, truly does have the best evolutionary advantage in resolving the current global warming emergency.

c. When one also looks at the evolution of the universe as a whole system, from its very beginning to the present, one sees recurring natural processes and patterns, which are also supportive of the idea that we as a species should be able to overcome the global warming challenge. Two of those reassuring deep evolutionary patterns are:

   1. Evolution seems to most often work out for the good of the evolving whole, and

   2. In spite of how it looks right now, the progress of evolution is currently the best it's ever been! (At least from what we know in our little corner of the universe.)

This suggests that alignment with natural evolutionary processes themselves should also help to preserve at least enough of human and other species on the planet so that our evolutionary process can go on and we can learn from the global warming challenge. Because evolution has in fact progressed to "the best it's ever been" and produced an amazingly adaptable and intelligent species—humanity—we *really do have* the best chance of any species in all of evolutionary history to meet this global warming challenge and cooperate in new ways to resolve it.

> "Evolution is science's greatest discovery, the most trial-and-error tested, time-proven sustainable success system that has ever existed, and it is the best documented 'theory of everything' that currently exists." — Lawrence Wollersheim, Executive Director at Job One for Humanity

Evolution tends to do everything simultaneously

Evolution tends to do everything *simultaneously*. In one place, it will move progressively forward; in another, it will be in a retrogression phase. In other places, it will appear to meander seemingly without aim.

In another place, it will be moving into a state of destructive creation. Destructive creation is defined as the breakdown and recycling of non-learning, non-adaptive or "non-cooperating" parts or wholes.

Nothing is wasted in universe evolution. This core meta-pattern of continuous breakdown and recycling allows evolutionary "failed experiments," retrogressions, or other failed adaptations, collapses, and extinctions to be reused later on in some other new evolutionary creativity and experiments— hence the term *destructive creation*.

In other places, evolution will appear to be holding a somewhat steady state. Elsewhere, it will appear to stop, stall, or fail (go extinct) in that line of evolutionary development.

Even though evolution is doing all of these things simultaneously, as a *whole system*, there is still a general and natural *progression* occurring within the whole universe system. Looking back over evolutionary history, evolution also appears to be naturally progressing in the direction of increased complexity, adaptability, learning, intelligence, and cooperation, etc.

All this leads to the following bit of good news. In what can initially appear to be failing or stalling activities within the natural progression of any of evolution's processes, there also are silver linings. Here are some of those silver linings as they emerge from the different processes of evolution as it concerns global warming. Each one will be expanded upon later in this chapter:

a. The *destructive creation* process of global warming can hasten and facilitate major structural and systemic changes that may not be possible by any other means than the complete destruction of non-adaptive parts or wholes.

b. The natural evolutionary *compression and retrogression* phases of escalating global warming can also facilitate or catalyze positive outcomes.

   "Every adversity...carries with it the seed of an equal or greater benefit."
                      — Napoleon Hill, personal success author

The destructive creation process of global warming can hasten and facilitate necessary structural and systemic changes that may not be possible by any other means.

Destructive creation is one of the key processes of evolution. Once all "non-learning," non-adaptive, and "non-cooperating" parts or wholes involved in the global warming emergency are recycled by natural evolutionary processes, their resources can be reused *later* in a new, more sustainable evolutionary experiments.

The following can seem a little complex and harsh, but there are practical applications and reasons for this time-tested evolutionary principle. For example, many individuals who have survived great catastrophes and collapses in their lives (periods of destructive creation) have said that the catastrophe or collapse gave them the chance to see aspects of their lives or their world that had been hidden behind *veils of denial*. They also said that their life catastrophe or collapse was *absolutely essential* at that time to finally give them the opportunity to change, restructure, and take more responsibility for what they had finally discovered behind the veils of denial.

Historically, great catastrophe or collapse (destructive creation) has often also preceded a period of great renewal, advancement, and growth. In the last Five Great Extinction Events occurring over the last 3 billion years on Earth, when 50-90% of all species died, some species always adapted and survived. A new apex species *always evolved* that was better equipped to deal with the new environment.

As a simple cultural example of this idea of how greater good can come out of catastrophic events, consider the Dark Ages and the Black Death—a combined millennium period ending in the 14th century. The great destructive creation of this bleak period was eventually followed by the great advances of the Enlightenment Age of human history where, among other wonderful advances, *modern science* was born.

If global warming continues to escalate unchecked, it will bring about its own natural period of evolutionary destructive creation. This destructive creation might be in the forms of a cleansing or re-aligning collection of superstorms, droughts, flooding, wildfires, soil degradation, changing growing seasons, and other global warming-related catastrophes. Maybe we will even enter into a new kind of *temporary* "Dark Ages" period.

After this destructive creation phase, it will be far more likely that whatever remains of humanity will finally be ready to *pay attention* and learn the hard global warming lessons humanity currently seems reluctant to face and learn. To say the least, these new lessons would include building green energy generation, good atmospheric stewardship, sustainability, and better global cooperation.

If we have to go through this "necessary" but painful destructive creation phase to resolve the global warming emergency, humanity will experience a simultaneous *collective Holocaust-like "never again" trauma*, but at a scale larger than any other in our history. This deep, excruciating collective trauma and memory would also act to help prevent such global warming-caused destabilization of the climate from ever occurring again.

Seeing life and evolution continuing on from a big-picture perspective is poignantly helpful in this situation. If our planetary civilization has become so fossilized in protecting the status quo that it has lost its ability to adapt and effectively resolve global warming, there is little doubt that a global catastrophe and meltdown of unprecedented scale will eventually occur, including the widespread ecological, social, economic, and political and biological collapses described in the later phases of the Climageddon Scenario.

If we do not pay attention and resolve the escalating global warming emergency soon, as a last resort to save the future, it may be necessary for human civilization to temporarily collapse under the weight of this unfolding, unresolved challenge. This then may finally allow a new and better civilization with adaptable political, economic, and social systems and values to emerge in the post-collapse, with remaining survivors now *very willing* to change to something new, less painful, and less dysfunctional.

Maybe only through a new and massive destructive creation episode in what is already being called the *Sixth Great Extinction* will we be able to bring about a restructured, realigned, and more sustainable global political, social, and economic order, as well as a new, more just, and appropriate way of living sustainably for *all of* Earth's inhabitants.

It is also reasonable to believe the destructive creation portended by our currently escalating global warming emergency will eventually also force us to resolve global warming's deepest underlying structural and systemic causes. In order to stop burning fossil fuels in time to prevent irreversible or near-extinction-level global warming, we will eventually have to face the structural and systemic roots supporting fossil fuel burning as well as our unsustainable paradigm of infinite economic growth.[171]

A few of the deeply-rooted problems that continue to support the fossil fuel energy generating paradigm are:

1. Rapidly rising population and overpopulation. We have far too many people for the Earth's carrying capacity. As our population escalates, so do our energy generation needs.

2. Unsustainable development in all its forms. As part of the long-term structural solution to global warming (as well as our other major current global challenges), we will eventually be forced to evolve sustainable development—more sustainable lifestyles, livelihoods, communities, and nations. We have already waited too long and we now need to activate a global warming emergency mobilization (GWEM) to enact far beyond Manhattan Project-scaled solutions in order to move rapidly from dirty fossil fuel energy generation to clean, green energy generation. Simultaneously, we will also need to quickly move away from our current

---

[171] Meadows, Donella H., Meadows, Dennis L., Randers, Jørgen, Behrens, William W. III. *The Limits to Growth.* (New York: Universe Books, 1972).
http://collections.dartmouth.edu/teitexts/meadows/diplomatic/meadows_ltg-diplomatic.html

unsustainable carbon/methane polluting associated with big agribusiness practices.

3. A lack of an empowered global government backed by verifiable and enforceable international law that can effectively manage and regulate cross-border meta-challenges like global warming-caused climate destabilization.The lack of effective global government represents a deep structural threat to the health, stability, and future of all of Earth's inhabitants and its future generations.

4. A global economic system and economic rules that do not work to support and sustain our critical human *life-supporting* ecosystems.[172] The Job One for Humanity Plan and the additional principles of *sustainable prosperity* found in Appendix 3 already contain many specifics of what changes need to be made to the world's current lifestyle and livelihood systems to make the resolution of global warming permanent. We can still get ourselves out of this emergency, but eventually we must also change the deepest structural causes of this emergency. Luckily we don't have to change *all* of these deep structural issues first to solve the global warming emergency.

To make these changes and adapt successfully, eventually we *will* be forced to engage in a massive restructuring and realignment of our economic, social, and political systems. (Maybe even some of our religious systems as well to deal with overpopulation and the moral duties of environmental stewardship.) In their current state of evolutionary development, some of the conditions, rules, assumptions, and

---

[172] Jason Hickel. "Clean energy won't save us – only a new economic system can." *The Guardian.* July 15, 2016. https://www.theguardian.com/global-development-professionals-network/2016/jul/15/clean-energy-wont-save-us-economic-system-can

values of these economic, social, and political systems are among the fundamental underlying causes that have fueled global warming, sustain it, and allow it to expand without resolution.

The silver lining here is that even if we continue to ignore or move too slowly to restabilize the climate, eventually the natural evolutionary process of destructive creation will come to our aid and force us to change or perish.

Cause-and-effect consequences and unbearable calamities will eventually force better evolutionary adaption upon those individuals or groups not paying attention to problems in their environments. It wonderfully and naturally does this by increasing the levels of painful consequences until the pain of the increasing calamity finally gets the individual's or group's attention focused back onto the denied, ignored, or unhandled problem.

This helps to get these individuals or groups to begin resolving their denied or deferred problems. Evolution has wisely discovered that many individuals and groups will not evolve and resolve what is challenging them until they deeply feel that the pain of going forward is less than the pain of staying where they are.

The natural compression and retrogression periods of global warming will also facilitate moving toward positive outcomes.

Evolution has natural "compression and retrogression" periods. Compression and retrogression periods are those times when things get pushed together tightly, creating increased tension. Sometimes those tensions do not resolve and the inaction causes a kind of temporary centralizing effect, compression, or retrogression.

Whether you are aware of it and in spite of how it appears to most people, we are in one of those natural evolutionary compression/retrogression periods. This particular natural evolutionary compression/retrogression period is being fueled by our many unresolved current global challenges such as resource depletion, global warming, economic inequality and instability, poverty, overpopulation, other environmental pollution and ecological degradation not caused by global warming, terrorism conflicts and wars leading to political and social instability, and even growing pandemic risks.

Of our current global challenges, escalating global warming should be seen as the Job One keystone challenge humanity *has to overcome* to survive. While there is much to be deeply concerned about in all of our other global challenges, accelerating global warming consequences and crossing more tipping points are the largest immediate *threat multiplier* for almost all of the other global challenges mentioned.

It is also important to grasp that these natural evolutionary compressions and retrogressions can serve to produce silver linings. When things are not adapting well, natural evolutionary compression and retrogression periods intensify the adaptive challenge's pain or loss.

Evolution does this "instinctively" so that the building pressure and pent-up "energy" of the compression period can be released (like releasing a compressed spring) to help break the existing change-resistant inertia to "energize" and mobilize the needed critical change and adaptation. Again, an example of this normally recurring evolutionary compression and retrogression cycle in history would be how after the previously mentioned painful compression and retrogression period of the European Dark Ages, humanity once again surged forward into the great European Renaissance period.

Our *current* natural evolutionary compression and retrogression period is defined by:

I.   How our global warming and other global challenges are still escalating and colliding into each other and potentially moving ever faster toward a *catastrophic mega-convergence*.

II.   How we still appear functionally unable to evolve the necessary effective global governmental mechanisms with appropriate enforcement and verification powers to resolve our escalating cross-border global challenges.

If left unresolved, this natural, intensifying evolutionary compression and retrogression process acting upon all of our current converging global challenges will catastrophically destabilize and regress most, if not all, of the planet to some less developed state.

The silver linings in all this seemingly bad news are:

I.   This hopefully should be a temporary compressive destabilization and retrogression period.

II.   It should also eventually lead to a great surge forward of positive growth for humanity.

III.   It's just another natural adaptive challenge in the great transformational, evolutionary adventure, and progress of evolving life on this planet and in the universe. And

IV.   Everything we have to do to restabilize the global climate on an urgent, first-things-first basis also directly or indirectly supports building more sustainable lifestyles and livelihoods and a *sustainable prosperity* for all. So none of our efforts in resolving global warming *will ever be wasted!*

There's a bit more helpful knowledge about evolutionary compressions and retrogressions. Sometimes, after a sudden or strong growth state, a natural evolutionary compression and retrogression will take place. If this compression/retrogression state is successfully adapted to, the compression lessens or stabilizes or even reverses itself into a new growth state. If the compression and retrogression state is not successfully adapted to, it usually results in a deeper *secondary* compression and retrogression period that may then finally have enough compressed and *pent-up energy* "coiled" within itself to *spring forward* out of the secondary deeper compression/retrogression to some new more optimal state.

How the cycles and phases of evolution relate to the current global warming compression/retrogression potentiality is telling for the future of humanity. If we do not adapt sufficiently to the global warming emergency, it is reasonable and probable to expect our various social, economic, and political systems will compress upon themselves, and possibly collapse and regress to some prior, less stable developmental state in an effort to re-establish a lower level *order* for survival. Failing to resolve this natural evolutionary compression and retrogression and continuing on the current global warming trajectory leads to a global evolutionary compression and retrogression *outcome* that no rational human being would ever want to allow or experience. It would be similar to taking society into a dystopian Mad Max-like world.

To many of society's thoughtful individuals, it appears our national and global cultures are entering one of those exciting and opportunity-rich destabilizing and retrogressing evolutionary periods—one that is also hopefully transitory. This period may develop into one, several or all of the following:

a. several natural compression and retrogression periods,
b. a second great evolutionary bottleneck,
c. a massive cataclysmic adaptive readjustment, or even possibly
d. a massive global systems collapse in an unfortunate and extreme act of self-induced destructive creation, resulting in an extinction-level event.

We have now entered into an age of potential destructive creation, a natural evolutionary compression and retrogression period, and a global mega-emergency far beyond the management capabilities of our fractionalized national interests and governments. This is a dangerous place. Hopefully, we will eventually adapt by evolving and ending the global warming emergency.

PART 2, CHAPTER 6

CLIMAGEDDON CONCLUSION

In *Climageddon* we have strived to make a fair, logical, and well documented case for the truth and importance of the premises we proposed in the first chapter. In the process, we hope we have provided you with an understandable new global warming prediction model that helps you visualize the complex and intertwined climate processes, time frames, and consequences to better plan your future using the daunting current realities of the global warming emergency.

Daunting realities

As the book makes clear, there is no sugar-coating the circumstances we are in. Among these key daunting realities, we now know:

- Today's global warming emergency is not a natural disaster or a natural cyclical climate phase. It is a human-made disaster caused mostly by the carbon released from burning fossil fuels since the Industrial Revolution.

- Life on Earth has flourished best when atmospheric carbon levels were in a range of 200-270 ppm in the preindustrial ages. Our current carbon level is 407 ppm—and rising. Due to carbon's "staying power" in the atmosphere, higher global temperatures will persist for generations. A 450 ppm carbon level (which will occur in about 10-15 years at present carbon pollution rates) could eventually increase average global temperature by 6° Celsius (10.8° Fahrenheit) in this century and end human civilization as we know it.

- Large-scale disruptions to our atmosphere, climate, and environment that normally happen over thousands of years are now happening over decades. These consequences will increase in scale, frequency, and severity and become ever more unpredictable.

- As we cross global warming tipping points, we increasingly lose control. Global warming catastrophes and crossed tipping points will amplify consequences and multiply existing weaknesses within the world's political, economic, social, and ecological systems.

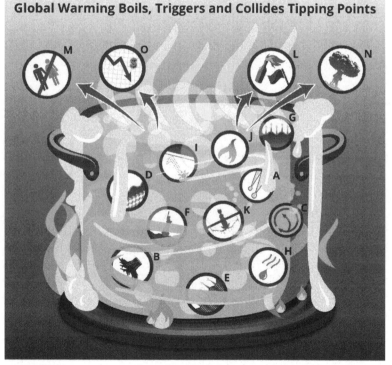

Global Warming Boils, Triggers and Collides Tipping Points

A - Melting Ice	**F** - Weight of Rising Seas	**K** - Plankton Dying
B - Forest Loss	**G** - Soils Overheating	**L** - National Instability
C - Ocean Current Change	**H** - Water Vapor Increase	**M** - Social Instability
D - Permafrost Pandemic	**I** - Albedo Effect	**N** - War & Conflict
E - Ocean Heating	**J** - Methane Release	**O** - Economic Loss & Collapse

- When you factor in the crossing of more global warming tipping points into consequence predictions scenarios, our world is in serious peril, not 40 or 80 years from now as we're being told, *but now and over the next 20-40 years.*

- If we reach the later phases of the Climageddon Scenario, no government, individual, or corporation— however strong or wealthy—will survive more than temporarily in the far north or far south.

- If we keep going as we are now, by the time the harsh facts about our global warming future become generally known and undeniable, it will be far too late to do anything about fixing it.

The following three illustrations are provided to help you see how escalating global warming emergency and the unfolding Climageddon Scenario create the *ultimate* security threat and greatest accelerating disruptor of the 21st century.

Escalating global warming is going to be expensive. Please review the following illustration and get a sense of just how expensive each incident will average in cost as we move through the Climageddon Scenario phases.

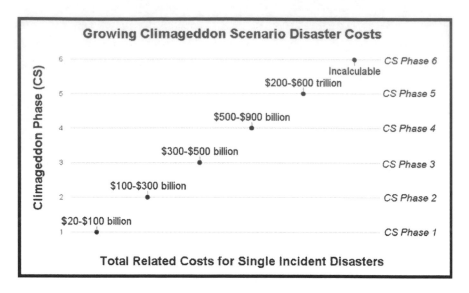

Knowing how fast temperatures will rise as we move from one phase to another will be invaluable in helping you to adjust you planning, adaptation, and migration strategies. Unfortunately, human history suggests that there will be little public demand to resolve global warming until its catastrophes reach unbearable cost thresholds.

Temperatures Above Preindustrial for Climageddon Scenario

CS Phase	Celsius	Fahrenheit
1	1.7°-2.2°	3°-4°
2	2.5°-3.2°	4.5°-5.8°
3	2.7°-3.5°	4.9°-6.3°
4	4°-4.5°	7.2°-8°
5	5°-6°	9°-10.8°
6	Unknown	Unknown

Knowing approximately when each phase of the Climageddon Scenario will occur will provide critical advance warning concerning steep increases in the many global warming consequences associated with entering each new phase.

Estimated Timetable for Climageddon Scenario

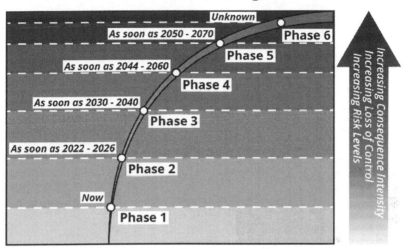

There is a last battle line and it acts similarly to a tipping point. If we cross the carbon 425-450 ppm battle line (as shown below,) and we fail to achieve carbon neutrality and a complete transition to green energy generation by 2026, the sufficient and necessary remaining control needed to manage our global warming future will drop off steeply.

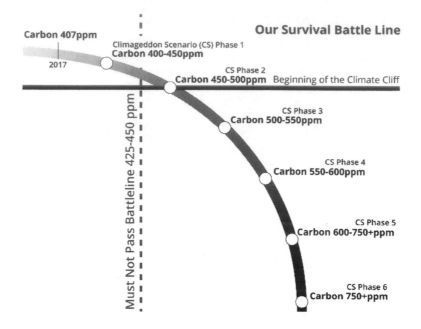

Our Survival Battle Line

Carbon 407ppm

2017

Climageddon Scenario (CS) Phase 1
Carbon 400-450ppm

CS Phase 2
Carbon 450-500ppm Beginning of the Climate Cliff

CS Phase 3
Carbon 500-550ppm

CS Phase 4
Carbon 550-600ppm

CS Phase 5
Carbon 600-750+ppm

CS Phase 6
Carbon 750+ppm

Must Not Pass Battleline 425-450 ppm

Viable solutions

The realities are stark. The challenges are intimidating. And there are no guarantees. But there are ideas with imagination and viability, as presented in the Job One Plan.

The key points of the Job One Plan to end global warming are:

- We must scale up and transition globally to nearly 100% renewable global green energy generation by 2026 and scale down fossil fuel use to ensure achieving carbon neutrality (net zero carbon) for all greenhouse gases by 2026.

- To resolve escalating global warming in time to save ourselves, we need mass mobilization from the top down using *verifiable and enforceable* global warming reduction laws and treaties to execute all of the simultaneous changes needed. We simply no longer have enough time left to adequately educate the public, mobilize enough political will, and sway politicians from the bottom up.

- We need financial incentives and penalties as proven facilitators for rapid and radical behavioral change. New national and international Fee and Dividend laws and treaties will help the world to change its fossil fuel behavior at the greatest possible speed.

- We need to entrust ongoing risk analysis and predictions for escalating global warming to national intelligence agencies as the most responsible, most qualified, and most influential entities.

- Because there are no guarantees this emergency can be solved before it becomes irreversible or moves into the later phases of the Climageddon Scenario, prudence dictates we have emergency survival plans for ourselves and loved ones, as well as ensuring that our businesses, community, and nation are fully prepared for what is coming.

- We must make the world's wealthiest corporations, individuals and celebrities (power centers) primarily responsible for resolving the global warming emergency. Average citizens simply do not have the necessary influence and control over our politicians. We have to persistently convince these power centers that there is no lasting escape, no matter how much money or power they might have. Once the world's power centers understand this is the ultimate no win game, they will follow their own highest self-interests which is always to save themselves <u>first</u> and, in doing so, they will save us all!

Imposing challenges

We still have many unique challenges to overcome.

- Three out of every 10 people will never acknowledge that the global warming emergency exists no matter how much valid science they read or how many painful global warming consequences engulf their lives. Often this is because the facts conflict with their deepest political, religious or social worldview, peer group values, or self-interests.

- At this moment, research into global warming in the United States has been blocked and has lost funding. Existing research is being removed from U.S. government websites. Purportedly to create more jobs, regulations are being gutted, many of which were working to reduce fossil fuel pollution. Blocking research on methane pollution is particularly dangerous, since it is one of the most destructive of all global warming gases and is steadily increasing, in part due to the relentless fracking boom.

- Despite being the world's most recognized authority on global warming, the United Nations Intergovernmental Panel On Climate Change (IPCC) has consistently underestimated consequence and intensity and timetables. The IPCC's general underestimation bias will create nightmares for those relying on that information and trying to do safe mid-term or long-term planning, whether it be on the personal, business, city, or national level.

- Many critical global warming system and subsystem tipping points are still not well researched. Without that vital information, we are in essence accelerating toward the *climate cliff* blindfolded.

Interacting Global Warming Tipping Points

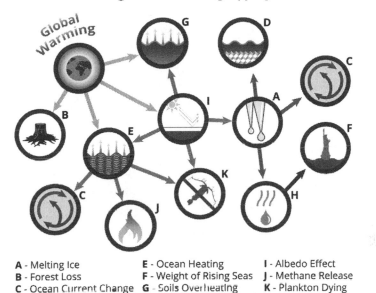

A - Melting Ice	**E** - Ocean Heating	**I** - Albedo Effect
B - Forest Loss	**F** - Weight of Rising Seas	**J** - Methane Release
C - Ocean Current Change	**G** - Soils Overheating	**K** - Plankton Dying
D - Permafrost Pandemic	**H** - Water Vapor Increase	

- By 2050, we may need as much as 40% more energy production to keep up with the world's population growth. This exerts additional pressures on the aim of replacing all existing fossil fuel-generated energy by 2026.

- The fossil fuel industry will not give up its lucrative profits to become good corporate citizens. They will fight to the death to protect their interests at the expense of our common well-being.

- Within a few decades, global warming-related catastrophes will consume at least 5% or more of the total U.S. GDP (gross domestic product) and that of many other countries. With most countries, including the U.S., already having substantial debt, maintaining solvency will be an intensifying challenge as global warming catastrophe recovery costs continue to escalate and eat up more and more of the GDP.

Worrisome unknowns

There are many known factors leading us to the truth of why there are no guarantees we'll resolve the global warming emergency in time to escape the Climageddon Scenario. In addition to the ones mentioned already within *Climageddon*, there are also other currently unknown or unpredictable factors.

- Average global temperatures could rise *much faster* than is "officially" being predicted. Around 9600 BCE, in what is known as the Boreal phase, Greenland ice core samples show global temperatures spiked 7° Celsius in less than a decade and sent sea levels soaring more than 12 feet over just a few decades. Very big temperature and sea level changes have happened in a very short amount of time before and they could happen just as quickly again!

- We could cross the last battle line of carbon 425 to 450 ppm and/or cross more points of no return and more global warming tipping points, making global warming irreversible.

- Sea levels could rise faster and to greater extents than expected.

- The growing methane leakage from fracking could lead to the "methane time bomb" starting to go off at a temperature increase of 5° Celsius from preindustrial levels. This could herald another Paleocene–Eocene Thermal Maximum-like extinction event.

- *Climageddon* itself (that is, this book) may fail to adequately illuminate the mostly invisible escalating global warming extinction threat in such a way as to trigger our evolutionary flight or fight mechanisms, or not reach enough people in time to motivate sufficient numbers to implement the effective last-chance Job One Plan actions.

- At a time when we need an unprecedented level of international cooperation, ultra-nationalism is rising rapidly around the world. This may set in motion countervailing forces to make a global warming resolution that much harder to achieve.

- Depending on whether we can scale up a full global green energy generation replacement in time, while we are also making all of the required drastic global fossil fuel use reductions, one unintended result could be a steep crash of the global economy that would destroy many nations, businesses and families financially.

Self-inflicted wounds

All the intertwining dynamics involved in the global warming resolution effort can lead to interesting, and perhaps pivotal, paradoxes. With its comparative global warming inaction, the U.S. may actually be harming itself long-term in unexpected ways. Consider just one.

China is the most likely nation to be the biggest economic winner in the run-up to Climageddon. China can quickly capture the market for manufacturing green energy generation equipment because of their existing manufacturing might, because they are a non-democratic, top-down directed economy, and because the United States is going in the wrong direction on regulating global warming and green energy generation incentives.

Meanwhile, the Europeans are still moving into the green energy generation transition far too slowly. As it appears now, China will acquire the greatest new energy generation transition financial benefit, which will be the rightful reward for whatever nation dominates the critical manufacturing processes for green energy generation equipment.

Hearing the call

Someone or something has to *make the call* for someone to *be called*. At first, you may think the unsettling facts of this book, the author, or the Job One organization are calling you to action to help resolve this emergency. You would be right, but perhaps only at a surface level.

Perhaps it is a call across time from future generations. Perhaps it is the call of our ancestors begging you to advance the 13.7-billion-year-old seemingly unstoppable impulse of universal evolution to go on. Maybe, if you are spiritual, the call is arising from the core values of your faith and the Great Mystery which your faith eternally serves.

It does not really matter what is calling you or how gently or strongly *this call is urging* you to act. It only matters that you act now, join others in action, and we wisely work together as one human family.

We *can* do this—because we *must* do this

If we provide enough creative influence and pressure at the points of maximum leverage as described in the Job One Plan, we can compel the world's politicians to enact all of the needed actions to save humanity in time. As we do this together, we will be overcoming humanity's greatest evolutionary challenge and engaging in humanity's greatest evolutionary adventure.

To assist you in getting into action, we listed a few additional things you can do in addition to the Job One for Humanity primary action steps found in Part 2, Chapter 2, and the scale up action list near the end of Part 2, Chapter 3. Here are a few short additional calls to action:

1. Get copies of *Climageddon* into the hands of people who should be reading it.
2. Please donate generously to support the people and organizations who are doing this critical work.[173]
3. Encourage other organizations to work on action steps compatible with the Job One Plan.
4. If you have a spiritual background, get your faith community out in front helping to resolve the global warming emergency through their great moral leverage.
5. Use your social media skills.
6. If you're working in an intelligence agency as an analyst, provide colleagues whatever they need to more fully understand the complexity, destructiveness, real deadlines and ever-diminishing control factor of this emergency.

If we fail to end the global warming emergency, it will be because we were unable to convince the world's wealthiest individuals, corporations, and power centers that only they have the necessary influence and power to solve this no win emergency before it becomes uncontrollable and descends into the last phases of the Climageddon Scenario.

Never forget many good things will happen in your life that you could not foresee when you act with Job One and the surging *global warming emergency mobilization* (GWEM) movement to help end global warming.

Always remember: you don't need anyone's permission to do good things in the world!

Thanks for reading *Climageddon*.

Lawrence Wollersheim

---

[173] Job One for Humanity. "Donate and Help End Global Warming." *JobOneforHumanity.gov.* Accessed March 23, 2016. http://factnet.nationbuilder.com/donate_job_one_for_humanity

FUTURE EPILOGUE

While writing *Climageddon*, I found my normal sense of peace and stability regularly disturbed by numerous unsettling research discoveries. As I shared bits and pieces of this information with friends and other environmental organizations, I soon discovered that those relationships would also experience levels of disruption as they tried to digest, reconcile, reject, or manage the alarming news I presented to them.

Right from the start, the unsettling information of *Climageddon* challenged the "elephant in the room" that no one really wanted to mention: the 30-year stalemate in resolving global warming and its quickly-approaching terminal consequences. These initial research discussions made even the most supportive friends and colleagues incredibly uncomfortable, because almost immediately, they too began to question the validity and meaning of their current lives and goals from within the new predictions, timetables and frameworks I was presenting.

This process was not dissimilar to how someone might question how to use their remaining time when their doctor tells them they have three months left to live. As you might imagine, it eventually got so bad that I was regularly asked not to be the "New Noah" or talk about *Climageddon* research at social events in order to "preserve the positive and social tone of the evening."

Discussing how escalating global warming has become the greatest threat to our collective survival and that, realistically, we have only had 6 to 10 years left to prevent a nearly uncontrollable process leading up to our extinction and the end of civilization as we know it, isn't exactly news anyone wants to ever hear.

In these passionate early discussions, I had unconsciously become an agent for the necessary disruption of our current inadequate global warming education. It has taken me quite a while to accept that prickly role.

After more discussions *Climageddon's* with friends, associates, and test readers, I was led to the idea that I should also provide a free post-publication epilogue for anyone who might want it. If you would like a deeper look into how *Climageddon* came into being, as well as additional insights as to where we are now in executing the Job One Plan post-*Climageddon* publication, go to this page http://www.joboneforhumanity.-org/climageddon_epilog after June 17, 2017 and follow the free epilogue instructions.

And finally, please do let me know anything you think would help make *Climageddon* more effective. I may not be able to answer every email because of volume, but I will always read every email and I will make adjustments or corrections to each new edition wherever necessary.

Lawrence Wollersheim, Lawrence@JobOneforHumanity.org

APPENDIX 1

THE JOB ONE PLAN ACTION STEPS MASTER CHECKLIST

The following checklist reflects the complete action step priorities of the Job One for Humanity Plan to end global warming. It is derived from the newly upgraded Job One for Humanity Plan found in *Climageddon*.

Use it to organize and coordinate your individual and collective Job One actions.

The Job One Primary Action and Primary Action Substeps

(Part 2, Chapter 2 of Climageddon)

❑ **Primary action step 1:** Demand an immediate emergency meeting of the world's politicians to:

   ❑ A. Declare a national and international "Global Warming State of Emergency" for the whole world.

   ❑ B. Declare the 2 critical new national and international goals and subgoals that, when reached by the 2026 deadline, will resolve the current global warming emergency.

   We cannot allow global warming to reach the carbon 425-450 ppm level.

Based on where we are now, the following are our only two valid *initial targets* that *must be* met:

1. Scale up and transition globally to nearly 100% renewable global green energy generation by 2026.

2. Scale down and reduce global fossil fuel use to ensure achieving carbon neutrality (net zero carbon) for all greenhouse gases by 2026.

3. Sign the petition[174] demanding an emergency global warming meeting of the world's leaders. Ask your friends to do the same.

❏ C. Create the new, verifiable, and enforceable national and international laws or treaties that will achieve adequate global warming reduction to meet the goals mentioned above and in time to save us as listed below.

❏ Demand the creation of a revenue neutral, Fee and Dividend-based global warming reduction program.

❏ Demand this fee and dividend income be used to:

---

[174] Job One for Humanity. "Declare a Global Warming State of Emergency." *JobOneforHumanity.org*. Accessed March 20, 2016.
http://www.joboneforhumanity.org/declare_a_global_warming_state_of_emergencyy

❑ Fund *appropriate* technologies [175] to help us rapidly achieve complete global green energy generation by 2026.

❑ Create employee retraining as well as a business and nation recovery fund that would assist all individuals, businesses, and nations that will suffer significant financial losses because of the rapidly falling use of fossil fuels.

❑ Fund global education and public relations campaigns on why we must comply with new, difficult, and costly global warming reduction laws or treaties and other changes that will be enforced by our governments.

❑ Fund other *appropriate* new technologies as an emergency back up if we fail to meet the two critical 2026 targets.

---

[175] Wikipedia contributors. "Appropriate technology." *Wikipedia, The Free Encyclopedia.* Accessed December 18, 2016. https://en.wikipedia.org/wiki/Appropriate_technology

❏ D. Demand world political leaders require their respective national intelligence agencies take immediate and full responsibility for re-analyzing current global warming research and rapidly reporting the updated security threats, predicted consequences, and new timetables.

❏ E. Have the world's political leaders demand *annual* global warming updates from their respective intelligence agencies, which going forward will always include projection scenarios for crossing more tipping points.

❏ F. Demand laws that will provide government subsidies and incentives for expanding green energy generation.

❏ G. Demand laws to increase natural carbon sequestration.

❏ H. Demand laws that will remove all government subsidies from fossil fuel energy generation.

❏ I. Demand new laws that will incentivize divestment from the dying fossil fuel energy generation industry.

❏ J. Demand new laws to tax all fossil fuel profits at significantly higher rates.

❏ H. Demand new international and national laws that mandate the creation of emergency recovery reserve funds equal to 5% of national GDP.

❑ I. Demand new laws mandating fossil fuel corporations pay for all present and past environmental damage from their product.

❑ J. Demand the International Monetary Fund and the World Trade Organization help call the emergency meeting of world's leaders and help facilitate the creation of verifiable and enforceable new global warming reduction laws or treaties.

❑ **Primary action step 2:** Scale up public education, collaboration and activism for individuals and organizations to work together effectively. (Partnerships and alliances as well.)

The Job One Supporting Action Steps
(Chapter 3, Part 2 of Climageddon)

❑ **Supporting action step A:** Begin contacting 1,000 celebrities to call for an immediate emergency meeting of the world's politicians to achieve primary action step 1 above.

❑ Decide which of the world's celebrities you want to contact. (The Job One Plan website will have some of this contact information and strategy.

Click here[176] to see this campaign's information and navigation page.)

❑ Find their contact information.

❑ Write or email the celebrities personal letters like those posted on the Job One For Humanity website.

❑ **Supporting action step B:** Begin contacting 1,000 of the world's wealthiest corporations through email and personal letters to call for an immediate emergency meeting of the world's politicians to achieve primary action step 1 above.

❑ Decide who you're going to contact first. (The Job One Plan website will have some of this contact information and strategy. Click here[177] to see this campaign's information and navigation page.)

❑ Connect with the recipient and make them care about your cause to call for an immediate emergency meeting of the world's politicians to achieve primary action step 1 above.

❑ Offer some positive strokes.

❑ Make sure you've researched the recipient.

---

[176] Job One for Humanity. "Climageddon Book Support Navigation Center." *JobOneforHumanity.org.* Accessed March 20, 2016. http://www.joboneforhumanity.org/climageddon_book_support_navigation_center

[177] Job One for Humanity. "Climageddon Book Support Navigation Center." *JobOneforHumanity.org.* Accessed March 20, 2016. http://www.joboneforhumanity.org/climageddon_book_support_navigation_center

❑ Request the recipient publicly declare their intent to help get the emergency meeting called and enact the necessary global warming reduction laws by lobbying politicians.

❑ Also ask the corporation to participate in the global planning and execution of the transition from fossil fuel energy generation to green energy generation and help the governments of the world in this area.

❑ Close with a personal appeal.

❑ If they respond, send a thank you and let the Job One for Humanity team know.

❑ **Supporting action step C:** Begin contacting 1,000 of the world's wealthiest individuals through email and personal letters to call for an immediate emergency meeting of the world's politicians to achieve primary action step 1 above.

❑ Decide who you're going to contact first. (The Job One Plan website will have some of this contact information and strategy. Click here[178] to see this campaign's information and navigation page.)

❑ Connect with the recipient and make them care about your cause of calling for an immediate emergency meeting of the world's politicians to achieve primary action step 1 above.

---

[178] Job One for Humanity. "Climageddon Book Support Navigation Center." *JobOneforHumanity.org*. Accessed March 20, 2016. http://www.joboneforhumanity.org/climageddon_book_support_navigation_center

❑ Offer some positive strokes.

❑ Make sure you've researched the recipient.

❑ Request the recipient publicly declare their intent to help enact global warming reduction laws by lobbying politicians.

❑ Close with a personal appeal.

❑ If they respond, send a thank you and let the Job One for Humanity team know.

❑ **Supporting action step D:** Maximize leverage by contacting the heads of your nation's intelligence agencies. Ask them to call for an immediate emergency meeting of the world's politicians to achieve primary action step 1 above. Also ask them to take full responsibility for the analysis of current global warming research as well as for reporting global warming's current security threat level, predicted consequences, and time frames to both politicians and citizens annually at the minimum.

❑ (The Job One Plan website will have some of this contact information and strategy. Click here[179] to see this campaign's information and navigation page.)

❑ **Supporting action step E:** Demand the International Monetary Fund and the World Trade Organization help call the emergency meeting of world's leaders and help facilitate the creation of verifiable and enforceable new

---

[179] Job One for Humanity. "Climageddon Book Support Navigation Center." *JobOneforHumanity.org.* Accessed March 20, 2016. http://www.joboneforhumanity.org/climageddon_book_support_navigation_center

global warming reduction laws or treaties. (The Job One Plan website will have some of this contact information and strategy. Click here [180] to see this campaign's information and navigation page.)

❑ **Supporting action step F:** maximize leverage by also contacting the heads of your nation's intelligence agencies. Ask them to call for an immediate emergency meeting of the world's politicians to achieve primary action step 1 above.

> ❑ (The Job One Plan website will have some of this contact information and strategy. Click here to see this campaign's information and navigation page.)

❑ **Supportive Action Step G:** scale up education, collaboration, and action fast.

There are numerous ways for you to help us scale up and quickly educate many others about the future-critical information of *Climageddon*:

> ❑ Click the following link to tell your friends [181] about the new *Climageddon* book and the Job One for Humanity Plan within it.

> ❑ Use our Spread The Word tool where you can automatically share the *Climageddon*

---

[180] Job One for Humanity. "Climageddon Book Support Navigation Center." *JobOneforHumanity.org*. Accessed March 20, 2016. http://www.joboneforhumanity.org/climageddon_book_support_navigation_center

[181] Job One for Humanity. "Spread the Word." *JobOneforHumanity.org*. Accessed March 20, 2016. http://www.joboneforhumanity.org/spread_the_word

book link [182] on Facebook, Twitter, LinkedIn, Gmail +, Reddit, Tumblr, and Digg. (Wherever you can, please add a personal note to your sharing of our link.)

❏ Go to Amazon, Itunes, *and* Google Play and write a book review. Start with Amazon as they are the biggest bookseller. This small action can make a big difference particularly because the well-financed fossil fuel climate denial propaganda machine will do everything it can to author many, false, horrible and insulting reviews at these websites designed exclusively to discourage anyone from evaluating the book's information for themselves.

❏ Sign up for our Global Warming Blog RSS feed[183] to get new global warming articles, and the latest news and progress. There are several thousand news articles already in this blog. (When you sign-up for the RSS feed on the Job One website, a Feedburner pop-up window may appear showing your email address asking you to enter the "no robots" code shown to prove you are not a robot. Once you enter the code, you will be sent an email to verify your email address with the email verification link in it. Once you click

---

[182] Job One for Humanity. "Climageddon Introduction." *JobOneforHumanity.org*. Accessed March 17, 2016. http://www.joboneforhumanity.org/book_intro

[183] Job One for Humanity. "Blog Signup Page." *JobOneforHumanity.org*. Accessed March 10, 2016. http://www.joboneforhumanity.org/blog_signup_page

the link in the email sent by Feedburner you will automatically receive regular Global Warming Blog updates.)

❏ If you know someone in any nonprofit or NGO that may be sympathetic to the information and action steps in *Climageddon*, talk personally with them about what you have learned and have them get a copy of the book. You might be the one who helps them refine and update their mission to the new global warming reality and then encourages them to join the emergency mobilization taking place.

❏ If you are already involved in any organization sympathetic to the ideas and action plan steps of *Climageddon*, your organization can help by becoming an independent collaborating partner or ally in the *Global Warming Emergency Mobilization* (GWEM) currently facilitated at the Job One for Humanity website. There is much your organization can do to collaborate and mobilize with Job One for Humanity on critical path actions to help end global warming. It will take nothing less than a massive emergency mobilization and collaboration between hundreds of thousands of organizations to end this crisis in time to keep us safe. Click here[184] for more *Global Warming*

---

[184] Job One for Humanity. "Mobilization Partners and Allies." *JobOneforHumanity.org.* Accessed March 20, 2016. http://www.joboneforhumanity.org/mobilization_partners_allies

Emergency Mobilization support, collaboration, and partnering information.

❏ If you know someone in any media-related organization that may be sympathetic to the information in *Climageddon*, talk personally with them about what you have learned and ask them to start covering information about how little time we have left in their media broadcasts. They are in the same boat as the rest of us. They and their families will suffer just as much as everyone else.

❏ If you are already involved in an organization sympathetic to the ideas and Job One actions of *Climageddon*, you or your organization can also buy the book in bulk at a substantial discount and distribute it wherever you think it will do the most good. (For current bulk purchase discounts, email us at manage@JobOneforHumanity.org.)

❏ If you are not already a member of an organization doing similar mission work to Job One for Humanity, please consider becoming a Job One volunteer and help us educate others. The Job One Plan needs all the volunteers it can get to be successful in the time we have left. To get started as a volunteer, fill in the online volunteer form by clicking here.[185] In the

---

[185] Job One for Humanity. "Volunteer." *JobOneforHumanity.org*. Accessed March 20, 2016. http://www.joboneforhumanity.org/volunteer

comments field, be sure to let us know about any special skills or experience you have or any specific projects that you would like to work on. One of our team members will get back to you with additional information. On the Job One Navigation Center[186] page you will also find a listing of positions that are currently open for volunteers.

❏ If you are not already a member of an organization doing similar mission work to Job One for Humanity, you can also set up and self-organize an independent Job One Plan meetup, study, and action group in your local area. We have website tools to help you do this, but you will be the main person creating and self-managing your own local area events and actions. Our newsletter and local area group coordinator will share planned larger scale actions and successful strategies as they become available.

❏ Donate to support the nonprofit tax-deductible mission of Job One for Humanity. Your financial support will be wisely and frugally used to end global warming and to spread the word and educate others. Your donations also help subsidize discounted or free books for students around the world. Never forget that well-financed vested interests in the

[186] http://www.joboneforhumanity.org/climageddon_book_support_navigation_center

fossil fuel industries and nations have nearly unlimited funds to impede our efforts. You can be certain they will use those resources against us as our new message gains traction. Help level the playing field by making an online or mail-in donation[187] to support our mission to *effectively* end global warming. All of your donations are tax-deductible if you are a US citizen.

❏ If someone has giving you your copy of *Climageddon* and, you can afford it, please make a donation to help us get more books into the hands of more people.

❏ Here are a few additional quick supportive actions. Like the Job One website, our Climageddon Facebook page, [188] and follow our Climageddon Twitter feed.[189]

There truly is no other way we will be successful unless we can scale up education and action globally! The Job One Plan website will have some additional scaling-up information and strategy.

---

[187] Job One for Humanity. "Donate and Help End Global Warming." *JobOneforHumanity.org*. Accessed March 23, 2016.
http://factnet.nationbuilder.com/donate_job_one_for_humanityhttp://www.joboneforhum anity.org/climageddon_book_support_navigation_center

[188] Job One for Humanity. "Climageddon." *Facebook*. Accessed April 10, 2017.
https://www.facebook.com/Climageddon/

[189] Job One for Humanity. "Climageddon." Twitter.com. Accessed April 19, 2017.
https://twitter.com/climageddon

❏ **Supporting action step H:** If necessary, contact individuals, corporations and celebrities as well as the WTO and the IMF directly at public events. The Job One Plan website will have some additional information and strategy relating to this supporting action step. Click here [190] to see this campaign's information and navigation page.

The Job One Secondary Action Steps Backup Preparation

(From Part 2, Chapter 4 of *Climageddon*.)

❏ Build the necessary emergency supplies and resilience for global warming catastrophe survival and recovery.

❏ Create a global warming emergency cash reserve fund equal to 5%-10% of monthly income.

❏ Plan now for how you will adapt and/or move critical resources, technology, and infrastructure to handle the escalating consequences of global warming.

❏ Create your long-term migration plan.

Find ways to enjoy your life each day in spite of the escalating global warming emergency.

---

[190] Job One for Humanity. "Climageddon Book Support Navigation Center." *JobOneforHumanity.org.* Accessed March 20, 2016.

APPENDIX 2

A SPIRITUAL TAKE ON CLIMAGEDDON

By Dan Shafer,
Chief Strategy Officer,
Job One for Humanity
and
Ordained Interfaith Minister

As this book has amply demonstrated, there is only a marginal amount of room for optimism as we engage the global warming crisis that is speeding toward us. We have, at best, a mere 10 years before it will be too late to avoid many of the most serious consequences of this emergency. As the author continues to remind us, even then we will need a certain amount of luck.

But for those of us who wish to take a more spiritual perspective on such things, there is another hopeful avenue that seems worthy of at least some consideration.

Every world religion encompasses, within its own sacred writings and/or in more modern-day pronouncements of its leaders, the idea of Man's responsibility for God's Creation. Moving beyond mere responsibility, humanity at its best and most aware understands the deep interconnections between us and Nature. Just as we depend upon clean air and water, safe and adequate food supplies, and energy from God's creation, so that creation in turn depends upon us for its continued ability to support us. This implies a stewardship responsibility that ensures we don't use resources faster than they can be renewed naturally.

This realization leads to an understanding that must be at the core of any spiritual approach to dealing with the global warming emergency that looms before us. As long as we believe that we are separate from Creation or, worse yet, destined to use what we need from Nature without regard for its impact on other creatures, we will find it difficult to be motivated to pay any serious attention to global warming. But the Truth is, we are not separate from Creation; indeed, we are an integral part of the Creation mythology that exists in all major religions. And that Creation is a deeply embedded part of who we are as well.

We know that, at some level at least, God — by whatever name we know It — is in charge and is always inclined toward good. That does not mean, however, that we can simply turn the global warming emergency over to God and brush our hands of the entire matter. There is an old Islamic folk saying: "Trust Allah, but tie your camel." In other words, let go and let God, but only after you've done all that you can. Within the Universe Community that lies behind this book and the work it undertakes, we have clear priorities. We will fully prepare for the worst, then forget about those preparations while we then focus and wholeheartedly work for the best!

What, then, are some specific ways in which spiritually-inclined individuals can contribute to the solution to the global warming emergency beyond those recommended in this book?

First, on a personal level, we can pray, meditate, contemplate, and visualize, applying the spiritual power of whatever our individual belief systems teach as effective applications of Divine energy to any problem. This may include praying for world leaders as well as the world's wealthiest individuals and corporations to awaken to the imminent danger facing the planet as well as for the general enlightenment of humanity to activate the centers of Compassion that all religions teach us are central to our nature.

Second, we can help organize our local, regional, and national religious establishments and communities to speak up and present the important values of the spiritual viewpoint that is so often lacking in public debate and discussion on this and other pressing issues. Particularly in the United States, with its First Amendment ban on any formal connection between religion and government, there is a tendency to try to separate politics from religion even when doing so makes governing more difficult or outcomes worse. We need to get beyond that.

Finally, we can get involved with Job One for Humanity in combating global warming. This organization, after all, has deeply spiritual roots even though we've chosen to minimize their visible influence in the interest of broadening the appeal of our critical message. Job One for Humanity grew out of the organization called Universe Spirit, which has the broader agenda of applying spiritual principles to sustainable prosperity in all of its many manifestations.

It is important to note that science and metaphysics today are converging around the idea that we humans can and must begin to engage in conscious evolution rather than allowing things to take their natural course. To do this requires paying attention on both mental and spiritual levels as we engage the world around us in an effort to understand the enemy, global warming, and ultimately defeat it.

There is hope. There is always hope. But hope doesn't solve problems; people taking action because they *have* hope is what solves problems. I hope and pray that your spirituality is in alignment with the needs of the Earth for consciously evolved humans to take the lead in rescuing ourselves from likely extinction and the planet from massive alteration. Together with the Power of the Divine, we *can* do it!

To read more of my spiritual and optimistic perspectives on the global warming challenges before us, click here.[191]

Dan Shafer

---

[191] Dan Shafer. "Cockeyed Optimist Blog." *JobOneforHumanity.org*. Accessed March 23, 2016. http://www.joboneforhumanity.org/global_warming_cockeyed_optimist_blog

APPENDIX 3

SUPPLEMENTAL ACTION STEPS

(Special Note: Appendix 3 of *Climageddon* does not need to be read until we see what happens in the next 6 to 10 years or, until you have done everything possible to successfully execute the critical action steps listed in Part 2.)

The Job One Plan Supplemental Action Steps

In Parts 1 and 2 of *Climageddon*, we have laid out the arguments behind the "must do now" action steps of Part 2. Many if not most of these action steps are non-traditional, because global warming is a crisis that demands *revolutionary* actions to combat it.

We've also applied a "war" analogy in pointing to a battle line that must not be crossed to have any hope of victory. As with other wars civilization has waged, there are mission-critical weapons and tactics that comprise the primary means of attack and defense. Any war is also supported by additional actions and strategies that serve specific *supplemental* purposes.

But, it is important to understand that in war, supplemental actions are not intended *on their own* to win the final victory. They cannot. Rather, they serve to complement or support some unique aspect of the larger victory plan or as back-up strategy in case of retreat or defeat.

So it is with the overall war against global warming. *Only* successfully executing the critical action steps found in Part 2—not the supplemental action steps of Appendix 3—can keep us from:

1. Crossing the carbon 425-450 ppm battle line, or
2. Crossing more global warming tipping points, or
2. Crossing into the later stages of the Climageddon Scenario and extinction.

As you read through the following supplemental action steps, never hide the fact from anyone that if we do not succeed in ending global warming emergency with the strategic understanding and action steps outlined in Part 2, the supplemental action steps in Appendix 3 cannot and *will not* fill the gap. Do not allow yourself to fall prey to the fatal illusion that any of the supplemental actions listed below either of themselves, or collectively --- even if done by hundreds of millions of us ---can end the global warming emergency in time. That's a false comfort that courts global catastrophe and the end of humanity.

Yes, there are specific uses and timing for the supplemental action steps. If we fail to resolve the global warming emergency, these supplemental actions may create temporary delays or a lessening of the worst of the global warming consequences, which could enable more emergency preparation or short-term refuge preparation (via migration) in the extinction face-off against the later phases of the Climageddon Scenario.

Additionally, if we do succeed and we avert a Climageddon extinction event, the following supplemental action steps done at the proper time and/or mandated by our governments can serve as a powerful preventative to keep any future global warming crisis permanently at bay.
Unfortunately, some of you may see the revolutionary action steps of Part 2 as too challenging or too difficult and you will be tempted to take the easy way out.
You may instead begin the supplemental action steps to either build some initial momentum, or at least do something because "everything helps" and they certainly can't hurt. If you take this misguided easy escape route, you will have made the same mistake that has been made repeatedly over the last 30+

years. We keep thinking an easier and gradual evolutionary solution will save us and then we do even less than what is needed for this new and more palatable gradual evolutionary solution to be effective.

The conditions and deadlines of our current emergency are long past allowing for any delusions of believing in any more gradual and insufficient *evolutionary* solutions. We are at the precipice of the carbon 425 to 450 ppm climate cliff. Only the radical, painful, and costly action steps of Part 2 have any honest hope of saving us in time.

It is important to acknowledge supplemental actions do have time and use-specific value, but it's vital to our collective survival not to misunderstand this. Keep this mission-critical information in mind if you attempt the following supplemental action steps as an individual or as a group. (If any part of the above cautionary notice still is uncertain to you, please re-read chapters 1-9 in Part 1.)

The Job One Plan supplemental action steps

For many people, some of these steps can be challenging to complete. You may skip over any of the action steps below if you feel it is not applicable to your situation or you feel you cannot do them. You also may do the steps out of sequence if that works better for you.

Supplemental Action Step 1: Divest out of fossil fuel investments and assets.

If you have any fossil fuel industry investments, divest and get out of all of your personal holdings in this dead-end industry. Next, do everything within your zone of influence to convince others within your networks to do the same. Next, work to convince businesses, pension funds, endowments, and national governments to divest completely out of the dying fossil fuel industry as soon as possible. Why?

1. The fossil fuel industry is a bad investment. Other than for limited use in the future for the military, air travel,

space exploration, and other limited applications, the age of fossil fuel energy generation has ended. No individuals or organizations should want to invest in an industry with its massive subsidies soon being removed, its profits being taxed at increasing rates, and with its growing legal liability to restore all of the damage it has done to the environment over the last 130 years. Get out before you get caught!

2. Money is real influential power! Money talks, and it talks effectively! One strong way to help convince our governments and the power elite that the age of fossil fuels is over and the age of green energy generation is here is to pull *all* financial support from the fossil fuels industry as soon as possible.

3. There is little future left for fossil fuel energy use. As mentioned in Part 2, global fossil fuel use has to be drastically cut while we rapidly move to global green energy generation to survive. Divesting quickly aligns beautifully and wisely with the many new fossil fuel use reduction laws that will be enacted.

> "Money does not just talk, it screams influence and power. If you want to see a change happen fast, properly incentivize it with strong monetary rewards or disincentivize it by removing its profit." — A Job One team member.

Click here to make your pledge to divest and join the divestment honor roll![192]

---

[192] Job One for Humanity. "Divest out of fossil fuels pledge." *JobOneforHumanity.org*. Accessed March 20, 2016.
http://www.joboneforhumanity.org/divest_out_of_fossil_fuels_pledge

For more information on why you should become a fossil fuel divestment promoter, please click here for a four-minute animation[193] that explains this tactic in more detail.

If you're still not convinced about the importance of immediate divestment, please watch this powerful 2-1/2 minute divestment video now by The Guardian.[194] See this article by Alister Doyle[195] for more information on why it's important to divest now.

When you have personally divested out of fossil fuels, let us know by emailing us at manage@JobOneforHumanity.org. You will be added to our Job One Plan divestment honor roll. If you have encouraged others to divest and they have done so, tell Job One your success story. Job One may share it in our Job One newsletter to help encourage others.

While you are divesting, don't forget that without all of the critical actions of Part 2 being done, divesting will not be enough to save us in time. If we fail, it will be due in part to our inability to grasp real deadlines and/or execute actions along a prioritized critical path as the Job One Plan outlines in Part 2.

Supplemental Action Step 2: Eat less animal and dairy products.

Yes, you read this correctly. The single most important *personal* action you can take to reduce global warming and fossil fuel use is *not*, as much popular thinking has it, to buy an electric car, insulate your house, or cut your hot water use by 60%. It is to eat significantly less meat and dairy products.

---

[193] "Global Divestment Day 2015." YouTube video. 1:25, posted by "Fossil Free," February 15, 2015. https://www.youtube.com/watch?v=ckJ9M56Ftbg

[194] "What is fossil fuel divestment and why does it matter?" Video. 2:40, posted by The Guardian, March 23, 2015.
https://www.theguardian.com/environment/video/2015/mar/23/what-fossil-fuel-divestment-why-matter-climate-change-video

[195] Alister Doyle. "Insurers call on G20 to phase out fossil fuel subsidies by 2020." *Reuters*. August 29, 2016. http://www.reuters.com/article/us-g20-climatechange-idUSKCN1142GN

This is because global food animal production and dairy agribusiness are leading causes of global warming, considering their total atmospheric greenhouse gas emissions.

The facts:

1. Animal agriculture *is* a major emitter of greenhouse gases. One report[196] has estimated global agribusiness is responsible for a whopping 17% of all global warming caused by greenhouse gas emissions. The *frequently incorrect* United Nation's IPCC uses a figure of 14% for agribusiness' share of global greenhouse gas emissions.

    Unfortunately, like many IPCC calculations, this reported 14% figure overlooks key agribusiness emissions contributors. The IPCC report also did not include *any calculation* for greenhouse gas emissions from fossil fuel-burning machinery needed for growing the almost 50% of the world's total crops that are used in animal feed. This would be for things like mechanical plowing, seeding, harvesting, processing, and shipping the crops used exclusively for animal feed. The total greenhouse gas emissions from agribusiness' *other systemic locked-in uses* of fossil fuel that are withheld from the calculations could be equal to all other agribusiness emissions the IPCC uses to calculate its 14% allotment. In other words, the percentage of global warming being caused by agribusiness could be underestimated by half or more.

    It might actually be much worse than that. Other reports listed below discuss the total greenhouse gas emissions from global agribusiness that consider *all direct and indirect* factors. These reports imply the real total greenhouse gas emissions attributable to agribusiness could be as high as 51% of all carbon and

---

[196] Veerasamy Sejian, Iqbal Hyder, T. Ezeji, J. Lakritz, Raghavendra Bhatta, J. P. Ravindra, Cadaba S. Prasad, Rattan Lal. "Global Warming: Role of Livestock." *Climate Change Impact on Livestock: Adaptation and Mitigation.* Springer India (2015): 141-169, doi: 10.1007/978-81-322-2265-1_10

methane greenhouse gas emissions. (See the following article by Martin Hickman [197] and this WorldWatch report [198] for more on this higher 51% estimate.) By comparison, the fossil fuel industry (all industries related to the mining, distribution, and use of petroleum, coal, or natural gas) is estimated to be responsible for 40% of all carbon and methane greenhouse gas emissions.

2. By comparison, even at the lower estimates global animal agriculture may be responsible for more greenhouse gas emissions than the combined exhaust from all transportation—private, public, commercial, and industrial.

3. Consistently eating a plant-based diet even just one day per week reduces more greenhouse gas emissions than buying local food *all year long,* and switching to a full-time plant-based diet results in greater greenhouse gas reductions *than switching from a gasoline-powered sedan to a hybrid vehicle.*

4. Vegetarian-only diets generate up to a whopping 42% fewer greenhouse gas emissions and lead to dramatically lower overall environmental impacts compared to non-vegetarian diets. (See this 1.5 minute video[199] that illustrates the above facts and adds more specifics on why reducing your animal products intake is so important to reducing global warming in our future.)

---

[197] Martin Hickman. "Study claims meat creates half of all greenhouse gases." *The Independent.* October 31, 2009. http://www.independent.co.uk/environment/climate-change/study-claims-meat-creates-half-of-all-greenhouse-gases-1812909.html

[198] Robert Goodland and Jeff Anhang. "Livestock and Climate Change." *WorldWatch Magazine,* 22, no. 6 (2006): 141-169, http://www.worldwatch.org/node/6294

[199] "The Most Shocking 1.5 Min Video the World Must See!" YouTube Video. 1:30, posted by "COWSPIRACY: the sustainability secret," November 17, 2015. https://www.youtube.com/watch?v=g1z1taw6yNw

If you cannot cut out all animal products and become a full-time vegetarian, at least start a program of eating fewer animal and dairy products, such as reducing your animal and dairy dietary intake first one day a week, then two days a week, and so on. You can start by eating less beef, which demands more fossil fuel resources to produce than chicken.

Everything counts. Begin by eating 20% less of the animal products than you are eating now within 6 months or less. You will save money and, according to recent studies, you will become far healthier, look better, and live longer. Once you hit your first target, keep reducing your animal intake by another 20% over the next 3-6 months and continue until you are either animal- and dairy products-free or you are eating very little of them.

Even though most people already know they are supposed to eat less animal and dairy products because of the many documented bad health impacts, this is a significant change for many people in their diet. Most of the time medical warnings don't change our behaviors, but when people also learn the hard science behind why reducing animal and dairy product intake is also important to their planet's future, many individuals are finally ready to make the commitment and change.

To help you understand the facts about how powerful changing your diet will be to reducing global warming, we strongly recommend you read this fact summary at: http://www.cowspiracy.com/facts/ and see this 1.5-minute trailer for the documentary here[200]. (*Cowspiracy* is also available on Netflix.)

If you still need convincing on why reducing your animal products food intake is important to help slow escalating global warming, please read these two amazing articles by

[200] "COWSPIRACY - Official Teaser 2 - HD." YouTube Video. 1:31, posted by "COWSPIRACY: the sustainability secret," December 6, 2014. https://www.youtube.com/watch?v=2SRPk6gB3g0

Khushbu Shah[201] and Felicity Carus[202] on how "voting" with your "low or no" animal and dairy products diet will help lessen global warming, as well as resolve other key global challenges to our shared future.

To help you make the change to eating fewer animal and dairy products, we also strongly recommend you read *Eat to Live* by Dr. Joel Furhman. You will not only discover how to have a tasty diet that will help save the planet from global warming, but you will also understand how this new low-to-no animal products diet will help you become healthier, look better, and live longer.

In summary, the most highly leveraged action any individual can take to reduce global warming is to reduce or eliminate consumption of animal and dairy products. When you have reduced your animal and dairy product intake, send us an email to manage@joboneforhumanity.org and enter the following in the subject line: "I am eating less animal products to reduce global warming." Job One will add you to our global warming dietary honor roll. If you have encouraged others to do the same, tell us your success story. Job One can share it in our newsletter to help encourage others.

Supplemental Action Step 3: Get your home and business converted to green energy generation systems.

Green energy generation can be solar, wind, hydroelectric, or some other alternative form of energy generation greener than fossil fuels. Today the reasons for converting to green energy generation in our homes and businesses are stronger than ever.

---

[201] Khushbu Shah. "UN says veganism can save the world from destruction." *Eater.com*. February 16, 2015. http://www.eater.com/2015/2/16/8048069/un-says-veganism-can-save-the-world-from-destruction

[202] Felicity Carus. "UN urges global move to meat and dairy-free diet." *The Guardian*. June 2, 2010. https://www.theguardian.com/environment/2010/jun/02/un-report-meat-free-diet

1. A massive scaling up of green energy generation is critical if we are going to stay below the carbon 425-450 battle line for meaningful control of our futures. It is also necessary to keep the world economy from severe recession or depression as we radically cut fossil fuel use to meet the last chance 2026 targets.

2. Green energy generation makes good economic sense by saving you money over the long term. Today, many individuals and businesses are converting to green energy not because they are sustainability advocates or want to save the climate from global warming but because going green saves money in their energy expenses over the long term.

3. Switching to green energy as soon as possible can also be seen as a patriotic duty and national security imperative. The U.S. and many other countries in the world still get a significant portion of their polluting fossil fuel energy supplies from areas of the world that are high-conflict zones where our energy supplies could be cut off, radically reduced, or priced so high that these changes would destabilize the productivity and economic stability of all countries in any way dependent upon importing those fossil fuels.

   Nations that import these fossil fuels from the high-conflict areas find themselves dragged into expensive, unending, or unresolvable conflicts in those fossil fuel-producing areas. These high-conflict fossil fuel-producing zones are also prime sources for exporting terrorism back out to the very parts of the world to which they sell their fossil fuels.

   A nation with *decentralized* green energy systems in use by most of its population is no longer dependent upon or held hostage by the fossil fuel producers from many of the world's high-conflict areas. Additionally, not having to send our military forces into these areas to protect our fossil fuel supplies and economic stability will also save lives and tremendous taxpayer costs in our national budgets. These savings can then be better used in other areas.

When you convert your home or business to green energy systems, you are making a *powerful* move to help build your national security. You are acting as a true patriot!

4. Green energy generation has become cheaper than ever due to manufacturing scale and the increasing number of people converting over. There are many improvements in green energy efficiency and in lowering costs for installing green energy in your home or business.

5. Green energy has come of age to such a degree that it is increasingly easier to finance in large and small green energy home and business installations. Soon it will be no more difficult to get financing to go green than it will be to get financing for a new car.

6. Green energy generation is still subsidized in many areas with either direct subsidy payments or tax deductibility.

7. Homes and businesses that are operating on decentralized green energy are far more prepared for any kind of emergency that would affect their current power systems and productivity. Having homes and businesses operating on *decentralized* green energy generation creates a high-level emergency reserve and a quick recovery resilience at both the local and national levels to any kind of emergency that would

affect our existing *centralized* fossil fuel-dependent energy generation and distribution systems.

8. Energy is power. When you go to green energy generation, often you can also decentralize power away from large utilities and international energy corporations. You bring real power and independence back into the hands of average citizens and small businesses.

Of all the steps listed, the step you just read is the *second* most powerful going greener step because it is about increasing green energy *generation,* which is essential to reaching our 2026 targets. Even if you don't own your own home or business, there is still something you can do here to advance national security and be a real patriot. You can convince those whom you are renting from or work for that converting to green energy generation as quickly as possible is the smart and patriotic thing to do for cost reduction, national security, reducing global warming, emergency preparedness, and protecting future generations.

Supplemental Action Step 4: Reduce your transportation-related energy use.

Tips to reduce your carbon footprint from driving:

1. In the U.S. 40% of all trips people make are 2 miles or less. 90% of those trips are taken by car. If the trip is longer than 2 miles and too far to bike, consider carpooling or mass transit. If you must drive alone, be sure to combine trips, completing as many errands in one trip as possible.

2. Drive a low-carbon vehicle. All vehicles now have an estimated miles-per-gallon rating [203] and pollution

---

[203] U.S. Department of Energy. "Find and Compare Cars." *Fueleconomy.gov.* Accessed March 22, 2017. https://www.fueleconomy.gov/feg/findacar.shtml

ratings. If electric cars are charged with *clean electricity*, they contribute no carbon dioxide to the atmosphere. After incentives and gas savings, it essentially costs nothing to switch to an electric car like the Nissan Leaf[204] or Toyota Prius. If you don't charge the electric car with your home's solar panels (or other clean electricity if it's available), you're better off with a high-MPG (miles per gallon) gas/diesel car or a hybrid. Here's why.[205]

- o Don't forget that "high MPG" doesn't always mean "low carbon dioxide emissions." Always check the emission ratings before you buy.

3. Take fewer vacations that are far away. Take more frequent and driveable "staycations" closer to home.

4. Use cruise control. Unnecessary acceleration and speeding can reduce mileage by up to 33%,[206] waste money and gas, and increase your carbon footprint.

5. Avoid traffic congestion. Being unnecessarily stuck in traffic creates unhealthy carbon dioxide pollution and wastes gas. Use traffic apps and websites to go a different way or wait for less congested times.

6. Tire inflation and engine tuning. Use the correct grade of motor oil and keep your engine tuned because some

---

[204] Carbon Offsets To Alleviate Poverty. "25+ Tips to Reduce Your Carbon Footprint." *COTAP.org.* http://cotap.org/reduce-carbon-footprint/

[205] Reid Wilson. "The states that will be hit hardest by the EPA's coal regulations, in one map." *The Washington Post.* June 2, 2014. https://www.washingtonpost.com/blogs/govbeat/wp/2014/06/02/the-states-that-will-be-hit-hardest-by-the-epas-coal-regulations-in-one-map/?utm_term=.3f5c6876f267

[206] U. S. Department of Energy. "Drive More Efficiently." *FuelEconomy.gov.* Accessed December 10, 2016. http://www.fueleconomy.gov/feg/driveHabits.jsp

maintenance fixes[207] like fixing faulty oxygen sensors can increase fuel efficiency by up to 40%. Properly inflated tires improve your gas mileage by up to 3%.

7. Remove excess weight from your car.

8. If 1 out of 10 people switched to an alternative form of transportation (biking, walking or public transportation), carbon dioxide emissions would drop by 25.4 million tons per year in the U.S. alone. If you are going a distance of less than 1 mile, walk instead of drive. If it's too far to walk, ride your bike. This will help you save parking and gas costs while reducing risks of obesity and improving health.

Air travel tips to reduce your carbon footprint:

1. Until petroleum-based aviation fuel is replaced, you should fly economy class, fly shorter distances, fly less frequently, and avoid flying altogether whenever possible.

2. Increase your use of video-conferencing tools like Skype and Facetime to reduce work-related travel.

Supplemental Action Step 5: Reduce your carbon footprint by buying local.

A basic diet of imported non-local ingredients can require up to four times the energy of an equivalent locally sourced diet. Where possible, buy from your local farmers' market or co-op. The typical meal in the U.S. currently travels anywhere from 1,200 to 2,500 miles from pasture to plate.

Buying local has a strong multiplier effect in the economy in addition to reducing the transportation carbon footprint. A

---

[207] U. S. Department of Energy. "Keeping Your Vehicle in Shape." *FuelEconomy.gov.* Accessed December 10, 2016. http://www.fueleconomy.gov/feg/maintain.jsp

10% increase in purchasing from locally owned businesses in lieu of national chain stores would yield nearly $200 million in incremental major metropolitan area economic activity and create 1,300 new jobs each year. A dollar spent on local products and services can circulate in the local community up to 15 times.

Supplemental Action Step 6: Reduce your carbon footprint by conserving energy at your home and business.

Once you have stopped adding to the carbon and methane pollution problem with your current fossil fuel use by going green, you can then look at the issue of home and business energy conservation. For every $1 spent on home or office energy conservation, $1.80 is saved over time. Home or office conservation also can reduce energy bills by 32%, and energy-efficient households save an average of $218 per year on their energy bills. In the U.S. 21% of all energy used is consumed in homes. 40% of home energy use goes to heating and cooling; 20% goes to water heating; and lighting and appliances, including refrigeration, use more than 15%.

The key to home and business energy conservation is simply finding those places where your home or business is losing energy or using existing energy inefficiently. The U.S. Department of Energy has a lot of information on "Do-It-Yourself Home Energy Assessments," including ideas for locating air leaks, inspecting heating and cooling equipment, perfecting insulation, and evaluating the lighting throughout your home or office.

No-cost energy conservation projects include closing blinds, shades, and curtains on cold cloudy days to retain heat; opening them on cold sunny days for solar warming; and closing them on hot days to hold heat out; making sure that your fireplace has a tight-fitting damper; and removing window-unit air conditioners in the winter to eliminate air leakage.

Low-cost and easy-to-do projects include blanketing your hot water heater, insulating hot water pipes, sealing holes around outlets with inexpensive outlet gaskets, and weather-stripping doors and caulking windows. Other projects include adding more ceiling and wall insulation, upgrading to energy-efficient units, insulating and properly sealing heating ducts, and sealing air leaks around doors, windows, and chimneys.

Once you have done all you can to conserve more energy in your home or business, you can hire a professional energy auditor to carry out a more thorough assessment. A professional auditor uses a variety of techniques and sophisticated equipment like infrared cameras to determine the energy efficiency of a structure and reveal hard-to-detect areas of air infiltration and missing insulation.

A word of caution: Regarding conservation, research has repeatedly shown that technology used to increase fossil fuel consumption efficiency more often than not increases overall fossil fuel use rather than reduces it. This is known as Jevons's paradox.[208]

This happens because of the economic savings that fossil fuel energy conservation provides, which then frees additional resources to buy or use more things dependent upon fossil fuels. Don't let your fossil fuel energy conservation increase global warming by accelerating fossil fuel in other areas. Just pocket the savings and use it elsewhere.

Supplemental Action Step 7: Do water conservation.

Another important energy conservation measure is water conservation at home or in your business. Up to 30% of a household energy footprint can come from moving water from its source to the home. (This water energy use would include

---

[208] when technological progress increases the efficiency with which a resource is used (reducing the amount necessary for any one use), but the rate of consumption of that resource rises because of increasing demand. From Wikipedia contributors, "Jevons's paradox," *Wikipedia, The Free Encyclopedia,* https://en.wikipedia.org/w/index.php?title=Jevons%27s_paradox&oldid=759401245 (accessed January 10, 2017).

transporting and processing the water from its original source to your home for safe home use.)

A faucet that is dripping just one drop per second will waste about four gallons of water in just one day, or 1,400 gallons in a year. The average household could conserve 34% of its water per year by installing water-efficient fixtures and appliances. You can also conserve water by installing faucet aerators, low-flow shower heads and low-flush toilets, and fixing leaks as soon as detected.

There are also easy water conservation behavioral changes you can make. In your kitchen, if you wash dishes by hand, fill a bucket or the sink first instead of letting the water run continuously. If you use the dishwasher, run it only when it is full. Run the clothes washer only with a full load. Take shorter showers. Turn off the faucet when shaving or brushing your teeth.

Cut down on outside sprinkler use. Landscaping alone accounts for 20-30% of all residential water use. Growing native plants can save more than 50% of the water normally used to care for outdoor plants.

Allow the grass to grow slightly taller. It will reduce water loss by providing more ground shade. Water your lawn in the late evening or early morning to minimize evaporation.

Supplemental Action Step 8: Buy energy efficient appliances and products.

Another good way to reduce your home energy consumption is to buy Energy Star™ appliances and products. Energy Star is a government-backed program using symbols that tell consumers if a product meets specific energy efficiency standards that will reduce greenhouse gas emissions and save energy.

The average home contributes two times the amount of greenhouse gases as the average car. In the long run, saving energy will save you money, as well as lessen your carbon pollution impact on our atmosphere and our planet. Many energy-efficient products such as windows and doors, water heaters, roofs, heating and AC systems, and solar energy systems qualify for a Federal tax credit of up to 30% of the cost. Click here for more information.[209] Visit www.energystar.gov/

You can also reduce your home and business energy use by powering down and unplugging electronics. It comes as a surprise to most people that appliances still continue to draw a small amount of power even when they are switched off.

75% of the electricity used to power home electronics and appliances is consumed in the average home while the products are turned off! When you are finished using any appliance you do not have to leave on, always unplug it.

To make things easy, plug an appliance (or several of them) into a power strip. When you are done, just flip the switch to cut off power. Gadgets like the SmartStrip[210] help by cutting the power to all electronics when it is turned off. Want more info? Visit www.energy.gov.

Although there are many types of subsidies and tax incentives for home and business energy conservation, do not put the energy conservation cart in front of the more important green energy generation horse. To prevent going over the carbon 425-450 ppm climate cliff, first we need to more effectively stop making the problem worse. Do this by reducing use of fossil fuels.

At this point in the global warming emergency, switching to *decentralized* green energy generation on a widespread basis will be a more cost-effective, time-effective, and successful strategy than trying to fix all of the much smaller energy loss

---

[209] Energy Star. "Federal Income Tax Credits for Energy Efficiency." *EnergyStar.gov.* Accessed December 18, 2016.https://www.energystar.gov/about/federal_tax_credits

[210] Bits Limited. "Smart Strip." https://www.bitsltd.net/

inefficiencies of homes and businesses everywhere. Want more info? Visit www.energysavers.gov.

Supplemental Action Step 9: Reduce your carbon footprint by investing in durable, reusable products.

The manufacturing of bottles to meet the American demand for bottled water requires enough oil to fuel 100,000 cars for a year (more than 1.5 million barrels). Every minute, 1 million disposable plastic bags are consumed worldwide (over 500 billion each year). Decreasing the number of disposable products in your life decreases your carbon footprint from manufacturing, transportation, and disposal.

To reduce your carbon footprint in this way, invest in durable, reusable bags, bottles, towels, mops, pots and pans, and anything else you need. Over the life of the products, you will reduce waste, reduce the energy-intensive extraction of virgin resources, and save money. Want more info? Visit http://www.newdream.org/water/.

Supplemental Action Step 10: Reduce your carbon footprint by planting an organic garden.

Planting and maintaining a garden reconnects us with the true value of food. Research suggests converting 10,000 small-to-medium-sized farms to organic production practices would store carbon in the soil equivalent to taking 1,174,400 cars off the road. Want more info? Visit www.plantingjustice.org.

Supplemental Action Step 11: Dive into additional green principles for creating a sustainable prosperity.

Much of what you have read in Appendix 3 is derived from the concepts and principles of *sustainable prosperity*. There is also a lot more to learn about going green not covered in Appendix 3, found within the sustainable prosperity principles.

Sustainable prosperity is about creating sufficient and sustainable abundance. It is about living within intelligent, realistic limits and boundaries. It is also about the new triple-bottom-line economics that will help create the thriving new lifestyles and livelihoods of the 21st century. If you would like to know more about the concepts of sustainable prosperity that underpin and expand upon Appendix 3 of this book, click here.[211]

Supplemental Action Step 12: If you are of a spiritual nature, work within your faith community to help educate others to end global warming.

Spiritually based motivations are among the strongest and most sustaining of all human motivations. If you are spiritual by nature, it is important to find additional support and motivation for this challenging advocacy work within your faith community.

Support from within your spiritual community will help you survive escalating global warming consequences as well as advance the Job One critical action steps. In this challenge, we absolutely need all the support and motivational resources we can find to resolve the global warming emergency before it's too late. Additionally, we also need to engage the amazing leverage of members of all the faith communities of the world to resolve this immediate threat to all people of the planet.

Unless more of the major religions quickly get on board, there will be few places left safe and stable enough for them to provide their spiritual services and other social benefit work for and with their members.

In addition to killing hundreds of millions of their members, the later stages of the Climageddon Scenario will also destabilize the resources and structures of the world's major religions *when they will be needed most* to help their migrating and trapped members deal with the extreme environmental, social, political, and economic chaos, which will occur as more global warming tipping points are crossed.

---

[211] Lawrence Wollersheim. "The Sustainable Prosperity Revolution: The New Good Life, Hope for the Economy and the Future of Job Creation." *JobOneforHumanity.org*. Accessed December 20, 2016. http://www.joboneforhumanity.org/sustainable_prosperity_booklet

It's easy to get started. Encourage your religious or spiritual group members to support and sign the global warming State of Emergency Petition,[212] as well as the other petitions and actions found on the Job One for Humanity website.[213]

If we succeed, it will be a time of gratitude. If we fail, it will be a time when spiritual persons will need their deep faith and prayer for the strength to endure what is coming.

Supplemental Action Step 13: If needed, refresh and revitalize your motivation with two inspiring short videos.

If you have not done so already, we strongly recommend you watch two videos to refresh your motivation. In a mildly humorous way, they also cover many of the key reasons why the escalating global warming emergency is also the greatest adaptive challenge and evolutionary adventure in human history. If you are confident you already understand global warming and why we need to address it, you can skip this step, but they are *great* videos.

> a. Watch The Most Terrifying Video You'll Ever See, Version 2.[214] (10 minutes) This video reconfirms the urgency of action needed to address global warming. It examines the arguments of the critics and those who deny the pattern of global warming, as well as those who believe global warming-caused climate destabilization is occurring. It brilliantly summarizes what will happen to us if we do not effectively confront

---

[212] Job One for Humanity. "Declare a Global Warming State of Emergency." *JobOneforHumanity.org.* Accessed March 20, 2016. http://www.joboneforhumanity.org/declare_a_global_warming_state_of_emergency

[213] Job One for Humanity. "Climageddon Book Support Navigation Center." *JobOneforHumanity.org.* Accessed March 20, 2016. http://www.joboneforhumanity.org/climageddon_book_support_navigation_center

[214] "The Most Terrifying Video You'll Ever See" YouTube Video. 9:33, posted by "wonderingmind42", June 8, 2007. https://www.youtube.com/watch?v=zORv8wwiadQ

the escalating global warming emergency. This video has been viewed over 1 million times.

b. Watch Wake Up, Freak Out - Then Get a Grip.[215] (11 minutes) Pay particular attention to the animation's excellent explanation of the various critical global warming tipping points.[216] This video has been viewed over 1 million times and has been translated into 22 different languages. One note: this video gives temperature degrees in Celsius. A rough Fahrenheit temperature conversion is double the Celsius amount. Near its end, the video presents a somewhat polarized viewpoint. Though the informational content is good science, Job One for Humanity, in principle, puts a higher priority on *collaborative approaches* in lieu of highly polarized ones.

As you can see, there are many supplemental steps of personal responsibility you can take to help the fight against global warming. But it bears repeating that these steps in Appendix 3 are just that—*supplemental*. Their value lies in either buying us more time if things go wrong, or maintaining a safe climate following successful resolution of the global warming emergency.

Without that resolution achieved through critical actions outlined in Part 2, supplemental steps can only temporarily delay catastrophe, but not prevent it. They cannot win the battle against global warming or stave off the the later stages of the Climageddon Scenario. That victory depends on completing the critical actions as presented in Part 2 of *Climageddon*.

---

[215] "Wake Up, Freak Out - then Get a Grip." Vimeo Video. 11:34, posted by "Leo Murray", September 11, 2008. https://www.youtube.com/watch?v=zORv8wwiadQ

[216] Job One for Humanity. "Climate Tipping Points." *JobOneforHumanity.org*. Accessed December 20, 2016. http://www.joboneforhumanity.org/climate_tipping_points

Summary

- The age of fossil fuel has already ended. No individuals or organizations should want to invest in an industry with its subsidies being removed, its profits being taxed at increasing rates, and growing legal liability to restore the immense damage it has done to the environment over the last 130 years. Divest and get out before you get caught! There is no future left for fossil fuel energy on a planet that has to rapidly move to green energy generation to survive and thrive.

- Going greener and lowering your avoidable carbon emissions related to fossil fuel usage is an immediate and practical way to take ownership for your personal responsibility to help reduce global warming. It is what we will all have to do by law once we have solved the global warming emergency. It is also what we will have to do if we fail to solve the global warming emergency to buy ourselves a little more time to prepare and migrate.

- It may be challenging, but continually eating less animal and dairy products is the single most powerful action you as an individual can take to reduce global warming and your carbon footprint.

- Although the action steps of Appendix 3 will not solve the escalating global warming emergency in time, each time we do them, we not only help to slow and lessen the rate of escalating global warming, but we also help to build the critical sustainability practices we will need to maintain a healthy temperature, climate and a sustainable and prosperous economy once we do finally resolve global warming. If we fail, these are the action steps that will buy us a little more time to prepare and migrate.

- If we succeed, the Appendix 3 supplemental actions will be needed to maintain a stable and safe temperature range and climate in the future and to prevent it from happening again. In fact, if we are successful in ending this emergency, many of these action steps will become mandated by law to ensure we never trigger a global warming emergency again. If we do not succeed with the primary and supporting critical actions of Part 2, what the Appendix 3 supplemental actions steps can do is help slow and lessen the total effects of escalating global warming enough for, hopefully, several billion of us to have time to prepare for what is coming, or to migrate.

- Some global warming educational organizations have not applied a rigorous prioritization of tasks by critical deadlines discipline to resolving global warming. Inadvertently they are keeping their followers busy doing only the kind of action steps described in Appendix 3. For those individuals, it creates a sense of comfort, but it's a false comfort that is derived from doing improperly prioritized actions. The non-critical path action steps of Appendix 3 also create a false sense of progress in terms of the critical 6-10 year deadline and the levels of action we must achieve to have any future at all. Not understanding this critical prioritization need and erroneously holding on to the unqualified "everything helps" mindset will inadvertently make our nearly impossible task even harder.

- The inability to either grasp or execute prioritized critical path action steps similar to the primary and supporting actions detailed in Part 2 of the Job One Plan will be one of the core causes if we fail. If you neglect the critical primary and supporting action steps of Part 2 in favor of the Appendix 3 supplemental action steps, you are simply rearranging the deck chairs on the Titanic when you should be changing the ship's course away from the iceberg.

- If you are of a spiritual nature, it is critical to work within your faith community to help end global warming through education and Job One compatible actions. The faith communities of our world, when committed, will exert the powerful leverage of collective moral force to help end the global warming emergency.

- Yes, everything helps, but non-critical path Appendix 3 actions will not save us in time. The primary action steps of Part 2 can still keep us from crossing the carbon 425-450 ppm battle line. The supplemental actions steps of Appendix 3 cannot!

APPENDIX 4

HONORING THE GOOD WORKS OF OUR MOVEMENT

"What is honored in a culture will grow there." —Plato

It is appropriate that after so much difficult news, there should be a part of *Climageddon* that also illuminates the global warming and environmental education and action good works of some of the leading individuals, corporations, and foundations supporting our movement. They are modeling important actions and behaviors that will help us end the emergency.

Please note the lists below do not re-mention the honor roll members of the global warming education movement already covered in the dedication and acknowledgments, and there are many more honor roll heroes and heroines than can possibly be included in the lists below.

1. *Political and religious leaders:* Former President Barack Obama, the United States EPA, Gov. Jerry Brown and the California EPA, Pope Francis of the Catholic Church.

2. *Celebrities:* Leonardo DiCaprio, George Clooney, Rahul Bose, Mark Ruffalo, Brad Pitt, Gul Panag, Matt Damon, Sean Penn, Robert Redford, Akon, Ted Danson, Natalie Portman, Rachel McAdams, Ian Somerhalder, Daryl Hannah, Emma Watson, James Cameron, Stella McCartney, Orlando Bloom, Willie Nelson, Thom Yorke, Edward Norton, Peter Coyote, and Ed Begley Jr.

3. *Corporations, foundations, and individuals:* Google, Patagonia, Facebook, the Bill and Melinda Gates

Foundation, the William and Flora Hewlett Foundation, Tom Steyer, Gordon and Betty Moore, Doug and Kris Tompkins, Ted Turner, Michael Bloomberg, David Gelbaum, Robert Wilson, Elon Musk, Donald Bren, Nathaniel Simons, David Gelbaum, Julia Robertson, Louis Bacon, Larry Linden, Hank Paulson, and Carl Ferenbach.

GLOSSARY

This glossary provides definitions for terms used in *Climageddon* that may be unfamiliar to the public. This glossary also describes climate, global warming, and other phenomena that may not have been precisely defined before, and/or clarifies limits or boundary ranges for complex conditions, processes or states that currently exist. Hopefully, these new or expanded definitions will make the complex conditions, processes or states of global warming in our climate easier to grasp.

- **45th parallel north:** A circle of latitude 45 degrees north of the Earth's equatorial plane. It crosses Europe, Asia, the Pacific Ocean, North America, and the Atlantic Ocean.

- **45th parallel south:** A circle of latitude 45 degrees south of the Earth's equatorial plane. It crosses the Atlantic Ocean, the Indian Ocean, Australasia, the Pacific Ocean, and South America.

- **Carbon dioxide equivalent (CO2e):** A standard unit for measuring all greenhouse gases in terms of the amount of warming they create compared to CO2.

- **Carbon parts per million (ppm):** The current level and concentration of carbon molecules in our atmosphere, as measured by the Keeling curve.

- **Carbon 425 to 450 ppm Battle Line (the Climate Cliff):** The critical tipping point of carbon 425 450 ppm marks the last battle line of maintaining meaningful control over stopping the processes that lead to irreversible global warming.

- **Catastrophic climate destabilization:** Term associated with a measurement of carbon 400-450 ppm (Climageddon Scenario Phase 1). The eventual temperature range commonly associated with catastrophic climate destabilization is an increase in average global temperature of about 1.2°-2.7° Celsius (2.2°-4.9° Fahrenheit). When global warming-caused storms, floods, seasonal disruption, wildfires, and droughts begin to cost a nation 30 to 100 billion-plus dollars per incident to repair (like the U.S. hurricane Sandy) we will have reached the level of catastrophic climate destabilization.

- **Celsius to Fahrenheit conversions:** The following list of temperature conversions are commonly used throughout the book. These amounts are usually used to represent temperature increases above pre-Industrial (1760-1840) average global temperatures.

- **Climate:** This is the statistics of weather, usually *over a 30-year interval*. It is measured by assessing the patterns of variation in temperature, humidity, atmospheric pressure, wind, precipitation, atmospheric particle count and other meteorological variables in a given region over long periods of time. Climate differs from weather, in that weather describes only the short-term conditions of these variables in a given region. (From Wikipedia.) Fossil fuel lobbyists like to confuse us by directing our attention to the shorter time cycles of weather and climate, whereas global warming cycles have occurred over hundreds of thousands and millions of years. When we compare current global warming to past global warming cycles and time frames rather than current weather, or 30-year climate cycles, we can see what's really happening and how dangerous current global warming is to our future.

Temperatures Above Preindustrial for Climageddon Scenario

CS Phase	Celsius	Fahrenheit
1	1.7°-2.2°	3°-4°
2	2.5°-3.2°	4.5°-5.8°
3	2.7°-3.5°	4.9°-6.3°
4	4°-4.5°	7.2°-8°
5	5°-6°	9°-10.8°
6	Unknown	Unknown

- **Climageddon:** This coined term combines the words climate and Armageddon. "Armageddon" is often used to refer to any end-of-the-world scenario. Global warming as described in *Climageddon* has evolved into an impending end-of-the-world scenario.

- **Climageddon Scenario**: A new analytical prediction and future planning model to better understand the complex and intertwined processes, contexts, relationships, transformations, and consequences of escalating global warming up to and including an extinction scenario.

- **Climagees:** Refugees from areas stricken by the various consequences of global warming such as famine, drought, and flooding. (Part 1, Chapter 3)

- **Climate destabilization:** According to Alexei Turchin, "[a] transitional state of escalating global climate instability...characterized by greater unpredictability, which lasts until the global climate eventually finds a new and different stable state of dynamic equilibrium and balance at some different level of temperature and other climate qualities from what it has held for hundreds or thousands of of years."

- **Climate change:** An intentionally misleading term forwarded by fossil fuel lobbyists to downplay and confuse the dangers of global warming to the public and media.

- **Climate cliff:** An atmospheric carbon concentration of 425-450 parts per million. This "cliff" marks the last the battle line of maintaining meaningful control over stopping the processes that lead to irreversible global warming.

- **Committed warming:** A "baked-in" average global temperature rise between 1.5° and 2.7° Celsius that will not change in meaningful human lifespan time frames no matter what we do. It is in part due to ocean warming, the removal of carbon soot particles, and unknown crossed tipping points. (Part 1, Chapter 5)

- **Complex adaptive system:** The collective whole of connected structures and processes (systems and subsystems) that are highly unpredictable, self-organizing, and often include spontaneous or unexpected outcomes and tipping points. They also contain nonlinear relationships, meaning that one area can affect a completely different system or subsystem where there seems to be no discernible cause-and-effect relationship. (Part 1 Chapter 4)

- **Destructive creation:** The natural evolutionary recycling pattern for parts or wholes of or in a system that are unable to adapt. This core meta-pattern of breakdown and recycling allows these parts to be reused and once again to support future experiments and the evolutionary process.

- **Extinction-level climate destabilization:** Term to describe when the amount of carbon in the air reaches carbon 600 ppm and global temperatures average between 5° and 6° Celsius, resulting in the eventual extinction of up to half or more of all species on Earth (Climageddon Scenario, Phases 5-6). Extinction-level climate destabilization occurs when life can no longer successfully exist. There is a possibility that extinction-level climate destabilization may never correct or re-balance itself to some new equilibrium level. If the climate were able to correct or re-balance itself from this level of destabilization, it could take hundreds of thousands of years.

- **Extinction-level global warming:** Term associated with temperatures exceeding pre-Industrial levels by 5-6° Celsius (9-10.8° Fahrenheit) or carbon ppm levels exceeding 750+, or the extinction of all planetary life, or the eventual loss of our atmosphere (Climageddon Scenario, Phase 6). If our atmosphere is also lost, this is referred to as runaway global warming. This occurs when the climate crosses a final keystone tipping point and destabilizes permanently. The result would be similar to what is thought to have happened to Venus 4 billion years ago, resulting in a carbon-rich atmosphere and minimum surface temperatures of 462 °C.

- **Global warming**: A term used for the observed century-scale rise in the average temperature of the Earth's climate system and its related effects. Scientists are more than 97% certain that most of global warming is caused by increasing concentrations of greenhouse gases and other human-caused activities.

- **Global warming emergency:** The current level of carbon parts per million (ppm) in the atmosphere and the continued exponential rise of carbon ppm in the atmosphere. We are currently in a undeclared global warming state of emergency and poised at the edge of irreversible global warming.

- **Global warming temperature prediction models:** To predict future temperatures, scientists use supercomputers to create many different models and simulations that incorporate current observational data. They also experiment with many different formulas and factors as there are many variables. There are climate inertia and momentum variables, as well as adjustment variables for the overall climate changing in the past slower than today. In the book, we frequently used Keeling curve observational data for temperature increase predictions where, for each additional 25 ppm of carbon added to the atmosphere, temperature would rise an estimated 0.27° Celsius (0.5° Fahrenheit). The length of time for that increase to be realized varies, but in general, the more cumulative carbon we add to the atmosphere, the faster the temperatures will rise. Additionally, although different climate researchers may use different formulas and factors in their models for determining their temperature increase time frames and these predictions may vary somewhat, what hasn't changed is that 97% of all climate scientists say human-caused global warming is real, dangerous, and an immediate problem for the future of humanity.

- **Great adaptive challenge, great evolutionary adventure:** A positive perspective for viewing the current global warming emergency and challenge.

- **Garrett global warming crisis:** If we do not scale up green energy generation as fast as we scale down fossil fuel energy generation, the global economy will collapse. If we do not radically shut down fossil fuel energy generation immediately, civilization will eventually collapse and humanity may go extinct. (Part 1, Chapter 8)

- **Greenhouse gases:** Gases like water vapor, carbon dioxide, methane, nitrous oxide, and ozone that absorb and emit heat radiation. (Part 1, Chapter 2)

- **First Great Evolutionary Bottleneck:** A drastic reduction in the global human population due to a supervolcanic eruption 50,000 years ago. This global disaster was theorized to have reduced the human species to 3,000-10,000 survivors and as few as 1,000 to 200 remaining mating pairs. (Part 1, Chapter 4)

- **Irreversible climate destabilization:** Term associated with a measurement beginning around carbon 425 ppm and going up to about carbon 550-600 ppm (Climageddon Scenario, Phases 2-4). The eventual temperature range associated with creating irreversible climate destabilization is an increase in average global temperature of up to 4° Celsius (7.2° Fahrenheit).

Irreversible climate destabilization is a new average global temperature range and a set of destabilizing climate consequences we most likely will never recover from—or that could take hundreds or even thousands of years to correct or re-balance. When global warming-caused storms, floods, seasonal disruption, wildfires, and droughts begin to cost a nation 100-billion-plus dollars per incident to repair, we will have reached the level of irreversible climate destabilization.

- **Irreversible global warming:** Term that describes the result of a _continuum_ of increasing temperature and escalating tipping point-triggered, self-reinforcing cycles that cause the global climate to rapidly change until it reaches stability at some new level and range of temperature that is irreversible on a practical human life span time scale. The eventual temperature range associated with triggering irreversible climate destabilization is an increase in average global temperature of 2.2°-4° Celsius (4°-7.2° Fahrenheit). Irreversible global warming inevitably leads to extinction-level global warming for most if not all species. In the Climageddon Scenario, irreversible global warming can begin as early as Phase 2.

- **Job One for Humanity organization:** A nonprofit social benefit organization whose mission is to provide strategies, leadership, and support for a global movement to end global warming and avoid the later extinction level phases of Climageddon. (JobOneforHumanity.org)

- **Job One for Humanity Plan:** A comprehensive "first-things-first" plan using innovative remedial strategies and the best science available. It is a fully prioritized sequence of action steps designed to first slow and lessen global warming, then eventually to end the emergency before we pass the critical thresholds where global warming becomes irreversible.

- **Keeling curve:** A graph plotting the ongoing change in concentration of carbon dioxide in Earth's atmosphere since 1958 as charted by Charles David Keeling. Keeling's measurements showed the first significant evidence of rapidly increasing carbon dioxide levels in the atmosphere.

- **Keystone tipping point:** A tipping point that triggers other dependent and interconnected tipping points. Crossing a keystone tipping point is one of the potential triggers for irreversible global warming leading into the later extinction phases of the Climageddon Scenario. (Part 1, Chapter 4)

- **Meta-systemic analysis:** Examining systems and subsystems involved in global warming from a perspective that considers them as stand-alone and individual systems *as well as* being interconnected and interdependent with and upon each other. Meta-systemic analysis involves detailed analysis of processes, contexts, relationships, and continual transformations occurring among and between interconnected and interdependent systems and subsystems within the selected area of analysis. (Preface)

- **Methane time bomb:** Popularly known as the clathrate gun hypothesis, an increase in sea temperature that triggers a sudden release of methane from seabeds and permafrost, leading to irreversible temperature rise. There is evidence of these occurrences in the Paleocene-Eocene Thermal Maximum extinction event

55.5 million years ago (see next) and the Permian-Triassic extinction event 252 million years ago.

- **Paleocene–Eocene Thermal Maximum (PETM) extinction event:** A warming event 55.5 million years ago in which gigatons of carbon and methane were released into the atmosphere after the global temperature rose 5° C. It resulted in the extinction of roughly 70,000 species and is the most recent and accurate event within Earth's geologic history to compare to today's global warming.

- **Parts per million (ppm) and parts per million by volume (ppmv):** A measurement of the concentration of pollutants in the atmosphere, "ppm" describes parts per million by weight, which typically accounts for one pollutant (such as carbon) and does not account for traces of other pollutants. Parts per million by volume (ppmv), on the other hand, includes other trace gases, such as methane.

- **Perfect storm of perfect storms:** The process of multiple global warming tipping points crossing over to degrade and destabilize climate, human, and biological systems and subsystems in a self-reinforcing positive feedback loop and meltdown.

- **Point of no return:** The point of directional motion and momentum at which a developing process thereafter *irreversibly* moves toward crossing its tipping point. (Part 1, Chapter 4)

- **Positive feedback loop:** A process that occurs as a self-reinforcing loop in which the effects of a small disturbance on a system feed back upon itself to increase its magnitude, furthering and increasing the disturbance process in an unending loop.

- **Precautionary principle:** Used by policy makers to guide discretionary decisions in situations where there is the possibility of harm from making a certain decision (e.g. taking a particular course of action) when extensive scientific knowledge on the matter is lacking. The principle implies that there is a social responsibility to protect the public from exposure to harm, when scientific investigation has found a plausible risk. These protections can be relaxed *only if* further scientific findings emerge that provide sound evidence that *no harm will result.* (from Wikipedia; Part 2, Chapter 1.)

- **Remaining meaningful control:** We have only the next 6-10 years (2026) to prevent crossing a carbon ppm level of 425-450, achieve carbon neutrality, and complete the transition to green energy generation to avoid crossing over the climate cliff and losing remaining meaningful control of our global warming future.

- **Runaway greenhouse effect:** Also referred to as runaway global warming or extinction-level global warming, this describes the circumstance in which the climate destabilizes catastrophically and permanently from its original state—similar to what happened on Venus when the planet lost its atmosphere out into space.

- **Second Great Bottleneck:** Our current human-caused evolutionary bottleneck that, due to steadily increasing carbon and methane pollution of our atmosphere and its associated temperature increase, may cause the extinction of the human species. (Part 1, Chapter 4)

- **Sixth Great Extinction:** Also known as the Holocene or Anthropocene extinction, this refers to the ongoing extinction event during our present Holocene epoch due to human activity, especially global warming. At present, the rate of extinction is estimated to be up to 140,000 species per year—the greatest loss of biodiversity since the <u>Cretaceous-Paleogene extinction event</u> 66 million years ago.

- **Second Industrial Revolution:** A period of innovation between 1870 and 1914 that introduced the combustion engine, the telegraph, radio, mass production via assembly lines, widespread usage of electricity, and the expansion of the usage of oil and steel.

- **Slowing and lessening actions:** Essential and critical actions required to have a meaningful chance of saving ourselves from irreversible global warming, such as achieving carbon neutrality and transitioning globally to renewable green energy generation by 2026.

- **Sustainable prosperity:** A set of new sustainability principles that create shared sufficiency as well as abundance for individuals, communities and nations in the vital and meaningful areas of life, and to have this qualified prosperity sustained over the long term.

- **Third Industrial Revolution:** A new industrial revolution based on moving out of fossil fuel energy generation and into green energy generation, as well as using new Internet and other digital technologies that will create hundreds of millions of new jobs. Like the mechanization of the textile industry in the First Industrial Revolution and the introduction of mass production via assembly lines in the Second Industrial Revolution, the Third

Industrial Revolution is occurring as manufacturing moves from fossil fuels to green energy and into digital innovations such as the Internet of Things. This term refers to Jeremy Rifkin's concepts from a book called the *Third Industrial Revolution*.

- **Tipping points:** The point where a process or stimulus experiences a sudden change, causing the process to jump from one state to a new, significantly different state—much like a tipped wine glass going from being full to empty. (Part 1, Chapter 4)

- **West Antarctic Ice Sheet:** A good example of the dangers of crossing a point of no return, this ice sheet has already begun the irreversible collapse process. Once this particular ice sheet melts completely, it will trigger the subsequent melting of most of Antarctica's ice, significantly raising global sea levels.

- **Wild card:** An unpredictable positive or negative factor that can drastically influence the outcome of a situation. (Part 1, Chapter 6)

REFERENCES

Basseches, Micheal. *Dialectical Thinking and Adult Development*. Ablex Publishing, 1984.

Beinhocker, Eric D. *The Origin of Wealth: The Radical Remaking of Economics and What it Means for Business in Society*. Harvard Business Review Press, 2007.

Berry, Thomas. *The Great Work: Our Way Into the Future*. Broadway Books, 2000.

Bhaskar, Roy. *Dialectic: The Pulse of Freedom*. Verso, 1993.

Butler, Octavia E. *Parable of the Sower*. Four Walls Eight Windows, 1993. This is part one of two sequential novels. Set in 2024, it gives a very human, detailed and unusually accurate description of the human suffering and migration consequences that will happen as the global warming emergency worsens in California. If you want *feel* what the global warming future is going to be like for individual human suffering, this duology is a compelling must read.

Butler, Octavia E. *Parable of the Talents*. Seven Stories Press, 1998. This is part of two of the Parable duology. Set in 2032, it gives a very human, detailed and unusually accurate description of the human suffering and migration consequences that will happen as the global warming emergency worsens in California. If you want *feel* what the global warming future is going to be like for individual human suffering, this duology is a compelling must read.

Carson, Rachel. *Silent Spring*. Houghton Mifflin, 1962.

Craven, Greg. *What's the Worst That Could Happen?: A Rational Response to the Climate Change Debate*. Perigee, 2009.

Diamond, Jared. *Collapse: How Societies Choose to Fail or Succeed*. Penguin Books, 2011.

Esbjorn-Hargens, Sean and and Michael E. Zimmerman. *Integral Ecology: Uniting Multiple Perspectives on the Natural World*. Integral Books, 2009.

Fisher, Len. *Crashes, Crises, and Calamities: How We Can Use Science to Read the Early-Warning Signs*. Basic Books, 2011.

Funk, McKenzie. *Windfall: The Booming Business of Global Warming*. Penguin Press, 2014.

Fuhrman, Joel. *Eat to Live: The Amazing Nutrient-Rich Program for Fast and Sustained Weight Loss*. Little, Brown and Company, 2011.

Greer, John M. *Dark Age in America: Climate Change, Cultural Collapse, and the Hard Future Ahead*. New Society Publishers, 2016.

Guzman, Andrew T. *Overheated: The Human Cost of Climate Change*. Oxford University Press, 2014.

Hansen, James. *Storms of My Grandchildren: The Truth About the Coming Climate Catastrophe and Our Last Chance to Save Humanity*. Bloomsbury, 2009.

Jantsch, Erich. *Design for Evolution: Self-Organization and Planning in the Life of Human Systems*. George Braziller, 1975.

Klein, Naomi. *This Changes Everything: Capitalism vs. The Climate*. Simon & Schuster, 2014.

LaConte, Ellen. *Life Rules: Nature's Blueprint for Surviving Economic & Environmental Collapse*. New Society Publishers, 2012.

Laske, Otto E. *Measuring Hidden Dimensions: The Art and Science of Fully Engaging Adults*. Laske and Associates, 2011.

Lovelock, James. *The Vanishing Face of Gaia: A Final Warning*. Basic Books, 2009.

Lynus, Mark. *Six Degrees: Our Future on a Hotter Planet*. National Geographic, 2008.

Macy, Joanna and Chris Johnstone. *Active Hope: How to Face the Mess We're In Without Going Crazy*. New World Library, 2012.

Meadows, Donella H. *Thinking in Systems: A Primer*. Chelsea Green Publishing, 2008.

Miller, Peter. "Cool It: The Climate Issue." National Geographic, November 2015. Print.

Newitz, Annalee. *Scatter, Adapt, and Remember: How Humans Will Survive a Mass Extinction.* Doubleday, 2013.

Pike, David. "The Job One for Humanity Global Warming Blog." Job One for Humanity. Last modified February 16, 2017. http://www.joboneforhumanity.org/blog. Many of The Global Warming Blog's 2000+ articles were referenced in the creation of this book.

Rich, Nathaniel. *Odds Against Tomorrow.* Farrah, Strauss and Giroux, 2013. This is a fictional novel based on the global warming catastrophe in New York City. An entertaining and easy read. Not as detailed as Olivia E. Butler's books, but a definite contribution to humanizing the effects of global warming.

Rifkin, Jeremy. *The Third Industrial Revolution: How Lateral Power Is Transforming Energy, the Economy, and the World.* St. Martin's Press, 2011.

Sahtouris, Elisabet. *EarthDance: Living Systems in Evolution.* iUniverse, 2000.

Salthe, Stanley N. *Evolving Hierarchical Systems.* Columbia University Press, 1985.

Stewart, John. *Evolution's Arrow: The Direction of Evolution and the Future of Humanity.* Chapman Press, 2000.

Tainter, Joseph A. *The Collapse of Complex Societies (New Studies in Archaeology).* Cambridge University Press, 1988.

Taleb, Nassim N. *The Black Swan: The Impact of the Highly Improbable.* Random House, 2007.

Wagner, Gernot, and Martin L. Weitzsman. *Climate Shock: The Economic Consequences of a Hotter Planet.* Princeton University Press, 2015.

Made in the USA
Columbia, SC
09 November 2018